| County or Shire | Date Formed | Formed From | References |
|---|---|---|---|
| Accawmack | 1634 | (Was an Original Shire) | H I, 224, 249. |
| Accomack | 1663 | Northampton | H.II, 122, 106 |
| Albemarle | 1744 | Goochland | H.V 266; H,VI 441 |
| Alexandria | 1847 | Dist. of Columbia | U.S.Statutes I, 130, 215 |
| Amelia | 1735 | Prince George and Brunswick | { H IV 467, H V, 379. { H XII 723, H XII 596 |
| Brunswick | 1732 | Surry and Isle of Wight | H IX, 77, H IX, 355 |
| Buckingham | 1761 | Albemarle + Appomattox | { H VI 419 ; H IX 559. { A (1844-5) 38. |
| Caroline | 1728 | Essex; King and Queen; and King William. | { H.B. (1727-30), 39; H IV 420 { H V, 185; H IV 20. |
| Charles City | 1634 | (Was an Original Shire) | H.I, 224; H III 253; H IV 94. |
| Charles River | 1634 | (Was an Original Shire) | H.I, 224; H I 249. |
| Chesterfield | 1749 | Henrico | H.B. (1742-3) 391; A (1849-0), 26 |
| Clarke | 1836 | Frederick and Warren | A (1835-6) 20; A (1859-0) 496. |
| Culpeper | 1749 | Orange | A (1831-2), 44; H.B. (1742-2) 346, H XIII 558. |
| Cumberland | 1749 | Goochland; Buckingham | H.B. (1742-3) 346; H X, 522. |
| Dinwiddie | 1752 | Prince George | H VI 254. |
| Elizabeth City | 1634 | (Original Shire) | H I, 224; A (1662-2), 43 |
| Essex | 1692 | Rappahannock | H. III, 104; H IX, 77 + 240 |
| Fairfax | 1742 | { Prince William { and Loudon | { H V, 207, H.III 148; S II, 107 { US.STAT.S I, 130, 214; II, 103, 115. { A (1845-6) 50; A (1846-7) 41; A (184-7) 48. |
| Fauquier | 1759 | Prince William | H VII, 511; A (1823-4), 82. |
| Fluvanna | 1777 | Albemarle | { H,st 225; H XII, 71; A (1835-7)53; A (1838)57, A IV76-7, 20, 224 { A (1855-C) 99; A (1861) 151, A (1471-2) 542, |
| Gloucester | 1651 | YORK | H.I, 374 ; H XIII, 162. |
| Goochland | 1728 | Henrico | H.B. (1727-40) 38 ; H IV 240 H V, AGG. H XII, 71. |
| Greensville | 1781 | Brunswick, Sussex | H X, 363; H XIII, 596, S. II 347 |
| Hanover | 1721 | New Kent | H.B. (1712-26), 281; H 95; H X 208, H XII 620 |
| Henrico | 1634 | (an oric. SHIRE) | H I 224; H II 440 ; H XII 620. |
| Isle of Wight | 1637 | Warrosquyoake; Upper | { H I, 228, 247, 423; { Norfolk; and Nansemond } H XIII 405, 602. |
| James City | 1634 | { Ong Shire { New Kent & York | { H I 224; H IV 35; A 1852, 31 { H III 208, 405, 419 |
| King and Queen | 1691 | New Kent | H III, 94, 211; H IV, 77, 240; H VII, 620. |
| King George | 1721 | Richmond; Westmoreland | H.B. (1712-26) 279. |
| King William | 1702 | King and Queen | { H III, 211; H IV 77, H IX; 240. H IV 95,303, H IX 244,132. |
| Lancaster | 1651 | Northumberland; York | H.I, 374. |
| Loudoun | 1757 | Fairfax | H.VII 148; S II 107; A (1823-4), 82. |
| Louisa | 1742 | Hanover | { H V,208; H XII, 419; A (1836-7), 33; { A (1838)57; A (1876) 20, 21, 228. |
| Lower Norfolk | 1637 | New Norfolk | H I 228, 247. ; H III 95 |
| Lunenburg | 1746 | { Brunswick, + { Charlotte | { H V,383, H V 383,441, 252; { H XIII, 41; H III, 327. |
| Mathews | 1791 | Gloucester | H XII, 162. |
| Mecklenburg | 1765 | Lunenburg | H XIII, 41. |
| Middlesex | 1673 | Lancaster | H II 327 |
| Nansemond | 1642 | { Formerly { Upper Norfolk | { H I, 321; (Va.Map of Hist. and Biog, { Vol XXIII, 259. H. VIII, 405, 602. { H XII, 69. |
| New Kent | 1654 | York + James City | H I 387,8; H IV 35; H. VIII, 208 |
| New Norfolk | 1636 | Elizabeth City | Norfolk County Records + Land Grants |
| Norfolk | 1691 | Lower Norfolk | H. III, 95 |
| Northampton | 1642-3 | Accawmack | H. I, 249. |
| Northumberland | 1648 | Chiccoun | H.I, 294, 299, 337-8, 340, 352 ; 7,353,36,& |
| Nottoway | 1789 | Amelia | H XII, 723; H XIII 561. |
| Orange | 1734 | Spotsylvania | H V, 450; H V 78; A (1838), 52. |
| Powhatan | 1777 | Cumberland; Chesterfield | H.IX 522; A (1848-9) 26, |
| Prince Edward | 1754 | Amelia | H VII, 379; A (1844-5); 36, |
| Prince George | 1703 | Charles City | H III, 223; H IV 467; H VI 254. |
| Prince William | 1731 | Stafford; King George. | H IV 303; H V, 207, H VII 311. |
| Princess Anne | 1691 | Lower Norfolk | H III, 95. |
| Rappahannock | 1656 | Lancaster | H I, 427; H. III, 104. |
| Rappahannock | 1833 | Culpeper | A (1832-3), 44. |
| Richmond | 1692 | Rappahannock | H III 104; H IV, 95. |
| Southampton | 1749 | Isle of Wight; Nansemond. | H. B. (1742-7) 371; H XII, 69. |
| Spotsylvania | 1721 | { Essex; King William; { King and Queen | { H IV, 77; { H IV 450. |
| Stafford | 1664 | Westmoreland. | H II, 259; 250; H IX 303; H III 244. |
| Surry | 1652 | James City | H I, 373; H III, 355. |
| Sussex | 1754 | Surry | H V, 304; S II, 347. |
| Upper Norfolk | 1637 | New Norfolk | H.I, 228, 247, 321, 423. |
| Warrosquyoake | 1634 | Original Shire | H I, 224, 249. |
| Warwick | 1642 | Warwick River | H.I, 249, 250; A (1661-2) 43. |
| Warwick River | 1634 | Original Shire | H.I, 224, 249. |
| Westmoreland | 1653 | { Northumberland, { and King George | { H I 321; { H IX 432. |
| York | 1642/3 | Charles River | H I 249; H XII, 405 419 A (1852) 31. |

CLARKE 1836

LOUDO 1757

WARREN 1836

PRINC

FAUQUIER 1759

RAPPAHANNOCK 1833

CULPEPER 1749

ST

ORANGE 1734

SPOTSYLVANIA 1721

LOUISA 1742

HA

FLUVANNA 1777

GOOCHLAND 1749

D

BUCKINGHAM 1761

CUMBERLAND 1749

POWHATAN 1777

CHESTERFI

AMELIA 1735

Appomattox River

PRINCE EDWARD 1754

NOTTOWAY 1789

DINWIDD 17

LUNENBURG 1746

GREENSVILLE

MECKLENBURG 1765

BRUNSWICK 1732

1781

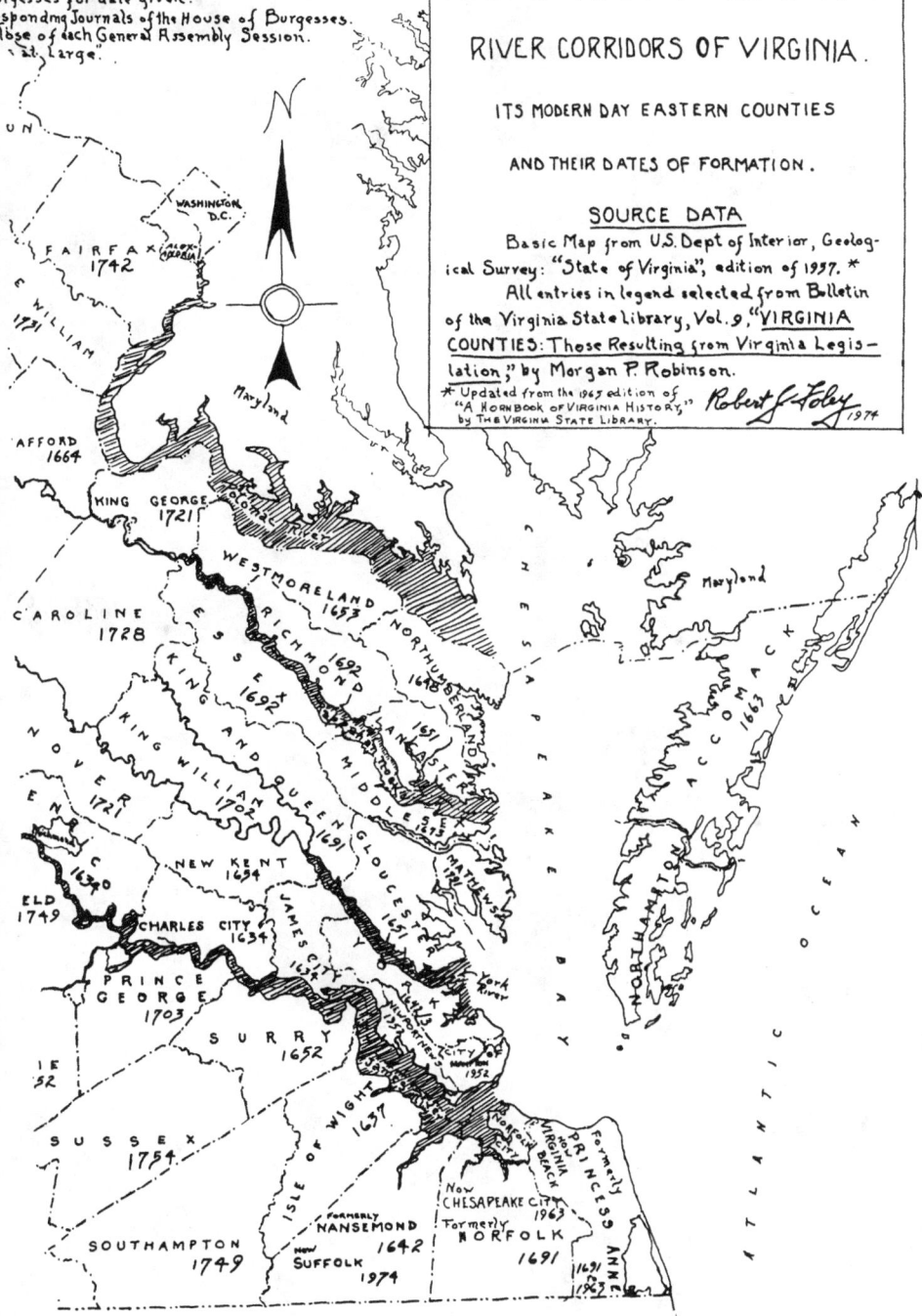

nces
ty of Virginia for date given.
"Statutes at Large" (volume given).
sses 1619 to 1776 (printed by State Library).
urgesses for date given.
espondng Journals of the House of Burgesses.
close of each General Assembly Session.
at Large".

# HIGHWAYS INTO NEW LANDS

## RIVER CORRIDORS OF VIRGINIA.

ITS MODERN DAY EASTERN COUNTIES

AND THEIR DATES OF FORMATION.

### SOURCE DATA

Basic Map from U.S. Dept of Interior, Geolog-
ical Survey: "State of Virginia", edition of 1957. *
All entries in legend selected from Bulletin
of the Virginia State Library, Vol. 9, "VIRGINIA
COUNTIES: Those Resulting from Virginia Legis-
lation," by Morgan P. Robinson.

* Updated from the 1965 edition of
"A HORNBOOK OF VIRGINIA HISTORY,"
by THE VIRGINIA STATE LIBRARY.

Robert G. Foley
1974

UN

WASHINGTON D.C.

FAIRFAX
1742

ALEXANDRIA

W I L L I A M
1731

Maryland

AFFORD
1664

KING GEORGE
1721

WESTMORELAND
1653

CAROLINE
1728

RICHMOND
1692

ESSEX
1692

NORTHUMBERLAND
1648

Maryland

KING AND QUEEN
1691

LANCASTER
1651

A C C O M A C K
1663

OVER
N E
1721

KING WILLIAM
1702

MIDDLESEX
1673

GLOUCESTER
1651

C
1670

NEW KENT
1654

MATHEWS
1791

NORTHAMPTON

ELD
1749

CHARLES CITY
1634

JAMES CITY
1634

PRINCE GEORGE
1703

SURRY
1652

YORK
York River

CITY
1952

IE
52

S U S S E X
1754

ISLE OF WIGHT
1637

VIRGINIA BEACH
Formerly

Now
CHESAPEAKE CITY
1963

PRINCESS ANNE

SOUTHAMPTON
1749

FORMERLY
NANSEMOND
1642

Now
SUFFOLK
1974

Formerly
NORFOLK
1691

1691

A T L A N T I C   O C E A N

C H E S A P E A K E   B A Y

Early Virginia Families
Along the James River

Their Deep Roots and Tangled Branches

Henrico County–Goochland County
Virginia

Compiled by
LOUISE PLEDGE HEATH FOLEY

VOLUME I

CLEARFIELD

Reprinted for
Clearfield Company, Inc. by
Genealogical Publishing Co., Inc.
Baltimore, Maryland
1992, 1993, 1994, 1996, 1999, 2001, 2002, 2003


Originally published: Richmond, Virginia, 1974
Reprinted: Genealogical Publishing Co., Inc.
Baltimore, 1979, 1983
© 1974 Louise Pledge Heath Foley
© transferred to Genealogical Publishing Co., Inc.
Baltimore, 1979
Library of Congress Catalogue Card Number 79-88216
International Standard Book Number 0-8063-0849-4
Made in the United States of America

To my parents

Edwin James Heath
and
Mabel Brown Heath

Their roots were deep

Their branches tangled

In Colonial Henrico County

Virginia

# Contents

# Errata

# Foreword

The purpose of this report is to assist in finding colonial and emigrant ancestors and, also, to assist in placing them upon their lands, all within the framework of events which influenced their lives as participants, and ours as their descendants. To this end this report includes a compilation of land records, historical information and maps as follows:

Selected historical background information to highlight certain events which led directly to the formation of Henrico, first as a city, then as a borough, and finally a shire, or county. The history is presented by making use of direct quotations from prime and original sources.

Explanations of boundaries. These also, whenever possible, have been taken from prime and original sources.

Abstracts of land patents from Patent Books No. 1 through 14 (1632-1732). Patent Books No. 1 through 5 have been taken from Nell Nugent's Cavaliers and Pioneers. Abstracts of Virginia Land Patents and Grants, 1623-1666. Patent Books No. 6 through 14 were also abstracted by Nell Nugent but her work went into litigation before it was published. The page proofs of her abstracts have been photo-copied and put into three volumes and are available at the Virginia State Library and plans are now being made to index and publish them. Your compiler appreciates permission from the Library to copy from these three volumes. These volumes have an index but only the names of the patentees are listed. The headrights and other named persons and places are not included. Consequently, the following report with a 34-page index of thousands of names should resurect many ancestors from their hitherto unindexed oblivion.

The Quit Rent Roll of Virginia, 1704-1705. This Roll contains the names of the patentees of new lands and their taxable acres. These alphabetized lists of names should be useful in the search for early land owners.

Map #1 shows the present counties of eastern Virginia with the dates of their formation and from which counties they were taken. As the population expanded along Virginia's great river highways new counties were formed, usually from western boundaries of earlier counties. Other boundary changes also occurred. In some instances a specific parcel of land had been a part of several different counties during the course of its history. Consequently, it is necessary to know the name of the county at the time research is to be made of the county records.

Map #2 shows the Curles of the James River as it appeared in colonial times, with colonial place names and names of many of the Henrico and Charles City County residents placed upon their lands. This map has been taken from a forthcoming publication by your compiler called The Jordan-Cocke Line of Henrico County, as it contains information pertinent to this compilation.

Every effort has been made for accuracy. However, in a compilation of this character errors are bound to occur and your compiler would appreciate having her attention called to any such errors. In this way any corrections can be made in future publications.

# Backward Glances

Tracing family histories through land patents can be richly rewarding. These records furnish valuable genealogical, historical and geographical information which is unobtainable from any other sources. History without people is lifeless; genealogy without history is statistical. Genealogy and history, along with geography are most compatable subjects, one adding luster and meaning to the other. These land patents give the name of the patentee, number of acres acquired and the date; the location giving the county; geographical boundaries such as rivers, creeks and branches; names of other family members in many instances, as well as names of adjoining neighbors; the number of persons brought to the colony as headrights and their names, with other incidental information.

It would be appropriate to briefly highlight certain geographical features of Henrico County, as its location bears directly upon its importance, second only to Jamestown during the earliest embryonic years of our nation's history. Henrico County is situated on the north bank of the James River about eighty miles upstream from the river's mouth and approximately forty two miles from Jamestown. It is bounded by Turkey Island on the east, Tuckahoe Creek on the west, Chickahominy River on the north and, of course, the James River on the south. It is bounded by the counties of Charles City on the east, Goochland on the west, New Kent and Hanover on the north and Chesterfield on the south. The city of Richmond is situated on the fall line of the river where the fresh water of the upper James flows from the Piedmont into the brackish tidewater of the lower James. The town was established in 1742[1] and is surrounded by Henrico County on the east, north and west, and of recent years the annexed part of Chesterfield County on the south side.

These present day boundaries differ greatly from those of colonial times. Consequently, for research purposes it is prudent to be aware of these variations and the dates of their changes. The boundaries of Henrico County extended on both sides of the James River from Turkey Island Creek and the Appamattox River westward from about 1629 until 1728. On the latter date Goochland was formed from Western Henrico. In 1749 Chesterfield was formed from Henrico's south side. (See pp xxi-xxiv; also Map #1.)

The land patents for existing Chesterfield County were too numerous in those early years, when it was part of Henrico County, to be included in this report. Some, however, are included because of their close association with persons on the north side. In fact, the parish lines of Henrico and later Varina extended on both sides, as the river offered relatively easy access.[2]

At the time Goochland County was formed from Henrico County it also extended on the south side of the James. The latter portion became Cumberland County in 1749 and was changed to its present name of Powhatan County in 1777. Patents of many of the south side Goochland County persons have been included because of the widespread interest in the Huguenots who were permitted to settle on lands assigned them at Manakin Town. Some other patents have also been included for reasons of close ties across the river. Charles City County lying east of Henrico County also extended across the James until Prince George County was formed in 1703. (See map #1). Here again, some few Charles City patents appear for the reasons given above.

Many topographical changes have occurred along the James River since our ancestors received their early land patents. This is particularly true along the "Curles" of the river from Curles Neck up the river to Dutch Gap. There has been considerable land erosion in this area as well as the entire tide-water lands, particularly along the north side. Its channel has been relocat-ed in several places, thus creating islands from peninsulas. West of Shirley Hundred a long narrow peninsula called Turkey Island was cut from the south side by Turkey Island Cutoff. The relatively wide peninsula to the west call-ed "Curles" gave its name to this entire meandering part of the river. West of Curles Neck, as it is known today, is another long narrow peninsula which was known as Rochdale Hundred, or Neck of Land, and is presently called Jones Neck. Meadowville Channel now separates it from the mainland on the south side. A short distance up river was located another narrow necked peninsula named Henricus (or Henricus Towne or Cittie, or Henrico) which became Farrar's Island. Directly beyond was Coxendale. A trench has been cut through both Coxendale and Farrar's Island's narrlw neck to form Dutch Gap.*

These unique geographical features were responsible for the early "peo-pling" of the Curles of the James very soon after the first settlers arrived in Virginia and had secured their precarious toe hold at Jamestown. Events of dramatic and historic importance took place in Henrico during those form-ative years. Locating these early settlers within the framework of their time and place in history, as well as upon their lands, should give us better knowledge and understanding of them as living, active human beings.

Henrico County was the first home in America for the ancestors of count-less living Americans. Early in the history of our country they settled along the Curles of the James River and there many remained, generation after gene-ration. Their roots grew deep into the alluvial soil along its banks and up its tidewater creeks, and in time their branches became tangled. Eventually the press of population, the devastation of battles of two wars upon its shores and the promise of fresh rich land lured later generations beyond the confines of Henrico County to frontiers of an ever expanding land. Tra-ditions and memories of their early Virginia heritage became hazy, but their names continued to speak eloquently of their early ties with the struggling Virginia colony.

On June 2, 1607[3] Christopher Newport with his band of twenty three other explorers arrived at Arrahattock (see map #1) marking the beginning of the history of Henrico County. Seventeen days after the "First Colony in Virginia" had been established at Jamestown on May 14, Newport, along with his mariners and sailors went "in his shallop to discover up the river as advised to do by the King's Council for Virginia. .... They reached a low meadow point about thirteen miles from Jamestown, that night, which they called

Wynauk (Tanks Weyanoke. See map #1. - ed.). The next day they passed up some
sixteen miles to an islet which they called Turkey Island (Turkey Island
Bend). ... They rested that night at a place about twenty-two miles farther
up the river, which they called 'Poore Cottage' or 'Port Cottage.' June 2
they feasted with the werowance Arahatec, in the country Arahatecoh, at a
place they called Arahatec's Joy. ...'They were so ravished with the admirable sweetness of the streame, and with the pleasant land trending along on
either side, that their joy exceeded, and with great admiration they praised
God.'" This landing at Arrahattock marks the first known occasion of Englishmen setting foot upon Henrico soil.

Newport and his men continued their exploration up the shoreline and
some "ten miles above Arahatec's Joy they came to 'the second islet on the
river (Drewry's Island), over against which, on Popham (north-ed.) side, on
a high hill, is the habitatyon of the great Kyng Pawatah (Powhatan-ed.),
which they called Pawatah's Tower.'... Some three miles above the islet they
came to an overfall of water ... long known to the colonists as 'The Falles,'
and to us as the site of Richmond, the head of tidewater. June 3 (Whit Sun-
day), they 'feasted King Pawatah giving him beer, aqua vite and sack to drink.
After dinner Captain Newport, upon one of the little ilets at the mouth of
The Falls, set up a crosse with this inscription: Iacobus, Rex, 1607, and his
own name belowe.' That night they returned to Arahatec's Joy, where they
found the king suffering from the effects of their 'hot drinks;' but he was
alright the next morning...Newport and his party then set sail back down the
river and arrived back at Jamestown on June 6."[4] When Newport left for
England several weeks later he carried with him "the first description of
the river, of the country and of the people."[5]

The history of Goochland County (western Henrico until 1728) began in
October, 1608. "Captain Newport, Waldo, Wynne, Percy, West, Mr. Scrivener
and others, made an exploration up James River above the Falls. There is no
reliable detailed account of this expedition, and the dates are uncertain;
but it probably began in October and ended about the 27th of November. Captain Smith, who was not in it, attempts to ridicule it in his history. It
was, however, an important expedition. The English went, for the first time,
into the wilderness for any considerable distance beyond the protection of
their ships. They marched 'four days journey' above the Falls, to the eastern gold belt of Virginia, and possibly to where 'this river devyds itselfe.'
In 1612, William Strachey, describing James River, writes: 'Forty miles above
the Falls, it hath two branches, or other rivers, that fall into it; the head
of the northermost (the Rivanna) comes from certaine steepe mountaines that
are said to be impassable; the head of the other (the Fluvanna, now the James)
comes from high hills afar of, within the land, from the topps of which hills,
the people (Indians) say they see another sea - and that the water is there
Salt.' In answer to a letter from Charles I., of November, 1627, the General
Assembly replied that, '19 years ago, a mine had been discovered four days'
journey above the Falls of the river.' In the map of 1610, 'Rossawich' is
given as the name of an Indian town in the fork of the rivers, present James
and Rivanna. No permanent settlement was made so high up the river for an

hundred years or more thereafter. The earliest settlers of this section called one of the chief tributaries of the Rivanna River 'Machumps' Creek, which was the name of an Indian who told the earliest settlers of Virginia much about the country; and a large creek flowing into the James on the north side above the present Scottsville was called Totiers (Tolere, etc.) Creek, which probably locates it as formerly in the region of one of the eastern Siouan tribes of Indians."[6]

The next date of importance in the history of Henrico was May, 1609.[7] It was on this date that King James I ordered Sir Thomas Gates, first Governor of Virginia, to remove the capital city of the Virginia Colony from Jamestown. Events in England were taking place which were to have a profound influence in the Virginia colony in general and in Henrico in particular.

The first two years at Jamestown were marked by squabbling, mismanagement, inefficiency and jealousy, considered largely the fault of the terms of the original charter of 1606. The king agreed to the drafting of a new charter which was "drawn up (probably late in January, 1609) ...'as every planter and Adventurer was to be inserted in the Patent, by name,' it was kept open to receive these names, and was not signed by the king and sealed until June 2, 1609."[8] The Virginia Company of London "at once shouldered the responsibility and took the matter well in hand. To reform the government in Virginia, they selected Lord De la Warr to be lord governor and captain-general, with Sir Thomas Gates lieutenant general, and Sir George Sommers admiral of Virginia, with Captain Christopher Newport vice-admiral."[9] "The general plan determined upon for securing a firm hold on the land was 'so to set and furnish out under the conduct of one able and absolute Governor, a large supply of five hundred men, with some number of families, of wife, children and servants, to take fast hold and root in that land ...'"[10] "To rectify the government - the first inconvenience - in Virginia, and to establish for the present a more absolute or strong form, it was finally determined to send Sir Thomas Gates first, and, after hearing from Virginia through him, then to send Lord De la Warr, who was slated to be the lord governor. As soon as the charter was signed and sealed Gates received his commission as sole and absolute governor, with the authority of a viceroy, and about June 8 hastened to join the fleet in the west of England, there staying for him. ... This was the first fleet sent by 'the Company for Virginia in London.'"[11] It was known as the third "supply."

Sir Thomas Gates' orders and instructions from "his majesties Counsell" in England were dated May, 1609, but they were not signed until June 2, the same date the king signed the charter, as was stated above. Of the 36 directives contained therein, #12 is particularly applicable as will be seen. It reads as follows: "In the distribution of your men according to these advises and relations which we have received, we advise you to continue the Plantation at James Town with a Convenient number of men, but not as your situation or City, because the place is unwholesome and but in a marsh of Virginia, and to keep it only as a fit port for your ships to ride before to arrive and unlade at, but neither shall you make it your principal Storehouse or Magazine either of arms victuals or goods, but because BUT BECAUSE

it is accessable, with shipping that an enemy may be easily upon you with
all the provision of ordinance and munition and it is not to be expected that
any fortification there can endure an enemy that hath the leasure to sit before it."[12] These instructions had a direct bearing on Henrico's future and
the important part she was destined to play in the expansion and strengthening of the Virginia colony. Due to unforeseen circumstances, however, the
time was delayed by many disheartening and tragic events.

"The first fleet sent out under the first company charter sailed from
Falmouth, England, June 18, 1609, in nine ships with the better part of 500
people, - men, women, and children." Their hopes ran higher than the tide
that started them on their journey toward a better life. Not only the emigrants and the joint stockholders of the Virginia Company, but also most
Englishmen shared the aspirations that Virginia would become a stepping
stone to the south seas and its glittering treasures. "They sailed via the
Canaries route; while in the tropic in the month of July many fell sick of
calenture or yellow fever, and out of two ships thirty-two persons were
thrown overboard. In addition to this the London plague is said to have
broken out on the Diamond. In the midst of this trouble, upon Saint James
Day (July 25) in crossing the Gulf of Bahama (the Gulf Stream near the Bahama
Islands) a most terrible tempest 'which endured fortie four hours in extrem-
itie' separated all of the fleet one from another. Five or six days after
the storm, the Blessing, the Lion, the Falcon, and the Unitie (on which ship
nearly all were sick) came together and laid away directly for Virginia and
fell into James River on August 21. A few days thereafter the Diamond arrived, and within three or four days the Swallow. The Catch was lost at sea,
and the Sea Adventure wrecked on the Bermudas."[13] " ... "the governor and
other principal officers appointed were all on the Sea Adventure; they did
not arrive at this time, and, of course, the first charter and the King's
form of government remained in force as the only legal authority in Virginia
until they did."[14] "Smith was to remain undisputed as president until September 20, and Captain Francis West was chosen to succeed him."[15]

The survivors found less than one hundred and nine remaining inhabitants
in Jamestown and the colony in pitiful condition. The fleet, which was to
have brought supplies for six hundred people for one year, brought only more
suffering to the already beleaguered colony. "The supplies for the most part
were ruined or damaged by the tempest. They fell upon the small corn crop
of the colony, 'and in three days, at the most, wholly devoured it.' Owing
to the scarcity and condition of the supplies, and the sickness of the colonists, Captain Smith ... for their better relief, divided them into three
parties."[16] "Captain Smith sent Captain Francis West with 'about 100 men'
up to the Falls, where the Indians soon killed and wounded some of them.
'So that in small process of Tyme, Capt. Smith did take his journey up to
the Falls to understand how things were there ordered.'"[17] "The end of his
stay in Virginia was, however, approaching and he was determined to find
some better site for a colony than the low marshy Jamestown. While there
he "bought of the natives a tract of land in that neighborhood near to where
Richmond now stands, - a range of hills salubrious and defensible. with so

fair a landscape that Smith called the place Nonesuch. On his way back to
Jamestown a bag of gunpowder in his boat exploded and wounded him so badly
that he was completely disabled. The case demanded such surgery that the
wilderness could not furnish, and as the ships were sailing for England early
in October he went in one of them."[18]

About the time that the remnants of the fleet were leaving, Captain
Francis West, with the survivors of his 100 men, were forced by the hostility
of the Indians to return to Jamestown from their attempt to settle at the
Falls.[19] West was determined to return to England with his ship. He sailed
about January 2, 1610, and after cruising about for some time finally
landed at Lyme in England in June, 1610 in the Swallow.[20]

"What is known in history as 'the starving time in Virginia' is generally
stated to have begun after Captain Smith left; but it really began during
his presidency in the spring of 1609, and (save for the temporary relief af-
forded by Argall in July and the arrival of the fleet in August) continued
until the arrival of Gates. It was one of the most disasterous periods in
the life of the colony."[21] "The Sea Adventure, under command of Captain Newport, vice-admiral of Virginia (with Sir Thomas Gates, governor, and Sir
George Somers, admiral; ... was driven by 'the Tempest' for several days."
On August 7 "they were wrecked (but 'not a hair perished') on 'the still
vexed Bermoothes.' ... On September 7, 1609, Richard Frobisher began building a large pinnace of eighty tons, called the Deliverance. December 7, Sir
George Somers began to build a small one of thirty tons, called the Patience.'
On May 20, they set sail for Virginia and arrived at Jamestown two weeks
later.[22]

"On the arrival of Gates, June 2, 1610, with the new commission, the
period of the royal government ended; but, as the colony was then in no condition to be benefited by the change, it seems more just to begin the estab-
lishment of the new order of things in Virginia, with the arrival of Lord
De la Warr on June 20, 1610. ... Lord De la Warr left London about March 12,
1610, and sailed from 'the cowes' on April 11 ... with supplies for the
colony and about one hundred and fifty emigrants ..." arriving at Cape Comfort on June 16th. On this same date Gates, having "reached the conclusion
that there was no way before him save to abandon the colony," was making his
final preparations for his voyage back to England with his approximately 200
remaining men. Fortunately, he was intercepted by one of De la Warr's party
and instructed to return to Jamestown, which he did. Lord De la Warr reached
Jamestown with his ships on June 20 and "Sir Thomas Gates caused his company
in arms to stand in order and make a guard ..." His commission was read
"which instituted him 'Lord Governor, and Captain General during his life,
of the Colony and Plantation in Virginia (Sir Thomas Gates our Governor
hitherto, being now stiled therein Lieutenant General),' upon which Sir
Thomas Gates delivered up to his lordship 'his owne commission, both patents
and the counsell seale.'"[23]

Gates, with Newport sailed for England on July 25, 1610,[24] arriving in
England in early September.[25] He immediately set about planning for a large

expedition of men and supplies to sail for Virginia in two or more sections as soon as possible. All word coming from the colony had been so discouraging that it was becoming increasingly difficult to get volunteers to settle in land so hostile, or for persons to venture the costs for their transportation.

Lord Governor Sir Thomas De la Warr was well aware that the Virginia Company of London had been a financial failure for its stockholders and that salable commodities would have to be discovered within a short time, or the attempt at colonization would fail. Anticipating the possibility that the "Councell of Virginia" would order his return home and thus "abandon the action," he sent a letter by way of Sir Thomas Gates to be read before the council extolling the land and its possibilities. He stated his willingness to sacrifice his life and fortune "upon the prosecution of the plantation." Gates also swore before the governing body as to the colony's great potential resources, "and lastly, that it is one of the goodliest countries under the Sunne; ... and that he longeth and hasteneth to go thither again."[26]

The rumor of gold fields lying beyond the Falls (in western Goochland County-ed.) was a straw to which De la Warr and the management of the enterprise, were tenaciously clinging as he set about organizing and strengthening his position at Jamestown. "The governor, now wishing to march towards the mountains to discover the mines of gold or silver which 'Faldo, an Helvetian,' (a Swiss-ed.) had persuaded the Council in England that he could locate, his people having been so reduced by death, felt obliged to order Captains Yeardley and Holcroft, the commanders of the two forts on Southampton River, to abandon them and bring their commands to Jamestown. The expedition soon set forward under command of Captains Edward Brewster and George Yeardley, being in number one hundred persons; but the Queen of Appamatuck invited some of them to a feast, and, while they were eating, treacherously massacred fourteen of them, including 'all the chief men skillfull in finding out mines.' ... By reason of this disaster the expedition went no further than the Falls of the river, where they built a fort and remained near three months, his lordship being there in person for most of the time." While there the Indians massacred several of his men, including Captain William West, his nephew. Trouble with hostile Indians, as well as his own declining health, decided De la Warr "to retire to Jamestown, giving order that the fort which we had built there whould be quitted and the troupe drawn down, which accordingly was done."[27]

"All three forts were now abandoned, and the colonists, reduced by sickness and by Indian massacres to less than two hundred, were concentrated at Jamestown and Algernoune Fort. When Dale attributed this state of affairs to the assertion that Lord De la Warr's object was 'rather the search after Faldoe's mines than the founding of the colony,' it was as an apology rather than as a fact. It is true, however, that he was sent to rescue the old colony rather than to settle a new one. He wished to find mines, of course, but the first thing he did (his first object) was to strengthen the colony. He did not really search for the mines at all, and the real cause why the end had not been more fully advanced was 'the sickness.' as Dale found out himself within less than two months after his arrival."[27]  Spring found De la Warr in too weakened a condition to endure another "sick season in Virginia" and he sailed April 7, 1611, arriving in England "towards the end of May."  He is believed to have left no more than about 150 persons in the entire colony.  "On leaving the colony the lord governor appointed Captain George Percy to act as his deputy governor until the coming of the marshal, Sir Thomas Dale (who was then expected daily), whose commission was likewise to be determined upon the arrival  of  Sir  Thomas  Gates."[28]

The expedition, divided into two sections, sailed from England in the spring of 1611.  Sir Thomas Dale, who had been appointed deputy-governor, left England "March 27, with the Starr (Captain Newport, vice-admiral of Virginia in charge of the voyage, and Captain Clark, pilot), the Prosperous, and the Elizabeth, and three hundred people ..."  "The men brought by Dale were classed as 'honest sufficient artificers,' 'honest and industrious men, carpenters, smiths, coopers, fishermen, tanners, shoemakers, shiprights, brickmen, gardeners, husbandmen, and laboring men of all sorts.'  Rev. Alexander Whitaker came at this time as one of their ministers, and the Rev. Mr. Poole as another."  He arrived at Point Comfort May 22, 1611 and left some of his men to repossess the two forts, Henry and Charles, which had earlier been abandoned, and also to build cottages and plant corn.  He proceeded to Jamestown where "Mr. Strachy read the commission which the Lord-Governor had left with him for Sir Thomas Dale, and Capt. Percy surrendered up his commission ..."  On May 31 at a meeting of the Council it was determined to "go up unto the Falls ward to search for and advise upon a seat for a new Town."[29] (Please see Sir Thomas Gates' orders and instructions from the council in England dated June 2, 1609 on page vi-vii.)

After the middle of June, Dale went up James River to search for a proper site for the new town which he had been instructed to plant in Virginia.  Every attempt to establish a settlement at the Falls had failed, even after Captain John Smith had purchased a tract of land from the Indians in that neighborhood of a range of hills near to where Richmond now stands. Dale and his men searched up to the Falls, but finally returned down the river to a narrow-necked peninsula near the Indian village of "Arahatec," or Arrahattock, as it became known.  "He wrote to the prime minister of England: 'I have surveyed a convenient strong, healthie and sweet seate to plant the new Town in, from whence might be no more remove of the principall Seate; and in that forme to build, as might accommodate the inhabitants, and become the Title and Name which it hath pleased the Lords (Privy Council), allreadie to appoint for it.'  It had been appointed by the Privy Council to name the new town Henrico for Henry, Prince of Wales, the patron of Dale and of Virginia."... "Dale thought that he saw good indications of mines about the Falls."[30]  On his return to Jamestown Dale put his men to work preparing timber, pales, posts, and rails "for the present impaling of the new town (Henrico), to secure himself and men from the treachery of the Indians, in the midst of whom, he was resolved to set downe;" being convinced of the importance of having the main settlement farther from the river's mouth and more inaccessible to the shipping of Spain.[31]

The second section of the expedition sailed from England toward the end of May, 1611 with Sir Thomas Gates, lieutenant-general of Virginia, "with three ships (the Trial, the Swan (and Sarah?) and three carvells (for cattle only), and two hundred and fourscore men and twenty women ..." The fleet arrived in Virginia the last of August. Sir Thomas Dale surrendered his commission and turned his attention to his final preparations for building a new town near the falls, "which purpose Lieutenant-Governor Gates approved." Dale "selected from 300 to 350 men, and about the middle of September, 1611, set out from Jamestown with the tide, and in a day and a half landed at the site selected."[32] Captain Bruster led most of the men overland and on his way to his appointed meeting place with Dale had a number of encounters and skirmishes with the savages.[33]

"Ralph Hamor, Secretary of the Colony, has left this account of its condition, and the founding of the City of Henrico and Bermuda City" and excerpts appear as follows: Having already prepared much of the material, Gates and his men set about fortifying seven English acres of ground for a town, "which in honor of the noble Prince Henry, of ever happy and blessed memory, whose royal heart was strongly affected to that action, he called by the name of Henrico. In four months' space, he had made Henrico much better, and of more worth than all the work ever since the Colony began therein done. It stands upon a neck of very high land, three parts thereof environed with the main river, and cut out between two rivers with a strong pale, which maketh the neck of land an island. (There was only one river, the James, which wound around this peninsula. It looked like two rivers, one on the east, and the other on the west side. - Sams.) There are in this town three streets of well framed houses, a handsome Church, and the foundation of a more stately one laid of brick, in length an hundred feet, and fifty feet wide, besides storehouses, watch-houses, and such like. There are also, as ornaments belonging to this town, upon the verge of this river, five fair (large - Sams) blockhouses, or commanders, wherein live the honester sort of people, as in farms in England, and there keep continual sentinel for the town's security. And about two miles from the town into the main, a pale of two miles in length cut over from river to river, (This pale seems to have run across the peninsula, south of the town, from the James to the Appomattox taking in a large area. - Sams.) guarded likewise with several commanders, with great quantity of corn ground impaled, sufficient, if there were no more in the Colony secure, to maintain with but easy manuring and husbandry, more men than I suppose will be addressed thither, the more is the pity, these three years.

For the further enlargement of this town, on the other side of the river, by impaling likewise, for we make no other fence, is secured to our use, especially for our hogs to feed in, about twelve English miles of ground, by name, Hope in Faith, Coxen-Dale, secured by five forts, called Charity Fort, Mount Malado, a Retreat or Guest-house for sick people, a high seat, and wholsome air, Elizabeth Fort, and Fort Patience. And here hath

Master Whitacres (The Rev. Alexander Whittaker - Sams.) chosen his parsonage house built thereupon, called Rock Hall.

I proceed to our next and most hopeful habitation, whether we respect commodity or security which we principally aim at against foreign risings and invasion, I mean Bermuda City, begun about Christmas last, (1613-ed.) which, because it is the nearest adjoining to Henrico, though the last undertaken, I hold it pertinent to handle in the next place. This town, or plantation is seated by land, some five miles from Henrico, by water fourteen, being the year before the habitation of the Ap-pa-ma-tucks; to revenge the treacherous injury of those people done unto us, taken from them, besides all their corn, the former before without the loss of any, save only some few of those Indians, pretending our hurt, at what time Sir Thomas Dale, being himself upon that service, and duly considering how commodious a habitation and seat it might be for us, took resolution to possess and plant it, and at that very instant, gave it the name of the New Bermudas, whereunto he hath laid out, and annexed to be belonging to the Freedom and Corporation forever, many miles of champion, and woodland, in several Hundreds, as the Upper and Nether Hundreds, Roch-dale Hundred, West's Shirley Hundred, and Digg's, his Hundred.

Rocksdale was also enclosed with a cross palisade near four miles in length; and there were many houses planted along the pale, within which their hogs and cattle had twenty miles circuit to graze in security."

Henrico and Charles City were the best fortified places in Virginia, until destroyed during the massacre of 1622. Both were built upon high cliffs. The fortification was by trench and palisade, with cleared land around them. Blockhouses were built 'upon passages,' that is, so as to control paths or roads, and for securing the palisades. At Henrico there were seven pieces of artillery.

A college was to be established at Henrico. Ten thousand acres of land were set aside for its endowment, to be worked by fifty men, 'tenants at halves,' that is, being furnished the land, half the profit of their labor was to be theirs, the other half, the colledge's. Mr. George Thorpe, a kinsman of Sir Thomas Dale, was the first superintendent, who had for his 'entertainment, and support,' three hundred acres, to be worked by ten tenants. The College was to be for education and religious instruction of the Indians as well as the English."[34]

Robert Johnson (the deputy-treasurer for Virginia-ed.), in 1612, describing Henrico as he saw it; ".. the colony is removed up the river forescore miles further beyond Jamestown to a place of high ground, strong and defensible by nature, a good air, wholesome and clear, unlike the marshy seat at Jamestown, with fresh and plenty of water springs, much fair and open grounds free from woods, and wood enough at hand."[35]

"Since the departure of Ralph Hamor from the colony John Rolfe had been the secretary and recorder, and although we have not his letters and records of particular events, his "Relation of Virginia " (written) in 1616 gives a fair idea of the condition of the colony from July, 1614, to March, 1616. The greatest portion of the colonists were seated or occupied in or about the fork of the James and Appomattox rivers, planting corn and tobacco, building, impaling, fortifying, etc."[36]

"John Rolfe gives us an account of the population of the Colony in 1615, as follows: The places inhabited by the whites, at this time, were Henrico and the limits, Bermuda Nether Hundred, West and Shirley Hundred, Jamestown, Ki-quo-tan, and Dale's Gift, places centering in a general way around the confluence of the James and Appomattox Rivers.**

At Henrico there were thirty-eight men and boys, of whom twenty-two were farmers. The Rev. William Wickham was the minister of this place. It was the seat of the college established for the education of the natives; they had already brought hither some of their children, of both sexes, to be taught. Captain Smaley was in command here.

At Bermuda Nether Hundred, Presquile (Turkey Island. Ref: Quadrangle map "Hopewell, Va."-ed.), the number of inhabitants was one hundred and nineteen. Captain Yeardley, deputy governor, and deputy marshall, lived here for the most part. The minister was Master Alexander Whitaker.

At West and Shirley Hundred there were twenty-five men under Captain Madison.

At Jamestown fifty under Captain Francis West, John Sharp being his Lieutenant and the Rev. Mr. Buck, minister.

At Ke-cough-tan Captain George Webb commanded; and the Rev. William Mease, or Mays, was the minister. (twenty men, Brown, p. 229-ed.)

Dale's Gift, the island on the sea-coast, near Cape Charles, was occupied by seventeen men, under Lieutenant Cradock.

The total population of the colony, at this time, was three hundred and fifty-one."[37]

"'So the number of officers and laborers are two hundred and five; the farmers 81; besides women and children, in everie place some,- which in all amounteth to three hundred and fifty one persons - a small number to advance so great a worke.' Probably less than fifty of these had arrived since the last coming in of Sir Thomas Gates (August, 1611); the rest belonged to that historic band long known as 'the old planters of Virginia.'"[38]

An analysis of these figures shows that of the total of 351 colonists in Virginia, 269 were men and 82 were women and children. Of these 269 men, 182 were up river in Henrico and surrounding environs, while only 50 remained at Jamestown.

Sir Thomas Gates had finally succeeded in complying with his orders and instructions he received two years earlier in 1609. He continued the plantation at Jamestown with a "convenient number of men" and removed most of the colonists, with his government, first to Henrico, and later, to Bermuda City, five miles removed. With emphasis away from Jamestown, the center of gravity had moved up the river to the "Curles of the James."

These first 10 years had been extremely critical ones for the survival of the colony. Of the approximately 1,650 persons sent to its shores, only about 350 had survived. "Probably about three hundred had returned to England at different times, and about 1,000 had died on the voyage or in Virginia."[39] "With the 'generallity' in England this period was the darkest hour in the life of the colony; but the managers held their faith in Gates and Dale and Argall. It was not in their plan to send any large number of people until those who had become acclimated had had time to prepare the ground and make ready to receive them. ... In the colony destiny was shaping its ends. John Rolfe was taking the pains to plant, tend, and cure the first crop of tobacco for export ever made by an Englishman in Virginia. And this 'vile weed' as some called it then and now, was in a few years to make virginia self-supporting, and in time, to all intents, an El Dorado."[40]

"Sir Thomas Dale sailed from Virginia on the Treasurer, and reached Plymouth on the last day of May, 1616. What documents, letters, etc., were brought I do not know; but he brought a very interesting party of people, including ... Pocahontas, Rolfe, and others ... Dale's time in Virginia is a wonderfully interesting period of our history ... Dale sent the following letter from Plymouth, soon after he arrived there. It was addressed "To the right Hoble Sr Ralfe Wynwood Kt, Principall Secretary to his Matie.' Plymouth, 3o Junix 1616, from Sr Thos Dale. (Sir Ralph Wynwood was also a member of the council of the Virginia Company, as well as having been his Majesty's principal secretary. For smoother and better understanding your compiler has modernized the spelling and punctuation from the following abstracts of this letter.-ed.) I am ... safely returned from the hardest task that ever I undertook ... and have left the Colony in great prosperity and peace, contrary to many men's expectations. This ship hath brought home exceptionally good tobacco, sassafras, pitch, potash, sturgeon and caviar, and such commodities as yet this country yields. How beneficial this admirable country will be for our State I know you are not ignorant of. ... I shall give your honor great encouragements that this Virginia affords to spur us forward to inhabit there, if his Majesty wishes to possess one of the goodliest & richest kingdoms of the world, & indeed so fit for no state as ours."[41]

The confidence and optimism Dale displayed in the future of the colony became justified and from that time on the colony progressed and expanded at a comparatively rapid rate. It is unfortunate, however, that so many official papers and personal letters pertaining to the government of Gates and Dale are missing. Little is known of the important events which transpired in Henrico and the other settlements along the Curles of the James and down the river at Jamestown. Although Jamestown was used primarily as a safe place for livestock, it remained Virginia's capital.[42] Sir Thomas Dale left the government to Captain George Yardley, who had been commandant at Bermuda City and Hundred. He continued to reside there for part of his time, but as governor he was obliged to reside partly at Jamestown.[43]

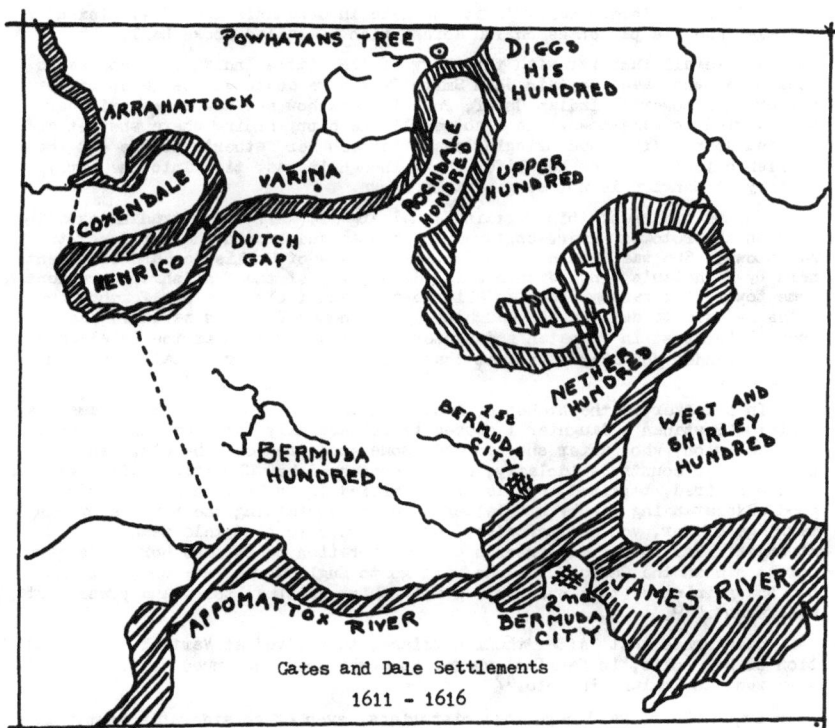

Gates and Dale Settlements
1611 - 1616

Within five years Dale had accomplished the almost miraculous task of having carved out of a hostile wilderness thousands of acres of mostly virgin forest land along the entire Curles of the James and firmly securing it as a part of the Virginia colony for the profit of the Virginia Company of London and the pride of the English people. This was accomplished by swift and very harsh military punishment. As soon as he had established Henrico for his chief city he expanded its boundaries westward across the river on its south side to another peninsula and named it Coxen-dale. The name is probably a combination of the family name Cox, who were early settlers in this region, and that of Sir Thomas Dale.[44] It was here in Coxendale that Rev. Alexander Whitaker had his parsonage on 100 acres which he called Rocke Hall.

We are all familiar with the story of the little Indian princess named Pocahontas who saved Captain John Smith from sure death at the hands of her father, the powerful Indian Chief, Powhatan and how she was taken prisoner and carried to Jamestown. We also recall the happy ending where she met and married John Rolfe, thus bringing peace between her father's people and the English colonists. How her life, short though it was, tied into the early history of Henrico is not so generally known.

In the spring of 1613 Captain Samuel Argall, while on a trading expedition on the Potomac River, captured Pocahontas and brought her prisoner to Jamestown. She was held hostage for the release of Englishmen and equipment held by Powhatan's men. Within a few days seven of the Englishmen were sent home toward her ransom but, as all the arms and tools were not forthcoming, Gates refused to deliver his daughter. Sir Thomas Dale, as marshal, had special interest in Powhatan's daughter and placed her under the tutelage of Rev. Alexander Whitaker[45] who, at that time, was minister of Dale's new church in Henrico.

In a letter to the Bishop of London, dated June 18, 1614, Sir Thomas Dale wrote: "Powtahan's daughter I caused to be carefully instructed in the Christian religion, who, after she had made some good progress therein, renounced publicly her country's idolatry, openly confessed her Christian faith, was as she desired, baptized, and is since married to an English gentleman of good understanding (as by his letter unto me, containing the reasons of his marriage of her, you may perceive,) another knot to bind this peace the stronger. Her father and friends gave approbation to it, and her uncle gave her to him in the Church. ... She will go to England with me; and, were it but the gaining of this one soul, I will think my time, toil, and present stay well spent."[46]

Sams wrote that "After their marriage, they lived at Varina, the plantation of Mr. Rolfe, in Henrico, where, no doubt they continued to reside until they went to England in 1616.[47]

It should be said here that historians, even of considerable stature, have been known to make positive statements at times based solely upon circumstantial evidence. Consequently, when substantiating evidence is lacking, such information should be viewed with caution. From the information above, however, it can be said with confidence that Pocahontas lived in Henrico from shortly after her capture in April, 1613 until her marriage to John Rolfe in April the following year. Philip L. Barbour, in his recent book, Pocahontas and Her World, expresses this fact clearly when he writes " ... it was obviously not long after Pocahontas' arrival at Henrico that John Rolfe met her. It may be that Rolfe experimented with his tobacco seeds in the neighborhood, for it is known that there was a 'great quantity of corn ground impaled' at Henrico and even more at Bermuda Nether Hundred, five miles down-stream."[48]

In the village of Heacham, Norfolk, England is an epitaph which reads, "He increased his property by merchandise. By exporting and importing such things as England abounded in, or needed, he was of the greatest service ..." These words appear on the tomb of John Rolfe (1562-1594), the father of John Rolfe (1585-1622), and they give insight into young Rolfe's later enterprise. [49]. The father had been a successful merchant and a self made gentleman. It is entirely possible that his son's interest in growing tobacco began before he left England and sparked his decision to become a Virginia planter.

Rolfe sailed from England in the ill fated Sea Venture which was wrecked on the Bermudas, "and while there a daughter was born to him ... the child soon died."[50] The parents reached Jamestown June 2, 1610 and the mother died shortly thereafter. Rolfe's experimentation with the growing of tobacco coincided with the arrival of Sir Thomas Dale in May, 1611. Seeds had been imported from Trinidad, probably through the arrangements of Rolfe, who was himself an ardent smoker.[51] "As the Indians and the colonists were so constantly at war, Rolfe was probably induced to cultivate a small patch for his own use as a means of obtaining a certain supply. Secondary to this motive was a desire to find some commodity that could be sold at a profitable rate in the markets of England, thus advancing the prosperity of the settlers, and promoting the success of the company. This condition appeared to be fulfilled in the case of tobacco, if it could be produced in quantities large enough, and of sufficient excellence in quality to allow an active competition with the Spanish leaf, which at this time met the demand in England."[52]

Dale "was eminently practical in his cast of mind, and soon formed a just notion of the conditions which had to be met in order to place the colonial settlements upon a footing of lasting prosperity." He "had established a vineyard at Henrico not long after the foundation of the settlement ... "[53], and also very likely encouraged Rolfe's tobacco endeavors. There could have been no better location for his tobacco plants than in the rich fresh soil within the safety of the Henrico palisade. Rolfe's little crop of tobacco had been planted in the spring of 1612, and after harvesting and curing, was shipped to England about July 8, 1613. "The most interesting news carried was of the capture of Pocahontas; the most important commodity was tobacco."[54] Of the crop, which Ralph Hamor described as owing its goodness to "Trinado or Cracus," he further claimed that there had as yet been no equal produced. Rolfe's tobacco compared so favorably with the fine, sweet, strong Spanish leaf that it immediately became a highly marketable commodity and did much to save the colony from failure.[55]

Above and east of Henrico Island on the river lies "Varina, so named, it is said, because of the superior character of the tobacco raised in the neighborhood, which resembled a high-grade Spanish tobacco, called Varina. This was long the county seat of Henrico, and here, it is said, resided, after their marriage, John Rolfe and Pocahontas."[56]

"In 1614, on the marriage of Pocahontas, a peace was concluded with the Indians which lasted for many years. The words of the peace had been stamped in brass, and at Opechancanough's request, had been fixed on one of his noted oaks. "Powhatan's Tree," on Powhatan Swamp, four miles from Jamestown, was probably this tree. There is a large tree in that vicinity, known to many as Cromwell's Tree, which may have been "Powhatan's Tree."[57] There was no need to seek a tree "which may have been 'Powhatan's Tree,'" as a "Powhatan's Tree" actually existed about two miles above Henricus Town and Varina plantation. Could this tree have been the one to which the historic brass marker was attached at the time of the marriage of Powhatan's daughter to John Rolfe? The surrounding area soon became known also as Varina (or Verinas).[58]

There is controversy as to whether this marriage took place in the church at Jamestown with the Rev. Buck officiating, or in the church at Henrico with Rev. Whitaker conducting the ceremony. Brown has stated that "The marriage was solemnized in the church at Jamestown, about the 15th of April, 1614, by the Rev. Richard Buck .. "[59] Brown also states that "He was married about the 5th of April, 1614, in the church at Jamestown, to Pocahontas, ... I suppose he was certainly married by Mr. Buck, the minister at Jamestown, and not by Mr. Whitaker, who was the minister at Henrico."[60] At another time Brown writes "It has been claimed that he (Rev. Alexander Whitaker) married Rolfe to Pocahontas; but I have not seen the evidence of it, circumstantial or otherwise. The only evidence that I have seen is circumstantial, and it points quite conclusively to the Rev. Mr. Buck, the minister at Jamestown, - where it is said the ceremony was performed, - the friend of Rolfe, and a witness to his will."[61]

Although this marriage has been well chronicled by contemporaries, no one mentioned where the ceremony took place. Pocahontas, Rolfe, Rev. Whitaker and Dale were all known to be in Henrico. Normally, a couple would be married in their own parish by their own minister. Brown mentions no unusual circumstances which would have taken them miles down river to another parish and minister. He unfortunately fails to give any hint of the "conclusive" circumstantial evidence on which he had posited his above statements. He does state that Rev. Buck was a friend of Rolfe's and was a witness to his will. It should be pointed out, however, that Rev. Whitaker was also a friend of Rolfe, he was his minister, as well as the spiritual counselor and instructor, of his intended bride; also, that Whitaker could not have witnessed Rolfe's will because he was dead before the will was drawn up.[62]

The Rolfe family - John, Pocahontas and their son Thomas, might quite appropriately be called the "first family of Henrico." Many persons living today have been able to trace their ancestors back to this family and to other "Ancient Planters" who were here in Virginia before the "coming away of Sir Thomas Dale" in 1616. They have been able to succeed in doing so to a great extent through the use of land records. Many others, however, share that honor unknowingly. Most of our ancestors arrived at a later date and these backward glances were their living history. Successful tobacco culture was a prime incentive for later Englishmen to cast their lot with the Ancient Planters and to gamble their futures on a better life in Virginia. Their story can be told through the medium of existing records but, due to lack of space, must be saved for another time.

# REFERENCES

1. Hening, Statutes, 191-193; A Horn-book of Virginia History. The Virginia State Library, 1965, 36.

2. Cooke, Charles Francis, Parish Lines-Diocese of Southern Virginia, The Virginia State Library, 1964, 128-131; Robinson, Morgan P., Virginia Counties, Vol. 9.

3. Brown, Alexander, The First Republic in America, 1969, 29.

4. Ibid., 28-30.

5. Ibid., 33

6. Ibid., 69-70.

7. Ibid., 84.

8. Ibid., 73-75.

9. Ibid., 76.

10. Ibid., 77.

11. Ibid., 84-85.

12. Kingsbury, Susan Myra, Records of the Virginia Company, Washington, 1906-35, Vol. III, 16.

13. Brown, Republic, 92.

14. Ibid., 93.

15. Ibid., 93.

16. Ibid., 97.

17. Ibid., 95.

18. Fisk, John, Old Virginia and Her Neighbors, Vol. 1, 178-179.

19. Brown, Republic, 97.

20. Ibid., 113, 124.

21. Ibid., 118.

22. Ibid., 114-117.

23. Ibid., 127-129.

24. Ibid., 134.

25. Ibid., 140.

26. Ibid., 140-142.

27. Ibid., 136-137.

28. Ibid., 138.

29. Ibid., 149-150.

30. Ibid., 151.

31. Ibid., 155.

32. Ibid., 156.

33. Sams, Conway Whittle, The Conquest of Virginia - The Third Attempt. 1610-1624, 152.

34. Ibid., 155-160.

35. Hatch, Charles E., Jr., The First Seventeen years - Virginia 1607-1624, The University Press of Virginia, Charlottesville, Va., 51.

36. Brown, Republic, 225-226.

37. Sams, Conquest of Virginia, 285.

38. Brown, Republic, 228-229.

39. Brown, Genesis of the United States, 1890. Reissued 1964, 782.

40. Brown, Republic, 173-174.

41. Brown, Genesis, 783.

42. Hatch, First Seventeen Years, 13.

43. Brown, Republic, 238.

44. Sams, Conquest of Virginia, 340-341.

45. Hatch, First Seventeen Years, 16.

46. Meade, Bishop, Old Churches, Ministers and Families of Virginia, Vol. 1, 78.

47. Sams, Conquest of Virginia, 258-260; Moore, History Henrico Parish and Old St. John's Church, 1904-Annals of Henrico Parish by Burton, Lewis W., 7.

48. Barbour, Philip L., Pocahontas and her World, Houghton Mifflin Co. Boston, 1969, 118.

49. Ibid.,113; Brown, Genesis, 986.

50. Brown, Genesis, vol. 2, 987; also Republic, 117.

51. Hatch, First Seventeen Years, 17.

52. Bruce, Philip Alexander, Economic History of Virginia in the Seventeenth Century, vol. I, 212.

53. Ibid., 219-220.

54. Brown, Republic, 190.

55. Ibid., 207.

56. Tyler, Lyon Gardiner, The Cradle of the Republic, 1900, 137.

57. Ibid., 108.

58. Page #1 of this report under Seth Ward.

59. Brown, Republic, 204.

60. Brown, Genesis, vol. 2, 987.

61. Ibid., 1050.

62. Ibid., 987; 1050.

* During the Civil War, General Butler tried to deepen Dutch Gap in order to make it navigable for war-ships, so that they could avoid a Confederate batter at the southern end of the peninsula. The Confederates prevented this. After the war, it was deepened by the United States Government in 1871-72. (Tyler's Cradle of the Republic, Second Edition, 11; Sams' The Conquest of Virginia, 340. Reprinted 1973 from a 1939 edition in the Virginia State Library.) This dredged away the neck of the peninsula where Dale's original Dutch Gap had been located, as well as much of the island, also carrying with it all possibility of archeological investigation of one of the most important historical sites in America. That which was left became located on the south side of the river in present day Chesterfield County. There are two monuments on this land, one acre of which still belongs to the County of Henrico. One was erected by the Colonial Dames of America in the State of Virginia on May 31, 1911. (The First University in America, a copy of an address delivered by W. Gordon McCabe, President of the Virginia Historical Society, and published by the Virginia Society of Colonial Dames, May 4, 1914.) The other, a Granite Cross, was erected in 1911 by the Churchmen of the Diocese of Virginia. "The inscription which was placed upon the Cross below an open Bible surmounted by an open book of Common Prayer, and which was removed by some seekers after copper, read: 'Near this spot was built Anno Domini 1611 the Church of Henricopolis under the Auspices of Sir Thomas Dale, High Marshall of Virginia, the Rev. Alexander Whitaker, M.A., Minister. This Cross is erected to commemorate the Foundation of the Protestant Episcopal Church in Henrico Parish. 1911.' On both monuments the town is named Henricopolis. This was an error based on Bishop Meade's use of the work. The name of the Town and the University was HENRICO. It so appears in the earliest writings. From the name Henrico is derived the name of our County and our parish." (Cleaveland, the Rev. George J., D.D., The Rev. Alexander Whitaker, N.A., Parson of Henrico, Apostle to the Indians, a Savior of Virginia, as it appeared in the Virginia Churchman, June 1, 1957.)

** Jamestown, Ki-quo-tan and Dale's Gift were actually many miles down river from the confluence of the James and Appomattox Rivers.

# Explanations

## 1611 to 1612

The first boundaries in Henrico County date back to the time  when Sir Thomas Dale,  with between 300 and 350 men, fortified seven English acres of land for a town which he called Henrico, in honor of Prince Henry.  This town, also called Henricus, and later Farrar's Island was built in September, 1611 and settled by March, 1612.  (Brown, Alexander, Republic, 157-158.)

The following information has been copied from Alexander Brown's The First Republic in America unless otherwise stated.

## February, 1614 - December, 1614

Hamour describes Henrico as standing "upon a neck of very high land, 3 parts thereof invironed with the main River, and cut over between the two rivers (Dale's 'Dutch Gap,' such as he had learned to make in Holland), with a strong pale, which maketh the neck of land an island (now called Farrar's Island)... And about two miles from the towne into the Main, a Pale of two miles in length, cut over from (James) river to (Appomattox)River ... They had also impaled ... the bend west of 'Henrico' which they called 'Coxendale,' and secured it with five forts, called 'Hope in(and?)Faith, Charity (and Wisdom?) Fort, Mount Malado (Malady?) ..., Elizabeth Fort, and Fort Patience.' The Bermuda city, town, or plantation, was seated, by land some five miles from Henrico, by water fourteen, and just below the present Turkey Island bend, 'with a Pale cut over from River to River, about two miles long, we have secured some eight miles circuit of ground, upon which pale, and round about, upon the verge of the River in this (Nether) Hundred, half a mile distant from each other, are very faire houses'... The first Bermuda incorporation (town or hundred) was on or about the present site of Bermuda Hundred, and "the chief citty," afterwards called Charles City (for Prince Charles), was at City Point." (pp. 208-210.)

## April, 1616 - May, 1617

By March, 1617 the "incorporation of Bermuda City" was known as "the corporation of Charles Citty." (pp. 254, 313.)

## April - November, 1619

In order to establish one equal and uniform kind of government over all Virginia, such as may be to the greatest benefit and comfort of the people, each town, hundred, and plantation was to be incorporated into one body corporate (a borough), under like laws and orders with the rest; and in order to give the planters a hand in the governing of themselves each borough had the right to elect two burgesses to the General Assembly. These plantations were located in four large corporations or general boroughs which were laid out as follows:-

I. THE CITY OF HENRICUS included Henrico (Farrar's Island), extending thence on both sides of James River to the westward, the pale run by Dale between the said river and the Appomattox River being the line on the south side. The corporation of Henricus was then only one "burrough," the old planters at "Arrahattock," "Coxendale," and "Henrico" uniting, electing Thomas Dowse and John Polentine. (Note: to the General Assembly - ed.)

II. CHARLES CITY. From the said pale, including the neck of land now known as Jones Neck, eastward, down James River, on both sides, to the mouth of the Chickahominy River. The corporation of Charles City contained five boroughs which chose burgesses; but those from Martin's Brandon ... were not allowed, thus reducing the number to four:- 1. The old plantations of Bermuda Hundred, Sherley Hundred, and Charles City ... 2. Smythe's Hundred ... 3. Flowerdieu Hundred ... 4. Captain Ward's plantation.

III. JAMES CITY          extended down on both sides of the river, with the same bounds near the river as the present James City and Warwick (afterwards formed ...) counties on the north side, and as the present Surry and Isle of Wight counties, or it may have extended to the Elizabeth River on the south side, as the south bounds are not definitely stated. The corporation of James City, also, contained four boroughs:- 1. James City ... 2. Argall's Gift ... 3. Martin's Hundred ... 4. Captain Lawne's plantation ...

IV. "THE BURROUGH OF KICCOWTAN" extended from James City corporation to the bay. The corporation of "Kiccowtan" was then only one borough ... (pp. 313, 314.)

I. In "THE CORPORATION OF HENRICO," on the north side of the river, from the Falls down to Henrico, containing about ten miles in length, were 3000 acres for the company's lands, 1500 acres of the common land for the corporatio and 10,000 acres for the university, with other land (1000 acres ?) belonging to the college. The university lands were partly of the lands already impaled in the bend across the river and above Aiken Swamp bend, which was then called Coxendale, and in which the 100 acres of glebe land were located, and partly of other lands extending up the river on the north side towards the Falls. These lands were set out for the planting of a university in time to come.

II. In the corporation of Charles City, the 3000 acres for the company was located on the north side below Sherley Hundred (Epes) Island, and the 1500 acres for the corporation on the south side below City Point.

III. In the corporation of James City, the 3000 acres for the place of governor under the order of the Great Charter were located on the lands formerly conquered or purchased of the Paspihas and other grounds adjoining. This was "old Paspaheghe," a little more than a mile from Jamestown, on the north side of the river, towards the Chickahominy.

IV.  In Kecoughtan, the 3000 acres for the company and 1500 acres for
the corporation were on the east side of Southampton (Hampton) River.
(pp. 322, 323.)

### June, 1624 - March, 1625

State of the Colony in Virginia when it was Received
by the Company from the Crown, in 1609

Form.  Monarchical or Aristocratic.  Between 70 and 130 English, probably
"about 80" living precariously, some at Jamestown, others near the oyster
banks below, and some among savages.  No landowners; no ministers....

State of the Colony in Virginia when it was returned
by the Company to the Crown, in 1625.

Form.  Popular, Republican, or Democratic.

### The General Condition of the Colony

I.  THE CORPORATION OF HENRICO.
Public lands.  3000 acres of company and 1500 acres of common lands; 10,000
acres for the university and 1000 acres for the college.

Private lands.  Prior to April, 1622, there had been granted to some 23 proprietors about 2800 acres; but as a result of the massacre this corporation
was almost depopulated in 1625, the only inhabitants then being on the college lands.  With the exception of Francis Weston (or Wilton) and Edward
Hobson, the landowners of Henrico were either dead or living elsewhere.

It had been hoped that the western bounds of Henrico might be the great South
Sea; but the Indians made it unsafe for the extension of the settlements to
the westward, and thus the corporation became so small that at some time
between 1625 and 1629 the bounds were extended down the river so as to in-
clude the upper part of Charles City, "the Neck of Land" and "the Curls of
the river" below, making the dividing line as it was when the counties were
formed in 1634.

Inhabitants.  18 free, 3 servants, and 1 child born in Virginia.  Total, 22.
Houses.  10 dwelling-houses.

II.  THE CORPORATION OF CHARLES CITY.
Public lands.  3000 acres of company and 1500 acres of common land.

Private lands.  There had been granted to some 70 proprietors about 20,000
acres of land ... After the massacre, in 1622, many entitled to lands were
probably in doubt as to where best to settle, as they did not locate their
land until 1627-1629, after the colony passed to the crown.  It seems that
all the grants then in Charles City had been made before 1624.  After the
massacre, that part of this corporation above the mouth of the Appomattox
(which was afterwards added to Henrico),like Henrico, was almost depopulated,
and the "neck of Land" was the only plantation or settlement reported therein
in February, 1625.

Inhabitants. 119 free, 84 servants, 26 children, and 7 negroes. Total, 236.

### III. THE CORPORATION OF JAMES CITY

Public lands. 3000 acres of company and 1500 acres of common land; 3000
acres laid out for the place of the governor (planted), in which were some
small parcels, granted by Sir Thomas Dale and Sir Samuel Argall (planted).
These lands were in "Pasbeheys" on the north side of the river, below the
mouth of the Chickahominy River. The names of the owners of the "small
parcels" are not given, but they were among the earliest landowners in Virginia. There were also glebe lands in each corporation.

Private lands. There were many parcels of land granted on Jamestown Island
and lots in the town. In addition to these there had been granted to about
seventy proprietors about 40,000 acres of land. With the exception of thirteen grants, the rest were probably issued prior to 1624.

Inhabitants. 204 free, 226 servants, 35 children and 10 negroes. Total, 475.

### IV. THE CORPORATION OF ELIZABETH CITY.

Public lands. 3000 acres of company and 1500 acres of common land, with the
several glebe lands. The company and common lands were on the eastern side
of Southampton (now Hampton) river.

Private lands. There were over thirty-five landowners to whom over 12,000
acres of land had been granted.

Inhabitants. 235 free, 157 servants, 43 children, 2 Indians abd 6 negroes.
Total 443. (pp. 616-624.)

---

## CALENDAR
### Old Style - New Style

"A document written at that time in London on March 16, 1612 (present
style), would have been dated by an Englishman, March 6, 1611; by a Spaniard,
March 16, 1612; by a Dutchman, March 6/16, 1611/12. The different dates
given for the same day under the different styles then obtaining have caused
vast confusion of dates in our histories. For this reason, and also because
I am writing for people of the present time, I have determined to use the
present style date throughout the book, save when otherwise deemed advisable,
and have written out in full the old contractions of words, etc., in the
original documents." (Brown, Alexander, The First Republic in America, 1969,
xxiii-xxiv.)

(By way of a further explanation, before 1752, the year in Great Britain
began March 21. All of March, however, was called the first month of the
year. In 1751 the Calendar was changed to conform to that adopted by the
Catholic countries on the Continent in 1582 under Pope Gregory. Beginning
1752 the New Year was January 1st. It has been customary in referring to
dates in the years before this if in January, February or March, as for in-
stance 1648/49, 1750/51, etc.-ed.)

# Abstracts of Land Patents
## of
## Henrico County and Goochland County

### INCLUDING SELECTED PATENTS FROM

## Charles City, Chesterfield, and Powhatan Counties
## 1624-1732

### Patent Book No. 1 - Part I

WILLIAM DAWKES, Planter, 250 acs. in the upper part neare the Neck of land commonly called Verinas, butting E. upon 2 Mi. Cr., W. towards land of THOMAS PACKER, (or PARKER), S. upon a Swamp adj. to the maine river. 20 June 1632, p. 107. Due in right of his father HENRY DAWKES & his uncle WILLIAM LEIGH for their per. adv. & by bill of adv. dated 14 July 1608 & granted to him by order of Ct. the 7 Oct. last past. His first devdt., to be doubled, etc.

WILLIAM DAWKES, of Verinas, within the Corp. of Chas. Citty, Planter, sonn & heire aparant of HENRY DAWKES, dec'd., 200 acs. within sd. Corp., 7 Sept. 1632, p. 114. Ely. upon 2 mi. Cr., W. towards land of THOMAS PACKER (or PARKER) & S. upon the Sw. adj. the maine river. Due as lawfull heire of his father, being an Ancient Planter, for his per. devdt., being 100 acs., & the other hundred acs. by bill of adv. of 12 Lbs. 10 Shill. in right of his father, dated 14 July 1608 & graunted him by order of Ct. 7 Oct. last past.

WILLIAM DAWKES, of Verinas within the Corp. of Chas. Citty, Planter, 50 acs., within sd. Corp., 15 Mar. 1632, p. 138. W. towards land of THOMAS PACKER (or PARKER), Sly. upon a Sw. adj. the maine river, & adj. his own land. 21 yr. Lease.

DANIELL SHURLEY (SHERLEY), Planter, of the Neck of Land within the precincts of Chas. Citty, 50 acs., 12 Apr. 1633, p. 143. 21 yr. Lease. Bordering upon land of WILLIAM DAWKES. Granted by order of Ct. 5 Dec. 1632.

LEONARD MOORE, Planter, of the Necke of Land in the upper part, 100 acs. on W. side of the 4 Mi. Cr. W. towards 3 Mi. Cr. & S. upon the maine river. 21 Yr. Lease. 21 Mar. 1633, p. 146.

JOHN WARD, Planter of Verinas, 25 acs. E. upon his own land, W. towards land of THOMAS PACKER (or PARKER), & S. upon the maine river. 21 yr. Lease. 21 Mar. 1633, p. 146.

SEATH WARD, Planter, of Verina in the upper part, 60 acs. in the upper part within the Corp. of Henrico, abutting W. upon land of DANIELL SHERLEY, E. towards a tree knowne as POWHETANS TREE, Sly. upon 3 Mi. Sw. & Nly. into the maine woods. 21 yr. Lease. 30 May 1634, p. 148.

HUGH COX, 500 acs. Chas. Citty Co., between Kimiges (?) Cr. & land in posses-
sion of WALTER ASHTON, 27 Aug. 1635, p. 282. Granted by order of Ct. to said
HUGH COCKES, 6 Dec. 1634 & due for trans. of 10 pers: HUGH POWELL, HEN.
CROSBYE, HEN. PATTISON, HEN. COLLINS, JAMES FOWLER, ROBT. MORRIS, GEO.
BROWNING, PETER HOLLOWAY, ASHER JOY, FRANCIS HARPER.

THOMAS HARRIS, 750 acs. Henrico Co., within Digs his hundred, 11 Nov. 1635,
p. 304. Swd. upon land of EDWARD VIRGANY, thence extending Nwd. upon land of
JOANE HARRIS his wife, W. upon the river & E. into the woods. 100 acs. due
him as being an Ancient planter & adventurer in the time of Sir THOMAS DALE
his Govmt., according to a Charter of orders from the late Treasurer & Co.,
18 Nov. 1618, & 650 acs. for trans. of 13 pers: WM. PURNELL, JON. GODFRYE,
JON. SEARLE, THO. KEANE, RICH. MASCOLL, NATH. MOORE, JON. EDWARDS, ANN
RIDLEY, WM. JONES, THO. MORGAN, WM. JONES; 2 Negroes, a man & a woman. Note:
Renewed & 70 acs. added. THO. COOKE, Clr.

THOMAS SHIPPEY, 250 acs., 14 Nov. 1635, p. 307. S. upon land of ROBERT GREENE,
W. upon the river over against the neck of land, N. upon the 4 Mi. Cr. & E.
upon the maine land. Trans. of 5 pers: THOMAS SHIPPEY, ELIZABETH SHIPPEY,
JEFFERY BREWER, ROBT. COLE, THOMAS BROOKE, JOHN CAWKER. Note: Renewed by
Sir JOHN HARVEY. Rich. KEMP, Secr.

THOMAS WARREN, 300 acs,. Chas. Citty Co., 20 Nov. 1635, p. 314. S. upon
BAYLIFFS ——— (Baileys Creek - L.H.F.), E. upon the maine woods,. W. upon
the river, & N. upon 4 Mi. Cr. 150 acs. in right of his wife SUSAN GREENE-
LEAFE, the relict of ROBERT GREENLEAFE; 50 acs. due for her per. adv. & 100
for sd. ROBERT her former husband, being an ANCIENT PLANTER in the time of
Sir THOMAS DALE; 50 acs. due sd. WARREN for his own per. adv. & 100 acs. for
the trans. of 2 servts: JOHN FOUKE, RICH. WHITFEILD.

ELIZABETH PACKER (or PARKER), Widdowe, 200 acs. in Varinaes, Henricoe Co., 12
Feb. 1635, p. 330. Between land granted to WILLIAM DAWKES on the E. & the
Gleab land on the W., abutting on the Long feild towards the maine river,
Sly. Nly. into the woods & S. W. adj. (land) in the tenure of the sd. ELIZ-
ABETH. 100 acs. in right of her first husband WILLIAM SHARPE, an Ancient
Planter in the time of Sir THOMAS DALE, & 100 acs. for trans. of 2 servts.
called GILBERT PLATT, JOHN NEWMAN.

THOMAS HARRIS, 700 acs. called by the name of the long feild, with Swamp,
Marshes & Creeks, 2 May 1636, p. 337. Beg. at a little Cr. over against
Capt. MARTINS, bounded Nwd. on the back side of the Sw., Wwd. on the maine
river, S. E. towards Bremoes devident. Trans. of 14 pers.*

ALICE EDLOE, Widdowe, 350 acs. Henrico Co., 10 Nov. 1635, p. 351. Between
Harrow Attocks & the falls on the same side of the river that Harrow Attocks
lyeth some 2½ mi. from thence or thereabouts joyning to the great Sw.,

N. W. upon the river, & E. upon sd. Sw. towards the falls. 50 acs. for her
owne per. adv. & 300 acs. for trans. of 6 pers.*

HANNAH BOYSE, daughter & heire of LUKE BOYSE late of Henrico, 300 acs. in sd.
Co., 11 Nov. 1635, p. 351. Bounded upon the river N. W. & joyning upon the
land of ALICE EDLOE her mother E. 50 acs. due in right of her father for his
per. adv., 50 acs. for her owne per. adv. & 200 acs. for trans. of 4 servts.,
by her sd. father:  THO. LEWIS, ROBERT HALLUM, JOSEPH RYALL, EDWARD HOLLAND,
OLIVER ALLEN.

JOHN BAKER, 50 acs. in Varinae, upon the 2 mile Cr., Henrico Co., last day of
May 1636, p. 352. Butting S. W. upon land in possession of sd. BAKER & WILL-
IAM DAWKES parted with the sd. Cr., S. E. towards the maine river, adj. N. E.
to land of SEATH WARD & N. W. into the woods. Due for trans. of 1 servt. called JOHN BALDWIN(BALDWYN). Note: Renewed 17 Nov. 1643 in the name of SETH
WARD & a pattent for 150 acs. dated 13 Feb. 1635 graunted to sd. WARD & 150
(acs.) added unto them. Test: SAMLL. ABBOTT, Clr.

NATHAN MARTIN, 500 acs. Henrico Co., being called the great feild, last day
of May 1636, p. 356. S. upon the river, N. into the woods, E. upon a Cr.
running by the great Swamp & W. upon the maine to a marked oake over against
the fallen Cr. 50 acs. for his owne per. adv., 200 acs. by surrender from
BENJAMINE CARRALL, to whom it was due for trans of 4 pers; 100 acs. by surrender from ROBERT HOLLOM, due to him for trans. of 2 servts., 50 acs. by
surrender from THOMAS HARRIS due for trans of 1 servt., & 100 acs. by surrender from WILLIAM FARRER, Esqr., due for trans. of 2 servts., whose names
as alsoe the aforementioned persons are mentioned under this pattent: NATHAN
MARTIN, EDWARD ELLIS, JONATHAN DAWSON, ELIZA. TALLY, ALEX. NOREY, RICH. GOOD-
ALL, JOHN HOLLOWAY, JOHN NORTH.

EDWARD OSBORNE, Gent., 400 acs. Henrico Co., 3 June 1636, p. 358. Sly. joyning upon the great Sw., Wly. upon the maine river, Nly. towards the falls &
Ely. into the maine woods. 50 acs. for his owne per. adv. & 350 acs. for
trans. of 7 pers:  ROBERT JAMES, WILLIAM HOWE, RICHARD HITCHCOX, LEON BOLOE,
ROBERT ELLOM, CHARLES STEWARD, RICHARD BUMPASS.

ROBERT HALLOM, 1000 acs. Henrico Co., 2 June 1636, p. 358. Sly. upon land of
EDWARD OSBORNE, Wly. upon the maine river, Nly. towards the falls & Ely. into
the maine woods, said land lying right opposite against the falled Cr. Trans.
of 20 pers:  JAMES PLACE, RICH. FERRIS, NOBA PERFITT, JON. NICHOLAS, RICHARD
BALY, EDWD. HOLLAND, THO. SMITH, URIAH CLARKE, FRANCIS VISSELL, HUMPHRY
GRIZELL, JOHN READ, RICH. DIXON, JAMES REDDEY, BARTH. COOKE, MARY ALLEN,
HUMPHRY CASSELL, JAMES HORMER, THO. MORETHORPE, & 2 Negroes, all servants.

THOMAS MARKHAM, 300 acs. Henrico Co., 11 July 1636, p. 371. N. upon the 4
Mi. Cr., W. upon the river, E. upon the maine, S. upon Curles joyning upon
BAYLYS land. 100 acs. in right of his wife SUSAN the relict of ROBERT GREEN-
LEAFE, to whom 100 acs. was due as being an Ancient Planter before the

3

Govmt. of Sir THOMAS DALE; 50 acs. for her own per. adv., 50 acs. for the per adv. of sd. MARKHAM & 100 acs. for his trans. of 2 pers: JOHN FOKER, RICHARD WALL. Renewed, by Sir JOHN HARVEY.

ELIZABETH PACKER (PARKER), Widdowe, 500 acs. Henrico Co., 12 July 1636, p. 373. Between Curles & Varinaes, S. upon the maine river, E. upon 4 Mi. Cr., W. towards the 3 Mi. Cr. & N. into the woods. Due in right of her late husband Serjeant WILLIAM SHARPE, whoe, as by certificate from the Ct. of Henricc dated 25 Apr. 1636, transported 9 servants & 2 Negroes: RICH VASE, JOHN THOMAS, LEWIS JONES, LEON. LAUGHTON, WILLI. COOKE, PETER WHADSEY, EDWARD JONES, JON. WARD, WM. WOOLLEY.

ALICE EDLOE, Widdowe, 50 acs. Henrico Co., 29 Nov. 1636, p. 403. At Harroe Attocks, bounding W. upon the maine river, Nly. to a little Cr. over against Kings land, adj. Sly. upon land of GEORG BOATE, runing Ely. into the woods. It being now in the tenure of sd. ALICE EDLOE. Due for trans. of WILLIAM BARTON.

WILLIAM COX, 150 acs. Henrico Co., 29 Nov. 1636, p. 403. About 2½ mi. above Harroe Attocks, W. by N. upon the maine river, Wly. upon the great swamp, Ely. into the woods & Sly. towards Harrow Attocks. Due for trans. of 3 pers: THOMAS BRAXTON, RICHARD BIRD, RICHARD HEWES.

JAMES PLACE, 550 acs. Henryco Co., 1 June 1636, p. 405. Upon a small cr. by a cleare feild called Pimasioes (?) feild otherwise porridges feild, bounded upon the maine river S. W., Sly & N. W. towards the falls of the great river & S. E. Ely. towards land of ROBERT HOLLUM, N. E. into the woods. Due in right of his now wife ELIZABETH, to whom it was due, viz: 250 acs. in right of her first husband GEORG BOATES, to whom it was due for trans. of sd. ELIZABETH & 4 servants: 300 acs. in right of her late husband JOHN WARD, to whom it was due Viz: 100 acs. for his per. adv. as being an Ancient Planter in the time of Sir THOMAS DALE, & 200 acs. for trans. of his first wife GRACE WARD & 3 pers: CORNELIUS DEHULL, VINCENT DEHALL, RICH. TOMBS, JON. MORGAN, THO. ROBINSON, RICHARD GREETE.

WILLIAM TUCKER, MAURICE TOMPSON, GEORG TOMPSON, WILLIAM HARRIS, THOMAS DEACON JAMES STONE, CORNELIUS LOYD, of London, Merchants & JEREMIAH BLACKMAN, of London, MARMAS PAWLETT, beg. at a small gutt that riner, & their Associates & Co., 8000 acs. Chas. Citty Co., being a tract of land comonly knowne by the name of Burckley hundred, 9 Feb. 1636, p. 410. Bounding E. upon land of Capt. THOMAS PAWLETT, beg. at a small gutt that runneth into the woods at the W. end of the Clift of Westover, W. upon Kimiges Cr., up to the head, N. into the woods & from the gutt from the water side. N. into the woods &c. Due by deed of sale from the Adventurers & Co. of Burckley hundred &c.

ELIZABETH BALLHASH, Widdow, 450 acs. at Curles, Henrico Co., 25 Feb. 1636, p. 412. At 4 Mi. Cr. lying N. & by W. upon the river, joyning to land late in possession of NICHOLAS BALLINGTON Nwd. & running into the woods E. by N. Due by order of Ct. at James Citty 8 Dec. 1636.

4

RICHARD COCKE, 3,00 (3,000-ed.) acs., March 6, 1636, Page 413. Easterly
upon land granted to JOHN PRICE now in the tenure of ROBERT HALLUM, Westerly
upon land of THOMAS HARRIS & Southerly upon the main river.  Due for the
trans. of 3 score pers: MORRICE ROSE, THO. PEARSON, SYM. MORLEY, ELIZ. GAR-
GAINE, VALENT. FLETCHER, WM. ROGERS, THO. LOVE, JON. MORLIN, DAN. EVANS, ANN
BARFOOTE, RICH. HILL, ANTH. WAKLIN, ERAS. HARRISON, JON. HEARNE, JOANE ELY,
JON. ANDREWS, WM. WHITE, JON. JONES, HUMPHREY BURCHER, HENRY POWNDLE, JON.
WILLIAMS, WM. HARRIS, JON. CHAPMAN, NICH. OLIVER, JON. COOKE, THO. PARCOST,
MARGARET POWELL, MARY HUFFE, WM. HASTINGS, ISAAC HORTON, GEORG HARRISON, JOHN
SMITH, JAMES TOMPSON, JOHN HEWETT, ROBERT CHEYNY, JOHN SHORE, KATH. SHORE,
RICHARD COOKE, ANTHO. WYYON, THOMAS TURNER, JOHN NORTHERNE, ROBERT LEWIS,
JOHN JOHNSON, JOHN BROWNE, JOHN BROWNE, JOHN WATTIN, JOHN BEADELL, ROBERT
BREWER, JOHN WEST, WM. HINTON, PHILLIP FOSTER, JAMES SHORE, MARGT. a Negroe.

RICHARD MILLTON, 75 acs. in Charles City Co., 26 May 1637, p. 432.  Being at
Westover, S. upon the main river, E. upon JOHN CLAY, West upon WILLIAM THOM-
ASON & N. upon Herring Cr., which land is half of a plantation formerly be-
longing to JOHN DAVIS & JOHN CLAY in equall portions with all buildings etc.
which sd. DAVIS sold to THOMAS STEGG, Merchant.  Due by deed of sale from sd.
STEGG.

ALICE EDLOE, Widdow, 350 acs. Henrico Co., 1 June 1637, p. 433.  Between
Harrow Attocks & the falls on the same side of the river that Harrow Attocks
lyeth some 2½ miles, from thence joyning to the great Swamp.  50 acs. for her
own per. adv. & 300 acs. for trans. of 6 pers: ROBERT CASTONS, ROBERT SALS-
BURY, CHRISTOPHER GOSSE, THOMAS BURTLETT, THOMAS WADE, SARAH GLOVER.

JOHN BAKER, 200 acs. Henrico Co., 12 July 1637, p. 434.  Neare unto Varinaes,
Ely. upon the head of land of SEATH WARD, Sly. upon land of sd. BAKER & WIL-
LIAM DAUXE, & W. toward Capt. DAVIS his bottome.  Trans. of 4 pers: JOHN
CLARKE, MORGAN WATKINS, JOHN MILLS, ELIZABETH WRIGHT.

HANNAH BOYES, daughter & heire of LUKE BOYES, late of Henrico, 300 acs., 13
July 1637, p. 435.  N. W. upon the river & joyning upon land of her mother
ALICE EDLOE on the E.  50 acs. due in right of her father, to whom it was
due for his per. adv. & 250 acs. for trans. of 5 servts. by her father: THO-
MAS LEWIS, ROBERT HALLUM, JOSEPH RYALL, EDWARD HOLLAND, OLIVER ALLEN.

MATHEW EDLOE, (EDLOWE), son & heir to MATTHEW EDLOE, late of Va., dec'd.
1200 acs. upon the N. side of James Riv. over against the Upper Chippokes
Cr., S. W. upon the maine river & N. E. into the woods towards Danceing
point.  12 July 1637, p. 453.  Due in right of 24 servts. trans. at the cost
of his father: MATH. EDLOE, HUGH TYDDER, WM. DEANE, EDWD. TOMPSON, WM. COX,
ELIZ. JAX (JUX?)  (Note: this may be intended for "ux" - wife), GRIFF. ROB-
ERTS, JON. LICHESTON, PETER HOMES, EVANS KENP, JON BUXTON, THO. MORRIS, THO.
ROGERS, STEP. PETTIS, CHRI   JONES, WM. MARSTEN (or MARSHEN), JOHN BETHONE,
THO. MARTIN, JON. SEATON, GEO. PRICKLOVE, FR. ROBERTS, THO. CROSBY, RAND.
HEYWARD, HEN. CROFT.

5

THOMAS SHIPPEY, 300 acs. Henrico Co., 11 July 1637, p. 436. About 2 mi. above Curles, S. upon a great br. of the 4 Mi. Cr., E. by S. upon the maine land, W. by N. by the side of sd. Cr. towards the head of the Cr. into the maine woods. 50 acs. for his own per. adv. & 250 acs. for trans. of 5 pers: ELIZA. SHIPPEY, JEFFERY BROWNE, ROBERT COLE, THOMAS BROOKES, JOHN CAWKER.

THOMAS MARKHAM, 300 acs. Henrico Co., 11 July 1637, p. 436. N. upon the 4 Mi. Cr., W. upon the river, E. upon the maine & S. upon Curles joyning upon BAYLYS land. 100 acs. in right of his wife SUSAN MARKHAM, the relict of ROBERT GREENLEAFE, to whom it was due as being an Ancient Planter, & 50 acs. for her owne per. adv.; 50 acs. for the per. adv. of sd. MARKHAM & 100 acs. for trans. of 2 pers: JOHN FOKER, RICHARD WALL.

WILLIAM FARRAR, sonne & heire to WILLIAM FARRAR, late of Henrico, dec'd., 2000 acs. Henrico Co., 11 June 1637, p. 436. Abutting Ely. upon the Gleab land of Varina, extending Wly. to the bottome of ——— Island, Sly. upon the maine river & Nly. into the woods. Trans. at his owne costs of 40 pers: THO. WILLIAMS, RICH. JOHNSON, JON. HELY, JON. FRAME (or FRANCE), EUSTACE DOWNES, JON. PEAD, EDWD. FEWSON, RICH. GREEKE, JAMES RIGSBY, JON. PRATT, ELIZA. FOSTER, JON. HUES, HEN. GYLLOM, WM. THOMAS, JON. BAKER, PATRICK ROBINSON, CHRISTO. PENHORNE, MATH. WARANER, JON. SMITH, WM. TOWERS, WM. BAKER, EDWD. HOOKE, MARY HEYNES, JOHN GARNER, WM. RICHARDSON, JON. HOWMAN, MATH. BROWN-RIDGE, RICH LEWD, JON. GIBSON, JON. PRICE, FR. POSEY, JAMES ROBERTS, ROBERT TURNER, WILLIAM DAWSON, GILES CRUMP, RICH. GARNER, HOWELL EDMONDS, MARTIN DIMOCK, HENRY HOWELL, ROBERT COLEMAN.

RICHARD GREETE, 300 acs. Henrico Co., 11 July 1637, p. 437. S. upon land of THOMAS SHEPPEY upon the 4 Mi. Cr. E. by S. upon the maine land & W. by N. by sd. Cr. to the head thereof. 50 acs. due in right of SARAH DALAHAY, wife of GRINGALL DELAHAY, whoe surrendered his claim for her trans. to sd. GREETE, & 250 acs. for the trans. of 3 wives & 2 servants: ELIANOR GREET, ALICE GREETE, MARGARETT THOMAS, his 3 wives, JOHN HOWELL & RICHARD ———, servants; SARAH DELAHAY.

Capt. THOMAS HARRIS, 700 acs. in Henrico Co., 12 July 1637, p. 438. Called by the name of Long feild with Sw. & Marshes, beg. at a little Cr. over against the land of Capt. MARTIN, bounded Nwd. on the backside of the Sw., Wwd. on the maine river, & S. E. towards Bremoes dividnt. Due as followeth: 400 acs. graunted unto EDWARD GURGANEY by order of Court 1 Oct. 1617 from the late Treasurer & Co. & bequeathed by ANN GURGANEY, Widdowe of sd. EDWARD, to THOMAS HARRIS as by her last will dated 11 Feb. 1619; 300 acs. for trans. of 8 pers.*

RICHARD WARD, 100 acs. in Varina, Henrico Co., 14 July 1637, p. 440. S. W. toward the 2 Mi. Cr., N. W. into the maine woods, Sly. upon land of JOHN BAKER & E. N. E. to the sd. Cr. 50 acs. due for his owne per. adv., & 50 acs. by purchase from BARTHOLOMEW FARTHING, to whom it was due for trans. of 1 servant called SARAH BREMAN.

ALICE EDLOE, 100 acs. Henrico Co., 14 July 1637, p. 441. Lying 2½ mi. above Harroe Attocks towards the falls on the same side of the River in a Sw. betwixt land belonging to WILLIAM COXE & 350 acs. graunted to sd. ALICE bounded W. by S. upon the maine river, E. by N. into the maine woods through sd. Sw., beg. 12 ft. on that side of a Cr. towards land of sd. COXE, running up the river & abutting her own land. Trans. of 2 pers: JOHN WILLIAMS, WILLIAM ATTAWAY.

ROBERT CRADDOCKE & JOHN DAVIS, 600 acs. Henrico Co., 15 Aug. 1637, p. 451. 300 acs. Nly. upon a great Sw., Sly. towards land of ALICE EDLOE, Widdowe, Wly. over the river & Ely. into the woods called the Longfeild & 300 acs. joyning upon the sd. Longfeild Nly. the land included in this pattent beg. next to land of sd. ALICE EDLOE. 300 acs. due by assignment from WILLIAM COOKE & RICHARD CARPENTER & 300 acs. for trans. of 6 pers.

Memord: That I JOHN BAUGH of Varina, planter, hath assigned unto WILLIAM COOKE & RICHARD CARPENTER all my rights and title that I have unto the land taken up by mee in this pattent being the 13th of June 1636. Signed: JOHN BAUGH. Witness: BENJ. CARRILL.

Memord: That wee WILLIAM COOKE & RICHARD CARPENTER, planters, doth assigne & sell unto JOHN DAVIS & ROBERT CRADDOCK of Harihatoxs, planters, all the right and title that wee the above named hath according unto this pattent. In witness thereof wee have sett our hands the 9th July 1637. Signed: WILLIAM COOKE, RICHARD CARPENTER. Witness: JOHN BAUGH. Page 452.

JOSEPH ROYALL, 300 acs. Henrico Co., 15 Aug. 1637, p. 452. At S. E. side of Turkey Island Cr., runing into the woods N. E. & to the mouth of the Cr. S. W. 50 acs. for his owne per. adv., 50 acs. for trans. of his first wife THOMASIN, 50 acs. for his now wife ANN, 50 acs. for his brother HENRY & 100 acs. for trans. of 2 pers: ROBERT WARWELL, JON. WELLS.

ELIZABETH PACKER, Widdowe, 950 acs. Henrico Co., 17 Aug. 1637, p. 454. E. upon 4 Mi. Cr., W. upon land of SETH WARD, S upon the river & N. into the woods. Due in right of her late husband Serjant WILLIAM SHARPE, & THOMAS PACKER, whoe at their own costs & charges trans. 19 pers: RICH. VASE, JOHN THOMAS, LEWIS JONES, LEONARD HOUGHTON, WILLIAM COOKE, PETER HUDSEY, EDWARD JONES, JON. WARD, WILLIAM WOOLEY, 2 Negroe servts. to Serjt. WM. SHARP. THOMAS BLANCKS, JACOB DEWITT, JOHN HAMAN, ANDREW PRATT, CHRIST. STEVENSON, CHRIST. BEARE, JON. SHADDOCK, FRANCIS STONE, servants to THO. PACKER. Note: Henrico County Index to Patents carried this name as PARKER.

Patent Book No. 1. Part II

ROBERT HOLLOM, 1000 acs. Henrico Co., 1 Nov. 1637, p. 491. Butting Sly. upon land of HANNAH BOYCE, Wly. upon the maine river, Nly. up towards the falls & Ely. up into the maine woods, being right opposite against fallen Cr. Trans. of 20 pers.*

WILLIAM COX, 150 acs. Henrico Co., 29 Oct. 1637, p. 492. About 2½ mi. above
Harrow Attocks W. by N. upon the maine river, Wly. upon the great Sw., Ely.
into the woods & Sly. towards Harrow Attocks. Trans. of 3 pers.*

THOMAS WHEELER, 200 acs. Chas. Cittie Co., 29 Sept. 1637, p. 495. Being a
neck of land between two creeks, E. upon the Cr. that parteth Weyanoke land
& W. upon Oldmans (or Old mans) Cr., N. upon the maine woods & S. upon land
of Mrs. PERRY. Due for trans. of 4 pers: JONE COLCHESTER, RICHARD PHILLIPPS
WILLIAM MATHERELL, WILLIAM BAKER.

ARTHUR BAYLY, 200 acs. Henrico Co., 16 Jan. 1637, p. 512. Over against the
upper end of Lord Island, Wly. on the river, Nly. towards the falls, Ely. in
to the woods & Sly. upon the uppermost Cr. next the falls. Trans. of 4 pers
HEN ROBINS, JON. DRINKWATER, JAMES EVANS, JONAS BOWERS.

ARTHUR BAYLY & THOMAS CROSBY, 800 acs. Henrice Co., 16 Jan. 1637, p. 512.
Sly. upon land of SAMUELL ALLMOND, W.y upon the river, Nly. towards the fall
& Ely. into the woods. Trans. of 16 pers: (ARTHUR BAYLY his servts:) JONAS
BOWERS, WM CALFE, JON. DUCH, WM. GREENE, MARY DOUBTY, JERIMIAH BURR, THO.
BUSBY, JON. HARRIS. (THOS. CROSBY his servts:) WILLI. RIDER, WM. RIDLY, RICH
CHILDS, ROBT. PHELPS, EDWARD EVANS, JON. BENNETT, WM. BARKER, CHARLES WHITE.
Note: CROSBYE assigned 400 acs. of this pattent to SAMUELL ALMOND.

ARTHUR BAYLY, 300 acs. Henrico Co., 15 Jan. 1637, p. 513. Bet. land of SAM-
UELL ALMOND & JAMES PLACE, bounded S. upon JAMES PLACE land, Wly. upon the
Riv., Nly. upon sd. ALMOND & Ely. into the woods. Due for his own per. adv.
& trans. of 5 pers: ARTHUR BAYLY, ROBERT SPINKE.*

Capt. THOMAS PAULETT, 2000 acs. Chas. Citty Co., 15 Jan. 1637, p. 514. Bound
ing to the River S., N. W. to the maine Ewd. to land of Capt. PERRY, W. upon
Berkeley hundred land & extending by the river side from herring Cr., to gut
of land deviding this from sd. Berkley hundred. Due for the per. adv. of
himself & brother CHIDDOCK PAULETT & trans. of 38 pers: JON. TRUSSELL, AND.
HORE, (or HOOE), EDW. SHIPPEY, THO. COX, WM. HAVERT, EVAN MORGAN, JON. LEW-
ELLIN, WALTER NICHOLS, JON. KING, PHI. MAJOR, JON. TOWELL, JON. LONG, RICH.
CARPENTER, JON. CUNINGHORM, JON. BELDAM, ELIZ. CLARKE, ELIAS TALLY, THO.
GREGORY, WM. COOPER, SUSAN HATE, WM. ROSE, DAVID FLOOD, PETER LOW, ROBT.
CHAPLYN.

ROBERT CRADOCK (CRADDOCK), 300 acs. Henrico Co., 29 May 1638, p. 537. Nly.
on a little Cr. towards Lilley Valley upon land of WILLIAM COX, & ISAAC
HUTCHINS & S. upon land of JOHN DAVIS. Trans. of 6 pers.*

ANN HALLOM, Widdow, & the heires of ROBERT HALLOM, dec'd., 1000 acs. Henric
Co., 6 May 1638, p. 547. Lying N. by E. into the woods, S. by W. upon the
river, W. by N. toward Bremo joyning land of Mr. RICHARD COCKE, E. by S.
toward Turkey Island Cr., joyning land of JOHN PRICE, etc. Due by bargain &
sale from ARTHUR BAYLY, Merchant.

ELIZABETH BALHASH, 300 acs. Henrico Co., 2 May 1638, p. 551. Within the 4 Mi. Cr. neare Curles, bounding S. by W. upon land of WILLIAM VINCENT. Due in part of 100 acs. granted by order of Ct. 9 Dec. 1636.

BRYAN SMITH, 140 acs. at Curles within Henrico Co., 2 May 1638, p. 552. Adj. land of THOMAS MARKHAM, and E. by S. into the woods. Due for the per. adv. of himself & wife & trans. of 1 servt.: JOHN LUPTON.

MATHEW PRICE, sonn & heire to JOHN PRICE, late of Va., Labourer, 150 acs. Henrico Co., upon Turkey Island Cr., 23 May 1638, p. 558. E. by S. upon sd. Cr., W. by N. toward Bremo, S. by W. upon land granted to his late father, now in possession of his mother ANN HALLOM, widdowe, towards the gr. river & N. by E. into the woods. Due in right of his father who had a pattent of 150 acs. granted 20 Feb. 1619, by Sir GEORG YEARDLY.

WALTER ASHTON, Gent., 590 acs. Chas. Citty Co., 26 July 1638, p. 578. Between land of Sherly hundred & land he purchased of NATHANIELL CAUSEY, Sly. upon WATKINS his Cr., Wly. upon the head of land of Sherly hundred. Due for the per. adv. of himself & his wife WARBOWE ASHTON & trans. of 10 pers: JAMES JEFFERSON, WILLIAM WARD, THOMAS SHEILD, RICHARD WILLIAMS, JON. WILLIAMS, WM. JOHNES, JOHN HOBBS, JOHN ESQUIRE, JON. ROBERTS, JOHN MACEY.

ELIZABETH GRAYNE, (or GRAYVE) Widdowe, 750 acs. Chas. Citty Co., 25 July 1638, p. 580. E. into the woods, W. upon the river, N. upon land of JOHN MORGAN, S. towards Doggins Cr., part of sd. land bounded with a br. of Turkey Island Cr. Due in right of trans. of 15 pers: ROWLAND GRAYNE, JAMES GRAYNE, NICH. CLIFFE, HEN. BENTLY, WILLIAM ROWLY, ROBERT HOLMAN, MARTHA FLUDD, JON. PARKER, ROBT. FUTE, FR. DOWNES, DANIELL ARRYE, JON. DOOBEES, SARAH KEELIN, JON. DALE, RICHARD FALCONER.

Capt. THOMAS HARRIS, 820 acs. comonly known by the name of the Long feild, Henrico Co., 25 Feb. 1638, p. 615. With Sw. & marsh, beg. at a little Cr. over against Capt. MARTIN, N. on the back side of the Sw., E. S. E. into the woods towards Bremo, W. N. W. on the maine river. 100 acs. for his own per. adv., 100 acs. for the per. adv. of his first wife ADRY HARRIS, as being Ancient Planters, & 620 acs. for trans. of 13 pers: WILLIAM PURNELL, JOHN GOOD-FRYE, JOHN SEARNE, THOMAS KEMP, RICHARD MASCOLL, NATH. MOORE, JOHN EDWARDS, ANN RIDLEY, WILLIAM JONES, THOMAS MORGAN, WILLIAM JONES, 2 Negroes - a man & a woman.

JOSEPH ROYALL, 200 acs. Chas. Citty Co., 4 May 1638, p. 631. In Diggs hundred & S. upon land of THOMAS OGGS. (Record incomplete.) Due for trans. of 4 pers: ROBERT WORNALL, JOHN WELLS. THO. SWIFT, RALPH HIGSON.

ALICE EDLOE, Widdowe, 150 acs. at Harrow Attocks, Henrico Co., 24 Sept. 1638, p. 599. W. upon the river, N. to a little creek over against Kingaland, adj. Sly. upon land of GEORG BOATE, due for trans. of 3 pers: THOMAS PONDER (or POUDER), GEORGE PHILLIPPS, MARY BILLAN.

9

MATHEW GOUGH, Gent., 350 acs., Henrico Co., July 25, 1639, page 658. W. upon the river, & S. on land of BALHASH. 100 acs. part formerly granted to WILLIAI VINCENT, deceased. Due in right of trans. of 7 pers: of whom only the following names appear: WILLIAM MORGAN, FRANCIS DERRICK, NICHOLAS NETT, MATHEW GOUGH.

HENRY PERRY, 2,000 acs. known by the name of Buckland, Chas. City Co., extending from the head of Herring Cr. unto the old mans Cr. and so high as it ebbeth and floweth up these creeks. March 9, 1639, page 702. Son & heir of Capt. WILLIAM PERRY, late of Va., deceased. Bequeathed to sd. HENRY PERRY by will of his father dated Aug. 1, 1637. Granted to Capt. WILLIAM PERRY by order of court dated Sept. 19, 1633, and also by pattent to said HENRY dated 18 Dec. 1637.

RICHARD COCKE, Gent., 2,000 acs. Henrico Co., Mar. 10, 1639, page 707. To be augmented, etc. 300 acs. lying at Bremo, E. & S. upon Turkie Island, S. by W. upon the river, W. by N. upon Curles, etc. 1700 acs. upon the head of Turkey Island Cr. called by the name of Mamburne hills, etc. W. by N. upon land of Mrs. HALLOM, etc. Formerly granted sd. COCKE by patent dated March 8, 1636, 1,000 of which 3,000 acs. was surrendered unto ANN HALLOM, widow of ROBERT HALLOM. The sd. 2,000 acs. due by order of Ct. 1 Dec. 1639, and also due in right of trans. of 40 pers: MORRICE ROSE, THOMAS PERSON, SYMON MORLEY, a Negro woman, ELLIS GARGAME, VALLENTINE FLETCHER, WM. ROGERS, THO. LOWE, JOHN MARLIN, DANIELL EVANS, ANN BURFOOTE, RICHARD HILL, ANTH. WAMBLIN (or WANKLIN), ERASMUS HARRISON, JOHN HEARNE, JOANE ELYE, JOHN ANDREWES, WILLIAM WHITE, JOHN JONES, HUMPHRY BURGHER, HENRY PANDLE, THOMAS WILLIAMS, WILLIAM HARRIS, ROGER CHAPMAN, NICHOLAS OLIVER, JOHN COOKE, THOMAS PARCROFT, MARGARETT POWELL, MARY LUFFE, WILLIAM HASTINGS, ISAAC HORTON, GEORG HARRISON, JOHN SMITH, JAMES TOMPSON, JOHN HUETT, ROBERT CHEYNEY, JOHN SHORE, KATHERINE SHORE, JONAS SHORE, RICHARD COOKE.

SAMUELL ALMOND (ALLMOND), 600 acs. Henrico Co., 16 Mar. 1639, p. 711. 200 acs. beg. at the cleare feild upon the E. side of the river over against the Lower Island about 2 mi. below the falls &c., running downward towards JAMES PLACE his devdt.: 400 acs. Sly. upon said land, W. upon the river, N. towards the falls & E. into the woods. 200 acs. graunted to him by pattent dated 21 Nov. 1637 & due for his owne per. adv. & trans. of 3 pers., & 400 acs. by bargain & sale from THOMAS CROSBY, 26 Feb. 1638, to whom it was graunted 16 Jan. 1637 & due for trans. of 8 pers. The following names appear: SAMUELL ALMOND, WILLIAM WOOD, BARNABY RICHESON, MILES COOKE, WILLIAM RIDER, EDWARD EVANS, WILLIAM RIDLEY, JOHN BENNETT, RICHARD CHILDS, WILLIAM BARKER, ROBERT PHELPS, CHARLES WHITE.

HENRY PERRY, Gent., son & heir of Capt. WILLIAM PERRY, Esqr., late of Va., deceased, 3,500 acs. Charles Citty Co., known by the name of Buckland, May 10, 1642, Page 771. Being a neck of land bet. the old mans Cr. & Herring Cr. rising into the woods as farr as said Creeks ebb and flowe, as alsoe 227 acs. of Sunken Marsh and Swampe. 2,000 acs. thereof bequeathed to him by his father, Aug. 5, 1637. 1,500 acs. by assignment from GEORG MINIFIE, esqr., of his right for trans. of 30 pers: HUGH FORSHEW, JOHN THOMAS, HUGH SEAVER, JOHN WEAVER, RICHARD NEWMAN, THO. LISLE, JAMES SMITH, GEO. ABRAHAM, ROBERT BARWOOD, WM. COOKE, PATRICK CANE (or CAVE), JOHN GARRETT, RICHARD FLOOD, RALPH HARRINGTON, WILLIAM HANCE, JOHN SALTREA, RICHARD WILLIAMS, RICHARD OWEN. 12 Negroes bought of Sr. JOHN HARVEY, Knt., Anno 1639. (Marginal note: These in the Shipp Dove of London Capt. BICKING Mr. (Master) 1638.

THOMAS CROSBY, of Curles Planter, 400 acs. to SAMUELL ALMOND, Feb. 26, 1638, page 712. One half of patent taken up by sd. CROSBY & ARTHUR BAYLY, of Curles, Merchant, in Henrico Co., S. upon ALLMOND, W. upon the river, & N. towards the falls. Witnesses: RICHARD COCKE & CHRISTOPHER BRANCH.

BRYANT SMITH, 100 acs. Henrico Co., Oct. 10, 1641, Page 783. Bounded W. upon the river, E. into the woods, S. on Capt. HARRIS' land & N. on ANTHONY BODYES land. Trans. of 2 pers: NICHOLAS PERKINS, GRINGALL DELAYHAYE.

JOSEPH ROYALL, 600 acs., Aug. 20, 1642, Page 790. Bounding on the land of EDWARD MADDEN above Sherley hundred, N. & by E. on the river to Dockmans Cr., adj. DANIELL LEWELLIN W. & by N. Trans. of 12 pers: RALPH HEXON, THOMAS SWEFT, HENRY SMITH, KATHERINE his wife, JOHN GUILHAM, MARTHA JACOB, NOWELL HURIM, ANN COLE, STAFFORD BARLOW, THOMAS GUILHAM.

JOHN DAVIS, 200 acs. Henrico Co., last of Oct. 1642, Page 842. Adj. his former patent called the Longfeild, extending N. W. towards land of CORNELIUS DE HULL. Due for trans. of his wife MARY DAVIS, and 3 servts: JON. DEVALL, JON. TALBOTT, JON. COX.

CORNELIUS DE HULL, Oct. 31, 1642, p. 842. 502 acs. known as Lilley Valley, beg. next to Mrs. EDLOS Swamp, near his own land & S. E. upon JOHN DAVIS. S. W. to the river, ending neare a place called the Seaven ———— . 250 acs. of this land was granted to WILLIAM COX in 1637. Trans. of 10 pers: THOMAS BLACKSTON, RICHARD BIRD, RICHARD HEWES, JAMES DUPEN, MARY HOWTREE, JON. DODD, ROBERT HAYES, SAMLL. WATERHOWSE, WALTER JONES, WM. THOMAS.

DANIELL LEWELLYN, Gent., 856 acs., the Northermost part beg. above Mrs. HEYMAN, N. on upper branches of Turkey Island Cr. & S. on the head of Mr. ASTONS land. The Southermost part extending on Mr. ASTON & W. upon JOSEPH ROYALL bet. Dockmans Cr. & Sherly hundred. Trans. of 17 pers: MICHAELL PEACOCK, CHARLES EDGAR, THO. MORGAN, JAMES FOSTER, ROBERT HOPPS, TEGO FRAYLE, HEN. HITCHCOX, ROBERT WARD, THO. RICHARDSON, THO. TAYLOR, MARKE CHETON, MARY DAVIS, JOHN TALBOTT, JOHN DEVALL, ROBERT HALLOME, FRANCES HALLOME, ELIZA. JACKSON. PAGE 845. Oct. 27, 1642.

SETH WARD, 350 acs. Henrico Co., Nov. 22, 1643, Page 946. N. N. W. up the 2 mi. Cr., S. S. W. over against Varina, E. S. E. upon 3 Myle Swamp, extending towards 4 Myle Cr. & bounded at the end with a running brook called roundabout. 150 acs. by former patent, 50 acs. by purchase from JNO BAKER & 150 acs. for trans. of 3 pers: JNO. WILKESON, ROBT. FLEETE, JNO. MILLER.

WALTER ASTON, Gent., 1,040 acs. Charles City Co., Aug. 12, 1646, Page 78. 200 acs. near Sherley Hundred, S. upon a cr. formerly called Wattkins Cr., E. upon HUGH COXE, dec'd. & W. upon land where sd. ASTON now lives. 500 acs. upon Wattkins Cr., W. upon Sherlye Hundred & E. upon land formerly belonging to NATHA. CAUSESEY, but now in possession of sd. ASTON; 250 acs. on the great river, E. on CAUSEYS plantation, S. upon Capt. EPPS' land in the island & N. on land of ROBERT PARTIN. 200 acs. by patent dated Dec. 10, 1620 unto NATHA. CASSEY & due ASTON by purchase from JOHN CASSEY by bill of sale Feb. 7, 1634; 590 acs. by patent for the per. adv. of himself & his wife WARBOWE & trans. of 10 pers.* 250 acs. the residue for trans of 5 pers.*

JOHN CAWSEY, Planter, of Chas. City in Va., unto WALTER AUSTON, Gent. of CAUSES Cleare, by estimation 200 acs. neare Sherley hundred, S. upon HENRY WATKINS Cr., N. upon the main land, E. upon the Company land & W. upon land of ROBERT BROWN. Consideration: 1,000 wt. of Tobacco & 1 cowe already to him delivered. Feb. 7, 1634, Page 78. Signed JOHN CAWSEY. Witnesses: RICHARD MILTON, DANIELL LUELLIN.

Mr. STEPHEN HAMELIN, 1250 acs. Chas. City Co., 26 Oct. 1650, p. 266. Lyeing at the head of Weyonoke, bounded S. upon the heads of Wionoke, E. upon Matshcoes (or Matsrwes ?) Cr. & land of Mr. CANTRELL, W. towards old mans Cr. and Queens Cr. Due sd. HAMBLIN for trans. of 25 pers: JOHN RAY, HENRY RICE, ARTH. CHANDLER, WM. PYLAR, WM. CHELDNEDGE, RICHARD ARUNDELL, THOMAS MASON, GEORGE HAYNES, SAMLL. PARRY, THOMAS POWELL, PETER MASON, WM. HURT, THO. HOWELL, SAMLL. GOODWIN, THOMAS HARRIS, ROBERT TAYLOR, THO. UP RICHARD (AP), JONAS ALPOTT, JOHN WOODSON, EDWARD BUCKINGHAM, ROBERT FRYTH, JAB. ROBINSON, CLEMENT WHIDOW, ROBERT CROUCH, EDWARD THURSTON,

DANIELL LUELLIN 270 acs. Chas. City Co., 26 Oct. 1650, p. 268. Lyeing on the head of Shirty (Shirly) hundred commonly known by the name of Richard Levell, bounded W. upon the head of Shirly hundred, E. by S. upon land of Mr. WALTER ASTON & upon a former devdt. of his own. Trans. of 6 pers: EDWARD SHEPPARD, SAM. PIDISTON, EDWARD BAKER, FRA. CLARKE, KATH. ALLEN. WM. BREMAN, JOHN BULL, WM. SUCKER. (Note: The last 2 names enclosed in brackets.)

DANIELL LUELLIN, 956 acs. June 4, 1645, Page 95. The Northermost part. beg. above Mrs. HEYMANS, N. on the up. branches of Turkey Is. Cr., S. on the head of Mr.ASTONS land; the Southermost part extending on Mr. ASTONS land & W. upon JOSEPH RYALLS bet. Dockham Cr. & Shirley Hundred; 100 acs. in Sherley Hundred, adj. ROBERT BOURNE & JOHN HARRIS. 100 acs. purchased of ROBERT PARTIN, the elder, granted sd. PARTIN Feb. 20, 1619, & conveyed by ROBERT PARTIN THE elder & ROBERT PARTIN the younger, his sonn, unto sd. LUELLIN by deed dated Apr. 13, 1642. The residue by former patent for trans. of 17 pers.*

Capt. THOMAS STEGG, son & heir of THOS. STEGG, Esqr., dec'd., 1698 acs. Chas.
City Co., 24 Nov. 1653, p. 7. 1,000 acs. part thereof being a neck of land
lying upon the N. side of the old man's Cr. & upon Queens Cr. & 698 acs. at
the head of Queens Cr. between Seder (or Seller) Run & Fishing Run. 1,000
acs. formerly granted unto his deceased father & descended unto him as sonn
& heir, & residue by order of the Quarter Court (blank) as alsoe for trans.
of 14 pers.*

WILLIAM JOHNSON, 550 acs. Henrico Co., 1? Mar. 1653, p. 11. On the N. side
of the river, known by the name of Harrahadocks, beg. next to land of Capt.
EDLOE, thence. S. S. E., thence W. S. W. to the river, thence as the river
bayeth to the place of beg. Trans. 11 pers: ED. ELTON, ELIZ. PATTENT, MARY
FRANKLIN, KATH. PRICE, JON. PHILPOT, JON. CARTER, JON. MAYDEN, DANLL. BERRY,
JON. WOOD, THO. LOCK, JAMES HUMPHRY.

Capt. DANIEL LUELLIN, 200 acs. lying in or neer Sherly hundred, which was
late in possession of EDWARD GARDNER, dec'd, bounding E. into the woods, W.
upon the river, N. upon 40 acs. purchased of EDWARD MADDIN, and S. upon
land lately belonging to serjeant JOHN HARRIS. Sd. land formerly granted
unto sd. LUELLIN by order of the Quarter Court dated —— and alsoe for trans.
of 4 pers: JON. WHITE, GEO. MIDLEMORE. 11 July 1653, p. 26.

Mr. RICHARD COCKE, 2,482 acs. Henrico Co., 10 Oct. 1652, p. 133. On N. side
of James River; 1860 acs. near head of Turkey Is. Cr., bounded from corner
tree of JOHN PRICE S. by W. &c. to head of Mr. HALLAMS land &c. 622 acs.
commonly called by the name of Bremo, bounded along the heads of Capt. HARRIS'
land & other devdts. belonging to Curles, N. & by E., thence along the Cart
Path, along Mr. HALLAMS land to the river &c. 100 acs. due by patent to
TEMP. BAYLEY, 20 Sept. 1620; 2,000 acs. by patent to sd. COCKE 10 Mar. 1639;
& residue for trans of —— pers: CORNEL.CANADIA, NEALE WHITE, LUCE DAVIS,
DAVID CLOBE, WILLM. SHOEMAKER, ROBERT BOANE, MEREDITH LANGFORD, HUMPH MILES.

JOHN GREENHOUGH, 400 acs. Henrico Co., on E. side of James Riv., known by the
name of Smiths Bay, 6 Dec. 1652, p. 143. From the Riv. alongst THOMAS MARK-
HAMS devdt., toward four mile Cr. &c. Trans. of 8 pers: EDWARD PALMER, WM.
WRIGHT, JOHN LUPTON, LUKE ANWELL, JAMES DOBBS, SAM. FUER, FRA. STREETE, JOHN
GREENHOUGH.

Mr. WILLIAM FRY, 750 acs. near the head of Chichamony Riv., on S. W. side
thereof, 7 Apr. 1653, p. 192. Beg. at Fleets quarter includeing a small indian feild &c., Trans. of 15 pers: GILES CARTER, RALPH SPENDLOWE, JANE WALKER,
MILES NOBLE, ANNE WILLIAMS, WILLIAM BROOKE, RALPH BURTON, ANDREW MILLER, ALICE
ARCHER, the sd. FRY's wife & his three children; DOROTHY MILLER, WM. HOCCADIE.

Capt. DANIEL LUELLEN, 636 acs. Chas. City Co., 10 Mar. 1655, p. 379. 270

acs. on the head of Sherly hundred, commonly known by the name of rich Level:
E. upon land of Mr. WALTER ASTON, & N. upon his own land; & 200 acs. in or
near Shirly hundred, which was in possession of EDWARD GARDNER, dec'd., N.
upon 40 acs. of land purchased of EDWARD MADISON, & S. upon land lately belonging to Serjant JOHN HARRIS; 63 acs. in Sherly hundred, beg. at land of s(
LUELLINS, lately purchased of ROBT. PARTIN, Senr. & ROBT. PARTIN, Junr., &
sold to Mr. JOHN MEARES; 63 acs. another part being in Sherly hundred or Bermuda hundred, lately belonging to MICHAEL TURPIN; 43 acs. next to land latel;
belonging unto JOSEPH ROYALL, dec'd., next towards Sherly hundred maine. 27(
acs. by patent dated 26 Oct. 1650; 200 acs. by patent, 11 July 1653; 63 acs.
purchased of DOROTHY BAKER, the relict of JOHN BAKER; 63 acs. purchased of
MICHAEL TURPIN; 40 acs. purchased of EDWARD MADDIN. All of which several pa:
cels were ordered to be included in one patent.

### Patent Book No. 4

Col. EDWD. HILL. 2476 acs. Chas. City Co., 8 Dec. 1660, p. ——, (450). 416
acs. lying in Shirley Hundred, bounded S. on the swamp that parts *** Island,
E. on Mrs. ASTON, N. on JOSEPH ROYALL & W. on the main river. The following
names and places are mentioned in this record, which is badly mutilated: JOHN
MEERES, Cameages Cr., Mrs. ASHTON, —— LEWELLIN, Turkey Island Cr., Mrs HAYMAN
land. 316 acs. by purchase; 850 acs. deserted by JOHN MEERES was granted to
sd. HILL 3 Oct. 1659, by order of the Quarter Ct., & due for trans. of 17
pers.* The residue likewise due for trans. of 26 pers.*

THOMAS LUDWELL, Esqr., 961 acs., 1 furlong & 26 perches, being an irregular
tract known by the name of Timber Slash, Henrico Co., 16 June 1663, p. 103
(599). Beg. at cor. tree between Mr. COCKE & Mr. CREWES, hard by a Cart path
&c., E. by the 4 Mi. Cr. &c. W. up on land of THOMAS TAYLOR, E. by land of
BRYAN SMITH &c. Trans. of 20 pers: PHILL. LUDWELL, WM. BROADRIB, WM. DRAKE-
FORD, ANN DRAKEFORD, WM. HUGHLETT, ROBT. JARRETT, RICH. CROME, RICH. TALBOT,
2 Negroes; THO. BARTON, JAMES DUCKETT, ROGER HEYWOOD, ROBT. WARD, JOHN VENNE,
DAN. CORMACKE, HUGH BERRY, RALPH PARKSON, SETH DOBSON.

Mr. JOHN BEAUCHAMP, 65 acs. Henrico Co., 9 Mar. 1664, p. 110 (607). N. side
of James Riv., bet. land of THOMAS MARKHAM & land formerly belonging to ED-
WARD BALLHASH, E. on land of Mr. COCKE & S. on his own land. The following
names appear under this record: ANTHONY BRIDGMAN, WM. TOMKINS.

### Patent book No. 5

JOHN COX, 550 acs. Henrico Co., on N. side of the Riv., known by the name of
Harristocks, beg. next to land of Capt. EDLOE. 29 Mar. 1665, p. 164, (44).
Granted to ARTHUR BAYLY, who sold to WM. JOHNSON, by whom it was assigned to
sd. COX.

JNO. GREENHOUGH, 400 acs. on E. side of James Riv., in Henrico Co., 5 Aug.
1665, p. 215, (119). Commonly called & known by the name of Smiths Bay;

bounded from the river into the woods along THOMAS MARKHAMS devdt., E. &c.
towards 4 mi. Cr. Renewal of patent dated 6 Dec. 1652.

WM. HUMPHRIES, 200 acs. Chas. City Co., 18 Mar. 1662, p. 218, (125). Upon
Ely side of Turkey Island Cr. opposite to the great or long meadow. Trans.
of 4 pers: THO. HUMPHRIES, WM. HUMPHRIES, FRA. HUMPHRIES, EDWARD WARD (or
WARE).

GEO. BULLINGTON, 503 acs. Henrico Co., 21 June 1664, p. 224, (133). On N.
side of James Riv., beg. at THOMAS FEELDS Cr. Trans. of 10 pers: JAMES CREWS,
JNO. TOMSON, MARY HUFFE, WM. HARDING, ELIZ. ARNELL, WM. ENGLISH, Negro,
MARGARET, ELIZ. HART, EDW. COOKE.

THOMAS TAYLOUR, 281 acs. Henrico Co., 20 Mar. 1662, p. 237, (155). N. side
of James Riv., commonly called Harrahatocks, over against Kings land, bounded
from the Riv. a little below the Orchard by land of Mr. ARTHUR BAYLY &c. granted to MATHEW EDLOW 8 Dec. 1653 & by him assigned to sd. TAYLOUR.

THOMAS STEGG, 1280 acs. on N. side of James Riv., 25 Jan 1663, p. (200). Beg.
about a mile above the falls, running into the woods N. by E. 320 perches to a
slash named Woodwards labour &c. Trans. of 26 pers.*

DANIELL CLARKE, 1698 acs. Chas. City Co., 28 Jan. 1662, p. 280, (233). 1000
acs. being a neck of land lying between Old Mans Cr. on N. Ely. side & Queens
Cr. on the Sly. side; 698 acs. at the head of Queens Cr. between Seller run &
fishing run in Charles Co. Granted to Capt. THO. STEGG, 24 Nov. 1653 & by him
sold to sd. CLARKE.

Major WM. HARRIS, 450 acs. Henrico Co., 22 Jan. 1663, p. 304, (278). N. side
of James Riv., Ewdly. side of the Poplar Cr. & Ewdly. run of 4 Mi. Cr. & called by the name of Slashes, bounded S. on the head of land formerly in possession of DANLL. LEWELLIN, E. on Maborne hills & S. W. on land of BRIAN SMITH.
Trans. of 9 pers: MORGAN WILLIAMS, ADAM ROSSE, MARGARY FORGOTT, MARY BOURNE,
NICH. GYLES, THO. DEERE, WM. BLACKMAN, MARGT. FLOYD, ANN GAY.

JOHN FEILD, 400 acs. Henrico Co., known by the name of Cham, 24 Mar. 1662/3,
p. 338, (344). Bounded from Almonds Cr. "upwards to Chenck Cr. or farther
soe far forth as the land shall extend upwards towards the falls of James
River." Being part of 1000 acs. granted to JOHN WHITE, by him sold to THO.
FRY & by the sd. FRY his Exors. sold to sd. FEILD.

Mr. JOHN BEAUCHAMP & Mr. RICHARD COCKE, Sr., 2994 A., 2 R., 35 p. 2093 acs.
part on S. side of Chickahomeny Sw., running S. &c. to a run called Col. Owins
Quarter, W. by S. to a run above the Pamunkey path &c. over the run called
Cow taile Quarter &c. 901 acs. 1 rod in Henrico Co., on N. side of James Riv.
known by the name of the forke of the Cattaile Run & bounded N. & by W. to
the head of land formerly surveyed for Mr. RICH. COCK, Sr., along his line
over the Western br. W. S. W. &c. to line of Mr. GREENE &c. 21 June 1664, p.
367, (399). Trans of 60 pers: CORN. CANIDA, NEALE WHITE, LUCY DAVIS, DAVID

15

GLOAD, WM. SHEWMAKER, ROBT. BROWNE, MARY DETH LANGFORD, JOHN ELKES, JNO.
GUNTER, JNO. BEACHAMP, WM. ANDREWS, HENRY BULLOCKE, HUMPH. MILES (or MILLS),
RICH. HAYWARD, JNO. PARKE, WM. PARTRIDGE, ELIZ. BRIDGES, RABECCA MOORE, ROBT.
SHERLY, RICH. DENNIS, HENRY ———, JNO. SANDERS, TIMOTHY ISAR, ROBT. MARSH.
WM. RAMSEY, SAMLL. KNIBB, GEO. PRICE, ESTER BARFEILD, HENRY WATKINS, KATH.
SMITH, WM. BALDIN, JAMES FOSTER, JNO. HINE (or HIND), ROBERT ———, ANN THOMP-
SON, SIMON OWIN, JNO. MYLES, SALSBURY LAND, GEO. HINTON, ED. LESTER, JNO.
SMITH, HENRY FLAG, OWIN DAVIS, WM. LOWDER, JAMES HICKMAN, WM. COXON, MARY
CREWS, MARGERY BAKER, EDW. CRUMP, WM. WALKNER, MARGERY SPENCER, MARY SOTONE,
DANLL. JORDAN, ANN JORDAN, GILBERT JONES, CLEMT. BAYLY, THO. GULLY, RICHARD
VARLING, PHILL. SPARKES, THO. READ.

THO. LIGON, & Capt. WM. FARRAR, 375 acs. Henrico Co., 3 Oct. 1664, p. 376,
(416). N. side of James Riv., beg. at the Round about slash, adj. MORGAN
PRICE, & running through another br. of sd. slash W. N. W. &c. Trans. of 8
pers: WALTER FELKES, SAM. RIGOT, ELLINOR WALLIS, JAMES HICKSON, ANN ARME-
STRONG, JONE DAVIS, THO. PELDON, WM. DODSON.

DAVID JONES, 479 acs. 2 R., & 19 P. with marsh adj., at the upper end of Weynock in Chas. City Co., 20 Oct. 1665, p. 434, (516)..N. side of James Riv.,
beg. at a stake that parts JOSEPH HARWOOD & DAVID JONES, S. by E. along the
marsh &c. to a br. that runs in Kittawan Cr., W. to sd. Riv., S. S. W. along
same &c. 279 A., 2 R., & 19 P. due & confirmed unto sd. JONES by order of
the Gen'll. Ct. dated 16 Sept. 1663, & 200 acs. for trans. of 4 pers: "BRINE
of Channell," MARY GOSLING, GEORGE HOUGHTON, JAMES GRAUNT.

JOSEPH HARWOOD, 42 A., 2 R., & 25 P., Chas. City Co., 20 Oct. 1665, p. 435,
(518). N. side of James Riv. in Weynock, beg. at a stake that parts HAMMON
WOODHOUSE, sd. HARWOOD, N. by W. 294 po. to Kittawan Br. &c., also another
parcell of land in sd. Co. & belonging to the bounds of Weynock conteyning 120
acs. beg at the river, extending into the woods E. ½ Nly.; 240 po., abutting
FARDINANDO FUSTINS land &c. Said land due & confirmed unto sd. HARWOOD by
order of the Genl. Ct. dated 16 Sept. 1663.

JOHN TATE, 80 acs. Chas. City Co., 20 Oct. 1665, p. 435, (518). N. side of
James Riv., & along line that parts this & land of PETER PLUMMER, N. &c. Due
& confirmed &c. as above.

RICHARD & HENRY BLANKES, 150 acs. at the mouth of Queens Cr., in Chas. City
Co., 20 Oct. 1665, p. 436, (519). N. side of James Riv., along same N. by W.
&c. to the cleare gound, N. W. 20 po. N. to the house of sd. RICHARD & HENRY
BANKS 9 po., then up the Cr. E. &c. Due & confirmed by order &c. dated Sept.
1663.

THOMAS CHAPPLE (CHAPLE), 80 acs. Chas. City Co., 20 Oct. 1665, p. 436, (520).
N. side of James Riv. & N. side of Kittawan Cr., beg. at a line parting this
& land of JNO. TATE, into the woods N. &c. Due & confirmed as above.

16

HAMMON WOODHOUSE, 42 A., 2 R., & 25 P. in Chas. City Co., 20 Oct. 1665, p. 436, (521). N. side of James Riv. in Weynock, beg. at a stake parting this, land of THO. CABLE & MARGTT. HOES (HUES-HIVES?), N. by W. to sd. br. &c. Due & confirmed as above.

DANIELL CLARKE, Gent., 2029 A., 2 R. & 20 P., Chas. City Co., 25 July 1665, p. 440, (525). 1000 acs. being a neck, lying in between Old Mans Cr. on the Nly. side & Queens Cr. on the Sly. side, crossing the head thereof, running N. Wly. &c; 698 acs. at the head of sd. Cr. between Sellar run & Fishing run; & 331 A., 2 R., & 20 P. on N. side of James Riv., at the lead of his own land, beg. on Sellar run, running W. along the head to nere the ponds of the Old Mans Cr. run, then N. &c. 1698 acs. granted to Capt. THOMAS STEGG, Esqr., 24 Nov. 1653, assigned to sd. CLARKE & granted to him 28 Jan. 1662 & the residue for trans. of 7 pers: PETER HARDING, WM. STEVENS, MARY STONE, ANTHONY KNOTT, JNO. GOFFE, THO. WHITE, MARIA a Negro.

Capt. THOMAS STEGG, 1850 acs. Henrico Co., according to ancient bounds thereof, 29 Dec. 1663, p. 441, (528). Granted to Capt. MATHEW GOFFE & lately found to escheat as by inquisition &c.

Mr. JNO. KNOWLES, 100 acs. Henrico Co., according to ancient bounds thereof, 30 Dec. 1663, p. 441, (528). Granted to Capt. MATHEW GOFFE, dec'd. & lately found to escheat, etc. (as above).

JOHN BROWNE & EDWARD HATCHER, 500 acs. Henrico Co., according to the ancient bounds thereof, 30 Dec. 1663, p. 446, (534). Granted unto JAMES PLACE & lately found to escheat to his Majestie as by inquisition dated 5 Sept. 1663 & now granted the abovenamed who hath made their composition to bee paid paid according to act.

ROBERT EVANS, 80 acs. in Weynock in Chas. City Co., 20 Oct. 1665, p. 461, (559). N. side of James Riv. & N. side of Kittawan Cr., beg. at a line parting THOMAS CHAPPLE & ROBT. EVANS, running into the woods N. &c. Said land due & confirmed by order of the Genll. Court 16 Sept. 1663.

ROBERT EVANS, 41 acs. & 23 po. in Weynock in Chas. City Co., 20 Oct. 1665, p. 461, (559). N. side of James Riv., beg. at a stake parting FRANCIS RADFORD & ROBT. EVANS, running N. by W. &c. Due & confirmed as above.

Same. 60 acs., 3 R., & 9 P., same location, date & page, (560). Beg. at a stake parting THOMAS CABLE & ROBERT EVANS, running N. by W. to Kittawan, then W. &c. Due as above.

WM. & JAMES LAWRENCE(LAURENCE), 95 A., 16 P., Chas. City Co., at the lower end of Weynock, next to land formerly known to bee WM. CLAYES on N. side of James Riv., 20 Oct. 1665, p. 462, (560). Beg. at a stake by the Persimon Island Sw. & running N. by W. to Kittawan Cr., thence W. N. W. &c. Due &c. as above.

PETER PLUMMER (PLUMER), 80 acs. Chas. City Co., 20 Oct. 1665, p. 462, (561).
N. side of James Riv. & on N. of Kittawan Cr., beg. at a line that parts RICE
HOE & sd. PLUMMER, running into the woods N. &c. Due &c. as above.

WILLIAM HUNT, 346 acs. 1 R., 4 P., Chas. City Co., 21 Mar. 1665/6, p. 471,
(574). Beg. at a pochikery marked with 4 chops by a small Indian feild about
a mile from the river on the N. side, adj. JNO. STIFF, running W. &c. Trans.
of 7 pers: ITALY HOPKINS, JNO. PENNULL, JNO. SHORNE, JNO. TAYLOR, JANE LONG,
EDMOND JENKINS, GEORG MEDLY.

JNO. BURTON, 700 acs. Henrico Co., 22 Mar. 1665/6, p. 479, (585). 300 acs.
Nly. on a great swamp, Sly. towards land of ALICE EDLOWE, Widdow, Wly. over
the river & Ely. into the woods, called by the name of the old feild; 300 acs.
another parte joyning on the head of the Long feild pattent, beg. at a white
oake marked 4 wayes at the extent of the deviding line of JNO. BURTON & JNO.
DAVIES running along the greate slash S. E. by S. &c. 600 acs. granted to
ROBT. CRADDOCK & by HOELL PRISE, his Atty., sould unto JNO. COX, who assigned
to sd. BURTON, & 100 acs. due for trans. of 2 pers: ANN COLEMAN, MARK WMS.
(WILLIAMS).

DAVID LUELLIN (LEWELLIN), 636 acs. Chas. Citty Co., 15 May 1666, p. 518,(635).
270 acs. commonly knowne by the name of Rich Levell, bounding W. upon the
head of Shirly Hundred, E. & S. upon land of Mr. WALTER ASHTON & N. upon his
own land; 200 acs. in or neare Shirly Hundred, which was late in the possession of EDWARD GARDNER, dec'd., bounding W. upon the River, N. upon 40 acs.
purchased of EDWARD MADDIN & S. upon land lately belonging to Serj. JNO.
HARRIS; 63 acs. in Shirly hundred, beg. at land sd. LUELLIN lately purchased
of ROBT. PARTIN, Sr. & ROBT. PARTIN, Jr. & sould to Mr. JNO. MERES; 63 acs.
another parte in Shirly or Burmody hundred lately belonging to Mr. MICHAELL
TURPIN; 40 acs. being next to and lately belonging to JOSEPH ROYALL, dec'd.,
next towards Shirly hundred. Granted unto Capt. DANLL. LUELLIN, dec'd., 10
Mar. 1665, & now become due sd. DANLL. as son & heire.

WM. JUSTICE, 21 A., 2 R., 11 P., in Weynock in Chas. Citty Co., on N. side of
James Riv., 20 Oct. 1665, p. 537, (657). Beg. at a stake parting his own &
land of MARGARETT HEWES, running N. by W. 300 po. then S. W. along Kittawan
Br. &c. Being due & confirmed by order of the Genll. Ct. etc. dated 16 Sept.
1663.

JOHN CANNON, 80 acs. upon Kittawan Cr. on the back of Weynock in Chas. Citty
Co., on N. side of James Riv., 20 Oct. 1665, p. 537, (658). Running along
head line of DAVID JONES N. &c. Due & confirmed as above.

THOMAS STEGG, Merchant, 1,000 acs. Chas. City Co., — 18th, 1640, page 694.
Being a neck of land between the old mans Cr. & Queens Cr. on the Sly. side,
etc. 200 acs. being formerly granted unto THOMAS WHEELER & later assigned
unto PATRICK KANNADAY, Mariner, by JAMES TURNER & THOMAS HARRIS, assignees &
attorneys of sd. WHEELER, & by KANNADAY to STEGG. Due by order of court dated

Oct. 15, 1640 & for trans. of 8 pers: RICHARD HOW, RICHARD JAMES, THOMAS
ROBINSON, JOHN GULTON, SILVESTER WARD, THO. BESSEN, (or BEFFEN), THO. OLIVER,
RICHARD RICROFT, RICH. HASLEWOOD, GEORG POTTEETE, THO. PATTMAN, NICH. WOOFED,
WILLI. FANELL, HUMPHRY CHAPMAN, ROWLAND DEMSON, THO. PENTON. P.B. 1 - Part II.

WALTER ASTON, Gent. 250 acs. Chas. Citty Co., p. 12. (No date.) W. on the
great river, E. on the plantation of Causeys Care (Cleare?), S. on land of
Capt. EPPS (in the island) & N. on land of ROBERT MARTYN, Granted by order
of court 15 Oct. 1641 & alsoe due for trans. of 5 pers: JOHN BAILY, JOHN
BULL, HEN. BRADSHALL, ELIZA. VAUGHAN, JUDITH SETTLE. (By WM. BERKLEY.) P.B.
No. 2.

FIRDINANDO AUSTIN, 1200 acs. Chas. City Co., 25 Feb. 1653, p. 369. On N.
side of James Riv. & E. side of Queens Cr., Ely. on Moses run, S. on Mr. HORS-
MANDINE & Mr. HAMBLIN. Trans. of 24 pers: JOHN SMITH, JAMES COCKRUM, DAN.
VALKER, EDWARD SMITH, WM. ROGERS, THOMAS WILKES, WILLIAM BROWN, FERD. AUSTIN,
JOS. ALCOCK, FRA. ALLEN, JONE ——, ALLESTER ——, THO. GREGORY, JA. GREG-
ORY, THO. KELWAY, MARGT. LEGG, PETER BERRARD, THOMAS ——, JOHN GRIFFEN,
JONE IRISH, TEAGUE ALLEN, JONE BRISTOLL, THOMAS GREEN, JO. MITCHELL. P.B.No.3.

WM. JUSTICE, 143 A. 24 po. in Weynock at the heads on the other side of Kitt-
awan in Chas. Citty Co., 20 Oct. 1665, p. 537, (658). Beg. at a stake parting
WM. JUSTICE & WM. LAURENCE, running N. by W. &c., joyning JNO. CANNON, thence
E. &c. Due & confirmed by order of the Genll. Ct. &c., dated 16 Sept. 1663.


Patent Book No. 6

THOMAS TAYLOR, 631 acs. Henrico Co. N. side of James Riv., commonly called
Harrahadockes, over against Kingsland, 23 Sept. 1667, p. 52. 281 acs. from
the riv. a little below the orchard from Mr. ARTHUR BAYLY's land, &c. to the
lower side of Harrahadockes Cr. mouth, &c. 350 acs. on the N. side of the
Roundaboute &c., to S. side thereof at a cor. of JNO. COX, &c., to 4 Mi. Cr.
old path, &c. 281 acs. granted to sd. TAYLOR 25 Sept. 1663, & 350 acs. for
trans. of 7 pers: FRANCIS TAYLOR, DOROTHY TAYLOR, JOHN YOUNG, JNO. BELL, JNO.
STEWARD, SYMON BALMS (or BALONO), WILL. STANAWAY.

SOLLOMAN KNIBB, 710 acs. Henrico Co., N. side James Riv., 24 Sept. 1667, p.
52. Beg. on the Ely. run of Baylyes Cr. &c. to COLL. STEGG's path, &c. Trans.
of 15 pers: SOLOMON ——, JNO. CARTER, JNO. HARTWELL, EDWARD GOOD, EDWARD
CURRELL, ELIZ. RUSSELL, ALICE ATKINSON, JNO. WORTH, ROBT. DAVIS, PHILL. SHER-
RINGHAM, ALICE HARRIS, MARY PIGGOTT, MARY GLAS, WM. ATKENSON, VINCENT SHUTTLE-
WORTH.

FRANCIS PERCE & WM. PERCE, 350 acs. Henrico Co., N. side of James Riv., 24
Sept. 1667, p. 53. N. N. W. on 2 Mi. Cr., S. S. W. against Varina, E. S. E.
upon 3 Mi. Cr. swamp, taking in the sw. N. N. E. towards 4 Mi. Cr. & bounded

with a running brook called the Roundaboute. Granted to SETH WARD viz: 150 acs. 13 Sept. 1635; 50 acs. purchased from JNO. BAKER, last of May 1636, & 150 acs. 17 Nov. 1643, for trans. of 3 pers; JONATHAN BLANSHARD, ELIZ. GIBBIN, HENRY CHADDOCKE.

JNO. LEAD, 75 A., 24 P., 24 Sept. 1667, p. 53. 50 acs. parte granted to WM. BAYLY, who assigned to THOMAS TAYLOR, who assigned to sd. LEAD; beg. on E. side of 4 Mi. Cr., along the river S. E. by S. &c. to the Southern run by BAYLIE's feild, &c. Trans. of 2 pers; EDWARD UNDERHILL, IZ. VINTER.

JOHN BROWNE, 110 acs. Henrico Co., N. side of James Riv., 29 Sept. 1668, p. 189. Adj. SEATH WARD, RADFORD's lyne, &c. Trans. of 3 pers: ELEANOR WILLIS, JONE DAVIS, PHILLIS ———.

JOHN BEAUCHAMPE, 82 A, 2 R. & 24 Po., Henrico Co., N. side of James River, adj. BARROW plantation; 17 Aug. 1668, p. 211. Trans. of 2 pers: JNO. BEAU-CHAMP, JOHN WAYLETT.

HAMMOND WOODHOUSE, 341 A., 3 R., 7 P., Chas. Citty Co., N. side James Riv., 20 Apr. 1669, p. 216. At the head of his own & land of JNO. WARRENER, nigh Seller run, &c. Trans. of 7 pers: ROBERT JERVIS, WM. MASON, PATRICK IZARD, MARY COLE.

Mr. HENRY RANDOLPH, 961 acs., 1 furlong, 26 perches, Henrico Co., known as Tymber Slash, 23 Oct. 1666, p. 224. Bet. Mr. COCKE & Mr. CREWE's yard by a CART path by E'ly run of 4 Mi. Cr., adj. THO. TAYLOR, BRYAN SMITH, &c. Granted to THO. LUDWELL, Esq., 16 June 1663, deserted, now granted by order, &c., & due for trans. of 19 pers.*

Mr. ROWLAND PLACE, 1228 A., 1 R., 26 P., Henrico Co., N. side James Riv., at Almond's Cr., 25 Aug. 1669, p. 233. 600 acs. granted to HUMPHRY LISTER in 1650, given to JOHN WHITE, as by records of James Citty, who sold to Mr. THO. HUNT, who sold to sd. PLACE; 628 acs. for trans. of 13 pers: WM. JEFFRIES, ABRA. JACKSON, TIM. WHITE, BERNARD MOOR, JACQUES JOHNSON, PETER ELLET, EDWD. HINTON, AND. BEALE, ROBT. CARY, ROBT. HAINES, WM. GARRETT, THO. YATES, RICH. HARWOOD.

FRANCIS REDFORD, 254 A., 3 R., 8 P., Henrico Co., on N. side of James Riv., 5 Aug. 1659, p. 241. Nigh the Round about slash; adj. his own land &c. Trans. of 5 pers: RICH. GERRARD, NATH. PERTUE (or PERLUE), WM. STILE, JNO. MILNER, MARKE CARTER.

ROBERT BULLINGTON, 100 acs. Henrico Co., N. side of James Riv., adj. Mr. JNO. FARRAR & FRANCIS RADFORD, 26 Oct. 1669, p. 260. Trans. of 2 pers: JNO. RICHARD-SON, WM. MERRITT.

Mr. RICHARD PARKER, 350 A., 3 R., 16 P., Henrico Co., S. side of James Riv., on the head of the 4 Mi. Cr., beg. at Harrowhaddox Path, 28 Oct. 1669, p. 279.

Trans. of 7 pers: GILBERT PLATT, JNO. NORRIS, JNO. HARDING, ELLENOR CREED, JOAN SNELLING, & 2 Negroes.

Mr. ROBERT WOODSON, 1192 A., 3 R., 32 P. Henrico Co., N. side James Riv., 26 June 1670, p. 287. Adj. THO. LUDWELL, Esqr., THO. LIGON, JNO. WOODSON, Col. STEGG & Mr. BALLARD. Trans. of 24 pers: WM. MARSH, JNO. YEATES, WM. NEWTON, PETER ALLERTON, JNO. AMYS, HEN. NORTH, AMY JOANES, JEREMY NORTON, MARG. BURCH, JNO. LESTRANGE, ABR. BENNETT, ROBT. WILKES, JNO. PORTER, SUSAN GREERE, ROBT. BOWMAN, WM. ARTON, HEN. BRUTONS, MARY EVELYN, THO. PHILPOTT, HUGH WRIGHT, ABRA. SPROSON, MARG. HENRICK, THO. HEWES, RICH. HYRES (or HYYES).

Mr. ROBERT BULLINGTON, 150 acs. Henrico Co., 6 Apr. 1671, p. 344. Granted to WM. DAWKES, Dec'd, & by inquisition under Mr. HENRY RANDOLPH, Depty. Esch'r., 7 Oct. 1669 &c. and now granted &c.

THOMAS LUDWELL, Esqr., 2994 A., 2 R., 35 P. on S. side of Chickahominy Swamp, 7 Apr. 1671, p. 352. 2093 A., 1 R., 25 P. at a run called Col. WYNN's Quarter, to a run above Pomonkey Path, over Cowtayle quarter run, &c., 901 A., 1 R. in Henrico Co., on N. side of James Riv., at the forks of the Cattayle run, at head of Mr. RICH. COCKE, Senr., to Mr. GREEN, &c. Surveyed for sd. COCKE & Mr. BEAUCHAMP, deserted & now due by order, &c. & trans. of 60 pers: THO. MOSS, JNO. GROUT (or GRONT), JNO. BREWER, JARVIS ROGERS, ROGER MEKES, JNO. SKITTLETHORPE, JNO. SCOTT, JEREMIE EVERINGHA (?), JNO. HEPER (?), ELIZ. LASHER, PETER SIDES, JNO. STEER, WM. WITHINGTON (or WILKINGTON), JNO. FISOLL, ELIZ. OSBURN, JNO. CARPENTER, BEATA FOWLER, MARY BOLTON, REBECKA BOUGH, FRANCIS ROBINSON, ROBT. HART, MARY PICKINER, WM. EVANS, ROBT. WRIGHT, ROBT. LITTLEFEILD, RICHD. MARSH, THO. HUTTON, NIC. CORBEN, SARA MESEM, FRAN. CARY, SARA CLEMENT, WM. WAITES, SYMON BENFORD, ADDAM ROSE, JNO. SYMONS, JNO. GRIMSON, JNO. LADRICK, JNO. STRINGER, ESTER MARSHALL, RICH. BRIDGES, NIC. MARTIN, WM. BAGSHAW, ELIZ. TRUELOVE, BARBARA CORDEROY, DANLL. RIDELY, THO. BURROUGHS, ABRAHAM ALLEN, MARGERY ROSE, RICHD. CLARK, HUMPHRY ELLIOT, JNO. HUNT, JNO. WORTHAM, JNO. GAINEFORD, WM. SHIRLEY, GILB. MAKEVARY (?), JNO. MACKERGOE, JNO. COTTON, JAMES BOWLIN: 2 Negroes.

WM. PORTER, 58 A., 3 R., Henrico Co., N. side of Riv., adj. devdt. granted to & lost by Mr. JNO. BEAUCHAMP, which was granted to Honbl. THO. LUDWELL, Esqr., Secretary, &c. 7 Apr. 1671, p. 367. Trans. of LYDDIA DRUNKARD.

WILLM. PORTER, 30 acs. Henrico Co., on N. side of James Riv., beg. at Mr. BALLARD his out seat at the Poplar brooke, adj. Mr. RICH. COCKE, &c. 7 Apr. 1671, p. 369. Trans. of JANE CHRISTY.

FRANCIS RADFORD, 629 A., 3 R., 8 P. Henrico Co., on N. side of James Riv., 1 July 1672, p. 409. 375 acs. at the Roundabout Slash adj. MORGAN PEIRCE, granted unto Capt. WM. FARRAR, & THO. LIGGON, who assigned to FRANCIS RADFORD 12 Oct. 1665, 254 A., 3 R., 8 P., granted sd. RADFORD 5 Aug. 1669.

HENRICO PARISH, 198 A., 3 R., 16 P., in sd. Co. being a Gleab at Varina on N.

side of James Riv., on the 16 Apr. 1666, and by the ancient neighborhood
shewed bounded, viz. beg. at the Riverside at a small oake & running N. W. by
N. 320 W. 100 po. along Capt. DAVIES' slash S. E. by S. ½ Sly. 300 po. to a
pohickery standing about two poles above the Court house, then Ea. 136 pole
to the place afore-mentioned (recorded 7 Oct. 1672, page 427.)

JOHN DAVIS (DAVIES), 500 acs. Henrico Co., 1 Oct. 1672, p. 426. 300 acs. adj.
JOHN BURTON; includ. nigh half the long feild over the brass Spring &c., half
of patt. granted ROBERT CRADOCK & by HOWELL PRICE, Atty. of sd. CRADOCK,
Sould to JOHN COX, who assigned to sd. BURTON; 300 acs. due sd. DAVIS; 200
acs. for trans. of 4 pers: ABELL GOWER, WM. GOWER, JOHN CLARKE, ANN MALBY.

RICHARD PERRIN, 740 A., 1 R., 24 P., Henrico Co., N. side of James Riv., 15
Mar. 1672, p. 445. 474 acs. called the Worlds End; from JOHN BURTON's house
down the riv. 12 ft. below Cornelius' Cr., granted to Capt. MATHEW EDLOE 2
Oct. 1656 & sould to sd. PERRIN; 266 A., 1 R., 24 P. at the head &c. Trans.
of 5 pers: STEVEN LEWIN (or LEWIS), THO. STANBRIG, NAN the maide, JONA.
FISH, THO. MASON.

FRANCIS RADFORD, 93 A., 2 R., 8 P., Henrico Co., N. side James Riv., 13 May
1673, p. 451. On line of the Orphans of GARRETT, at the Roundabout, on JOHN
BROWNE, & his own land, &c. Trans. of 2 pers: RICHARD GERRARD, JOHN MILNER.

EDWD. MATHEWES, sonn of EDWD. MATHEWES, dec'd., 1536 acs. Henrico Co., on N.
side of James Riv., 26 May 1673, p. 454. Near the head of a Deep Bottom on W.
side of the 4 Mi. Cr., nigh a path, belowe the Wading place; to a br. of GRIN-
DALL's run, to JOHN LEAD, on division bet. THO. LUDWELL, Esq., Secretarie, &
Capt. MATHEWES, &c. 600 acs. granted to Mr. WALTER ASTON 20 Dec. 1651, who
sold to Mr. JOHN DIBDELL, who sold to ELLIS ELSE, who sold to JNO. WATER-
RIDGE, & ROBT. WILD, who married the relict & adms. of WATERIDGE, sold to Capt.
EDWD. MATHEWS, his father. The residue for trans. of 19 pers: JOHN, ELIZ-
ABETH, MARY, SARAH, JOSEPH & WM. FISHER; MARY DRURY, SARAH CARTER, WM. FISHER,
WM. FLESH, RUTH HEWANNO (?), WM. FISHER, JAMES & JOHN WHITE, THO. EDMONDS,
RICH. FOSTER, WM. BRIDGER, JNO. LAD, RICH. TUNSTALL.

Mr. CHARLES ROANE, 401 A., 40 Ch., Chas. Citty Co., 7 Aug. 1667, p. 109. Beg.
upon N. side of Kittawan Cr., &c. to the Oystershell Landing in Moyses Cr. &c.
Trans of 9 pers.*

MARTIN ELAM(ELLAM), 453 acs. Henrico Co., S. side James Riv., on Proctor's
Run; adj. Mr. CHRISTOPHER BRANCH, &c., 27 Oct. 1673, p. 81. Trans. of 9 pers:
MARGARET & MICHAELL WHITTY, JOHN STUART, MICHAELL ADKINS, EDWARD NELLEI (?),
MONGO, LONGO, HONGO, AMBO Negroes. (Marginal notation: 463 acres.)

MARY, JOSEPH, EDWD. & MARTHA TANNAR, 650 A., 2 R., 8 P., Henrico Co., S. side
James Riv., 30 Oct. 1673, p. 486. At the Middle Spring bottome; nigh Mr.
BAUGH, to mouth of Hell Garden Bottome, at the Landing, at the house &c. 450
acs. granted JOSEPH TANNAR, dec'd. 24 Mar. 1662, & given to his children above
named. 200 A. 2 R., for trans. of 4 pers: ELIZ. ROGERS, CHRIS. HATTON.

MATH. LINSLEY, NORGES (?).

HENRY TRENT, 200 acs. Henrico Co., N. side of James River, 7 Nov. 1673, p. 495
Beh. at Mr. PLACE, halfe a mi. from the river, at the head of COLESON's.
Trans. of 4 pers: CHARLES TYRE, HENRY TRENT, MARGARET RAYES, ALICE SLEEK.(?)

Major WM. HARRIS, 1202 A., 2 R., 4 P., Henrico Co., N. side of James Riv., 7
Sept. 1671, p. 496. Beg. at the Middle Spring bottom adj. Orphants of TAN-
NER, Mr. WM. BAUGH, to Ashen Sw., along the maine Sw., to the head of the Red
Water, to the head of the Dry bottome, &c., adj. THO. LIGGON & WM. FARRAR,
over mouth of the Ware Bottome, &c. Trans. of 24 pers: MORGAN WILLIAMS, ADAM
ROSSE, MAR. HORGOTT, MARY BRONE (BROWNE), THO. DEER, WM. BLACKMAN, WM. LINNEY,
MARG. FLOYD, ANN GUY, WM. ASCOTT, ELL. WHITE, JOHN JONES, HUGH LEADING, NICH.
CHILES, MATHEW ALLEN, WM. BUTLER, JNO. NORTH, NICE. MOORE, EDW. EVANS, JNO.
EDWDS. (EDWARDS), EL. MANACLITH, DOROTHY CAREY, WM. JONES, WM. BATTERSEE.

JOHN ROGERS, & JOHN LEWIS, 400 acs. Henrico Co., N. side James Riv., adj. WM.
HUMPHRIES, on E. side of Mill Run; 7 Nov. 1673, p. 497. Trans. of 8 pers:
WM. WILKINS, MICHAELL TRENCHMAN, EDWD. NICHOLS, THO. MOORE, JNO. STEWARD,
GARRATT WARREN, NICHOLAS ————, WILL. RICHARDS.

NICHO. PERKINS, 537 acs., 3 R., 20 P., Henrico Co., N. side James Riv., adj.
RICHARD PARKE; 26 Sept. 1674, p. 530. Trans. of 11 pers: HACKALIA HARNER,
MARGARET HARNER, HEN. FLEGG, MARGAT. FLEGG, ROBT. DAY, JANE SCOTT, MARY DIGGS,
JNO. BROWNE, JNO. HALL, ELIZ. DRUMMER, SCIPIO, Negro.

Mr. THOMAS COCK, 1983 A., 3 R., in Chas. Citty Co., on N. side James Riv., 4
Oct. 1675, p. 563. Beg. uppon Gyllie's (Gilles) path neare Merridaes path,
over Mongoies Run, to W. Br. of Herring Cr. to a run of Chickahominy &c. Trans.
of 40 pers: DORCAS YOUNG, ANN CHANDLER, RALPH CHANDLER, RALPH JENINGS, HUGH
JONES, ROBT. MERCER, ROBT. GREY, MATH. TERRELL, JA. WRAGG, JONE HARRISON, JNO.
EDWARDS, JNO. ALMAND, HEN. TYRE, WM. BAKER, MARG. (Or MARY) SMITH, MARY SLY,
REBECCA JACKSON, RICH. BEAKE, JNO. GLOVER, HEN. PETERSON, ISAAC WARREN, DANLL.
HUGH, MORRIS NEALE; 4 Irishmen: BRIDGETT CARTER, WALTER FLOYD, JANE ALDER,
THO. MANN, BERNARD WINN, THO. CASTLE, EDWD. RICHARDSON, HEN. HICKS, MARG.
SWANN, THO. CARY, JNO. CADDY, EPER. PACKENTON, ROGER DORMAN, RICHD. CLERKE.

Mr. THO. COCK, 3087 A., 3 R., Henrico Co., N. side of James Riv., 4 Oct. 1675,
p. 564. Beg. on S. side of Chickahominy Sw., at land taken up by Mr. BEAUCHAMP
Trans. of 62 pers: JNO. SMITH, SARAH CARTER, JNO. ROBINSON, DAVID WILLIAMS,
JNO. LAMBER, JNO. WATTS, THO. WEBB, MARY WEBB, JNO. FISHER, ELIZ. HAMES (or
HAINES), JONE ASHBROOKE, THO. MORY, ANN GRAY, JA. WILE, AND. MORE, JNO. MORE,
CATH. KYTE, ABELL DAVIS, THO. SORRELL, XPER. BOBBLETT, JNO. BAYLY, THO.
SPRING, JNO. GARRETT, JEFFERY HARRIS, WM. STOREY, GODFREY BAYLY, THO. HEWES.
CHA. JAMES, THO. EVERTON, JNO. HENRY, WM. ALAMAN, TEM. WAKER, HERC. BAKER, AND
FLOIDE, SAR. JACKSON, ALICE PETERCUE (?), CORN. YEURNON, JNO. PETERSON, ABIG.
THOMAS, PETER RUDDS, JO. MASON, THO. WILD, MATHEW WILD, ABRA. GOOSE, ANDREW
SHEERER, JOANE MARSTON, WM. RICHARDS, SARA CARTER, MARY DURING, THO. FOSTER,

GEO. ASHBROOKE, THO. WINTER, WM. JOHNSON: BUNGO, HECTOR, HERCULES, SANTE, TOMELINE, SANCHA, SALLO, GEORGE, TONEY.

NICHOLAS & WM. COX, 273 acs. Chas. Citty Co., N. side of James Riv., 4 Oct. 1675, p. 561. Adj. Mr. JNO. STITH, nigh a br. of Herring Cr., &c. Trans. of 6 pers.*

EDWD. HATCHER, 1300 acs. Henrico Co., N. side James Riv., 6 Oct. 1675, p. 570. Next to Lilley Valley; nigh Cornelius' Cr. over Mr. BEAUCHAMPTS path &c. Trans. of 26 pers: JNO. SOUTHFEILD (or STUTFEILD), MARY GAGE, ELIZ. RICHARDS, JNO. SMITH, ELIZ. HAWARD, JNO. CLEER, SAMLL. GREENE, HOPKIN POWELL, SUSAN WILSHIRE, MARG. BROWNING, JNO. HOSOCK, THO. FILBROUGH, AND. MARTIN, BEN. SALT, ELIZ. CURTIN, PETER SOUTH (or SOUCH), MORRIS MATTHEWS, THO. WATSON, JNO. WHITE, KATH. FOSSETT, GEO. GROKER, JNO. HOSOCK, CHAS. WHITE, BENJA. SALT, THO. DEACON, PETER SOUCH (?), MORRIS MATHEWS, HENRY HATCHER.

Capt. WM. BIRD, 7351 A., 2 R., 24 P., Henrico Co., N. side James Riv. 15 Mar. 1675/6, p. 604. Beg. (at) Shoccores Cr. mouth, up the river bet. W. & N. W. &c. 1280 acs. granted him 27 Oct. 1673; the residue for trans. of 122 pers: JOHN WILLOUGHBY, MARY STRINGER, THO. HUCCOBY (?), THO. BROWNE, ELIZ. PIRNELL (?), WM. BRANARD, WM. WHITTINGHAM, THO. LOWDER, ABRA. HODKINS, ANTHO. WHEELER, WM. HOWARD, THO. KYTE, ARTH. MILES, JNO. DACRES, THO. ARDELL, PETER SIMONDS, ROBT. BALL, JNO. GARDNER, ANTH. STRANGE, JNO. BULL, THO. NEW, ROBT. PENFEATH-ER, WM. KEY (?), ROGER KENISTON, WM. MILLER, JNO. PICK, WM. HARDING, JNO. PAR-SONS, ROBT. TEMPLE, DARBY ENROTY, JNO. BECK, JA. BECK, ELIZ. HOLLINSBY, MARY CARTER, RICH. FOSSELL, XPER. MEADS, JNO. LILLEY, JNO. WALLIS, WM. WILE (or WILD), JNO. WITTEN, PETER MERIE (?), JNO. WARREN, HANA GOODWIN, BEN. BEAN, DORO. WILLIMPH, MARY THORNEHILL, ESTHER JNOSON, MARY COOKE, JNO. DRURY, THO. CHAPELL, W. DROWGEN, MARY COX, MA. SHORTER, WM. WEST, JNO. HEDGPATH, THO. WHARTON, THO. HAYLES, WM. LOVEDERE, CHA. PISTOTE, ISA. BATES, JNO. SMITH, GEO. TOPPIN,HUGH BUCKINS, JANE HAYDENS, JANE LAURENCE, ALEX. MACKWELL, OTHELR. WRI-GHT, BARBA. HATH, ELIZ. HOLLINSBY, ELIZ. ARCHER, WM. WHEELER, WM. STITH, ELIZ. CRISPIN, THO. DAVIS, HEN. BARNARD, JA. MACKARY, WM. ELAM, JA. THOMPSON, BEN. HUDSON, WM. BIRD, JNO. HAMPTON, HEN. HARMAN, ROBT. ESTLY (?), ANN SIMSON, SARA BROWNE, RICH. TERRELL, JNO. DAWBY (DAWLY), WM. OTME, HEN. PARSONS, JNO. TERNDEN, GEO. LISSE, CHA. COOPER, OBED. BAY, ELIZ. PAGE, SAMLL. WELCH, ROBT. STOCK, FRA. LEECH, THO. DICER, BRA. BOODEN (or PRODEN), JA. HOWARD, WM. STANARD, MARY WAKAM, WM. HOLDEN, MA. JOHNSON, GEO. SHARPNELLS, WM. PALMER, JOH. HARRINGTON, WM. GYLES, ISAC CRESWELL, WM. WATERS, JNO. COULCHESTER, JAS. SHIPPY, AN. DUNCUM, JNO. SEABRIGHT, PHILL. DYER, JNO. NORTH, NATH. SHURBUN, THO. HALES, FRANCIS (?), DIXON, JACK, TONY, CATE, Negroes.

JOHN WATTSON, 478 A., 3 R., 1 P., Henrico Co., on N. side James Riv., at White Oak Br. or Sw. which falleth into Chickahominy (Sw.); 2 Jan. 1677, p. 632. Adj. Mr. THOMAS COCKE (COCK), over New Kent Road, &c. Trans. of 10 pers: ELIZA.DORMER, JON. COLE, ROBT. DAY, WILLIAM CLEFT, WILLI. MILNER, WILLI. HOW-ARD, JON. HUNT, ANNE ADAMS, ANNE NOBLES, GRACE SAVAGE.

THOMAS WELLS, 296 A., 3 R., 19 P., Henrico Co., N. side James Riv., 3 Jan.

1677, p. 632. Adj. Mr. THOMAS COCKE & JOHN WATTSON; neare Cedar Br. which falleth into White Oake Br., neare New Kent Roade, &c. Trans of 6 pers: WILLIAM RANDOLPH, WILLIAM SEAWELL, THO. EDWARDS, ELINORE BUTLER, PETER DANGERFEILD, JOHN LAWNE.

ROBERT BULLINGTON, 244 A., 1 R., 4 P., Henrico Co., N. side James River, 10 May 1678, p. 642. At head of Capt. JNO. FARRAR's land; along Capt. DAVIS' to JNO. COX at the path goeing to Harrahadox neigh the Spring, neare BAILY's path; to the Roundabout, &c. Trans. of 5 pers: RICHD. PAGE, MORRIS AKETON (or AHEREN), JANE CASE, BEN. ADAMS. ANN HOUSE.

REBECCA GYLES, 162 A., 2 R., Henrico Co., North side of James Riv., 26 Sept. 1678, p. 653. Beg. at Capt. JOHN KNOWLES', on Cornelius Run, to Cornelius Cr., &c. Trans. of 4 pers: HENRY HARMAN, JNO. EMERSON, THO. CARMELL.

JNO. GREENHAUGH, 446 acs. Henrico Co., known by the name of Smith's Bay, 26 Sept. 1678, p. 663. E. side of James Riv., by land of THOM. MARKHAM, W. by the gr. River, N. by land of SOLOMON KNIBB, & E. on land of Mr. THOMAS COCKE. 400 acs. granted him 6 Dec. 1652, renewed 5 Aug. 1665, & renewed & included in this present patt: 46 acs. by order of the Gen. Ct. 26 Oct. 1666 & due for importation of: JNO. GREENHAUGH.

BENJA. HATCHER & JOHN MILNER, 350 A.,.2 R., & 14 P., Henrico Co., N. side James River, in the fork of Cornelius Run, 30 May 1679, p. 687. Neare the maine branch, along BEAUCHAMP's path, &c. Trans. of 7 pers: WM. STANLEY, EDWD. FERNETT, MARY GAY, JNO. LEATH (LEACH), RICH. COOPER, ROBT. SOUTH, JNO. LANTTHORPE.


Patent Book No. 7

JOHN PLEASANTS & JNO. HADDELISEY, 548 A., 3 R., 20 P., Henrico Co., N. side of James Riv., 1 Oct. 1679, p. 12. On the maine brook of 4 Mi. Cr., adj. Capt. MATHEWS, &c. Trans. of 11 pers: MELCH RICHARDSON, MATH. MOCK, FRA. MAYBURY, MARY CLARK, SAMLL. ANDERSON, HEN TURNEY (or TURNER), JOS. WELLS, SUSAN PERROTT, JNO. KEMPTON, ABRA. GOFF.

Mr. FRA. WARREN, 647 acs. upon S. side of the main run of Chickahominy. Henrico Co., 1 Oct. 1679, p. 11. Adj. Mr. WYATT, to OUGHNOM Brook, &c. Trans of 13 pers: ELIZ. THRIFT, JACOB WAREING, JA. DANIELL, RICHD. JONES, MARGT. JONES, THO. COOPER, ROBT. HABORNE(?), JA. MORANT, JNO. DAVIES, FRA. BANKES, ELIZ. BROADRIB, MILL. BLEIZE, MARY COCK.

HEN WATKINSON, 170 acs. Henrico Co., N. on James Riv., in Verina Parish, 29 Nov. 1679, p. 17. Adj. JOHN LEWIS, near a br. of 3 (mile) run, & land of Mr. COCK & BECHAMP. Trans. of 4 pers.*

Mr. GEORGE BROWNING, 37 A., 2 R., 8 P., Henrico Co., in Varina Par., 23 Apr.

1681, p. 75.  Adj. Mr. LIGGON; ABRAHAM WOMACKE; THOMAS SHEPPEY; THOMAS JONES; &c.  Trans of 1 pers.*

LYONELL MORRIS, 860 A., 20 P., Henrico Co., Varina Par., S. side Chickahominy Maine Sw., 23 Apr. 1681, p. 84.  Beg. at Mr. HENRY WYATT; to Powhite Path; to Reedy Br., &c.  Trans. of 18 pers: JANE COX, NICH. BARDY, HUM. ROBINSON, JNO. SPEARMAN, ED. BOOMER, REB. RICKASON, THO. WEARE, JOS. TROWELL, ALICE CARLES, JNO. COLE, SAMLL. BUGGE, ISABELL RITE (or RICE), EDW. FINCH, FRA. CATETOPE, PETER CROSSE.

Mrs. FRANCES IZORD, 1036 A., 5 P., Henrico Co., Varina Par. on S. side of Chickahominy Maine Sw., 23 Apr. 1681, p. 86.  Beg. upon Uffenum brooke; crossing Widdows runn, &c.  Trans. of 21 pers: JNO. STARLING, THO. WARE, ELIZ. FISHER, THO. MEELER, RICH. BROOKE, ELIZ. BROCK, GEO. ALEES, GEO. BASE, REBECCA NICCOLS, FRA. LITTLE, ELIZ. ROGERS, THO. STANLY, ROBT. SPINLUGG, JNO. OAKELY, WM. ROGERS, THOS. BOEMAN, NATH. JONES, NEDD ——, GUNNY ——; THO. WORLY; PEGG a Negro.

ROBERT WOODSON, Mr. JOHN WOODSON, Mr. THOMAS EAST, Mr. ROBERT CLARKE, Mr. WILLIAM PORTER, 531 A., 1 R., 4 P., Henrico Co., S. side of White Oake Sw. Varina Par. 28 Sept. 1681, p. 102.  Adj. Mr. THOMAS COCKE; Madam BLAND, THOMAS WAILES, &c.  Trans. of 11 pers.*

WILLIAM GILES, 100 acs. Henrico Co., 28 Sept. 1681, p. 108.  Escheate land of HENRY ALFORD; inquisition under WILLIAM BYRD, Esche'r, &c.

Mr. WILLIAM PORTER, Senr., 315 acs. Henrico Co., Verina Par., on S. side of James River; adj. JOHN WADSON, & HENRY WATKINS (WADKINS); 20 Apr. 1685.  p. 433.  Trans. of 7 pers.*

WILLIAM PORTER, Junr., Mr. NICHOLAS AMOSS & Mr. RICHARD FERRES, 459 acs. Henrico Co., in Verina Par., N. side of the White Oake Sw., 20 Apr. 1685, p. 435.  Adj. Mr. THOMAS COCKE, crossing Bares Hill Branch, & New Kent path, &c.  Trans. of 10 pers.*

LEMON CHILDERS, 406 acs. Henrico Co., Varina Par., on N. side of James Riv., on Grindon's run; adj. Mr. JOHN PLEASANTS; & EDWARD MATHEWS; 20 Apr. 1685, p. 454.  Trans. of 9 pers: JOB. ——, THOMAS LYBORNE, PETER PROUT, JOHN LEYDEN, WM. HOWSE, JON. HARRIS.

Mr. THOMAS BRANCH Junr., 760 acs. Henrico Co., in Varina Par., on S. side of James Riv., 4 Nov. 1685, p. 489.  Beg. at Mr. ABELL GOWER, crossing Myry Run; S. the Deepe Bottome, to JOHN CLARKE; to Mr. THOMAS BRANCH, Senr., &c. Trans of 16 pers.*

SAMUEL BRIDGWATER, 333 acs. Henrico Co., Virina Parish, on N. side of James Riv., 27 Apr. 1686, p. 508.  Beg. at GILLIES' land, crossing Gillies' Cr., &c.  Imp. of 7 pers: PHILLIP ELON(?), ARTHUR BRYANT, JNO. RICH, KATH. KALIN JNO. HAYMAN, DANLL. FLINCH, JNO. DARBY, ELIZ. HOLLY.

Mr. ABELL GOWER & Mr. EDWARD STRATTON, 487 acs. Henrico Co., 27 Apr. 1686, p. 508. Granted to GEORGE BROWNING, dec'd., & found to escheat, by inquisition under WILLIAM BYRD, Esqr., Eschr. Genrll, &c.

Mr. ROBT. HANCOCK, 600 acs., Henrico Co., Virina Par., on S. side of James Riv., 30 Oct. 1686, p. 534. Beg. at his own land S. on bottome of the Cattaile run, &c., Trans. of 12 pers.*

FRANCIS CARTER, 622 acs., Henrico Co., in Virina Par., on S. side of James Riv., 30 Oct. 1686, p. 534. Beg. at Mr. ROBT. HANCOCK, to TIMOTHY ALLEN, &c. Trans. of 13 pers.*

Honbl. WILLIAM BYRD, Henrico Co., 20 Apr. 1687, p. 548. N. side of James Riv. beg. at mouth of Shaccoe Cr., down the river 250 po. to Gillie's Run, the division line bet. this & GYLLY GROOMAMARIN; N. to Kickinoky Road, to Shacko Cr., &c. 500 acs. included in a patt. to Honbl. STEGG, Esqr. & from him derived to Col.BYRD; the residue adj., included in the bounds, S. due for trans. of 10 pers: KATH. WITCHELL, JAMES SANDS (?), WELCH DAVY, WALTER SQUIRE, WM. GOLD, JAMES DARLOW; CALLE, DIANA, NAN & BESS, Negroes.

Mr. THOMAS COCK, Junr., 671 acs. Henrico Co., Virina Par., on N. side of James Riv., 20 Apr. 1687, p. 556. Adj. Mr. ROBERT BURTON & Mr. JOHN DAVIS; crossing the Round about br., to EDWARD HACKER, etc. Trans. of 14 pers: SARAH CARTER, ANNE NOBBS, JNO. ROBINSON, GRACE SAVAGE, DAVID WILLIAMS, PETER DANGERFIELD, JNO. WATTS, HEN. HICKS, JNO. CUDDY, JNO. SMITH, RICHD. CLARK, THO. CAREY, MARGARET SWINE, ROGER DORMAN.

Mr. THOMAS COCKE, 296 A., 3 R., 19 P., Henrico Co., N. side of James Riv., 20 Apr. 1687, p. 557. Adj. his own, & land of Mr. JOHN WATSON; neer Cedar Br. neer New Kent Roade, &c. Granted to THOMAS WELLS, 3 Jan. 1677, deserted, & now granted by order, &c. Trans. of 6 pers.*

JOHN BAYLY, 736 acs. Henrico Co., Virina Par., N. side of James Riv., 20 Apr. 1687, p. 560. Beg. at HENRY PRUETT & JOHN FIELD; to GILLES Cr., on SAMUELL BRIDGWATER, &c. Trans. of 15 pers:* Note: 15 rts. being part of a certificate for 20 rights granted by Mr. EDWD. CHILTON, 23 July 1686 to WALTER SHIPLEY.

Mr. SAMUELL BRIDGWATER, 404 acs., Henrico Co., Virina Par., N. side of James Riv., 20 Apr. 1687, p. 560. Adj. line of Esqr. PLACE. Trans. of 9 pers: ISAAC SHEFFIELD, JNO. WILLIAMS, ISAAC JONES, WM. SMITH, THO. SMITH, RACHEL YOUNG, ALICE WINGFEILD, THO. STEPHENS, JNO. EVANS.

GILLY GROOMERIN, 539 acs. Henrico Co., Verina Par., S. side of Chickahominy Sw., 20 Apr. 1687, p. 562. Beg. on the Cattaile Br., in line of Mr. HENRY WYAT (WYETT); to head of Holey Br., to LIONELL MORRIS, &c. Trans. of 11 pers: JOHN SMITH, AVIS COLLING, HEN. HICKS, ANNE COLLING, JNO. BESLE, MARGT. SWAINE, ROGER MORRIS, EDWD. RICHARDS, THO. CARY, THO. CHARLES, HENRY BROADSHA, JNO. CADDY, XPHER. PECKINGTON; MARIA a Negro.

JAMES LYLE, 156 acs., Henrico Co., Verina Par., on S. side of Chickahominy Riv., 20 Apr. 1687, p. 562. Adj. FRANCIS WARREN; on Ufnom Cr., Trans. of ———. pers.*

Mr. HENRY PRUETT & JOHN FIELD, 440 acs. Henrico Co., Virina Par., N. side of James Riv., 20 Apr. 1687, p. 569. Beg. at THOMAS FIELD's cor. on Almond's Cr., along SAMLL. BRIDGWATER; to Esqr. PLACE's line, &c. Trans. of 9 pers: THOMAS STEPHENS, WM. GOWRY, JNO. SIMPSON, WM. COSBY, ELIZA. GRYER, JANE FERNE, JNO. HUBORT, ANNE STREET, PORTER CRANNY.

MICHAELL TURPIN, 215 acs. Henrico Co., Virina Par., N. side of James Riv., 20 Apr. 1687, p. 570. Beg. at THOMAS TAYLER; to maine br. of the Roundabout, in the fork, to NICHOLAS PERKINS, &c. Trans. of 5 pers.*

FRANCIS REDFORD, 775 acs. Henrico Co., N. side of James Riv., 21 Oct. 1687, p.590. Beg. on N. side of one of the windings of a gr. slash or Sw. called the Roundabout in ROBERT SHARP's line; to TAYLER's cor., to sd. REDFORD's house, to land of BAKER, &c. 630 acs. by patt., 1 July 1672, which was grounded on 2 former pattents, which lines enterfering with adj. lands are now rectified; 145 acs. adj. due for imp. of 3 pers: SUSAN DALE, GEO. WALKER, RICHD. FRANKLIN.

Mr. JOHN EVERETT, 162 A., 2 R., Henrico Co., N. side of James Riv., adj. Capt. KNOWLES, on Cornelius Run, 21 Oct. 1687, p. 596. Granted to REBECCA GILES, 26 Sept. 1678, deserted & now granted by order, &c. Trans. of 4 pers: ALEX. ROBINS, JAMES DUDLY, JANE MORGROVE, WALTER ALLEN.

Mr. JAMES BLAIRE, Clerk, 453 acs. on N. side of James Riv., bet. E. br. & the Maine br. of Cornelius Run; adj. Mr. HUTCHER's line; Beauchamp's path, &c; 21 Oct. 1687, p. 600. 350 acs. granted to Mr. BENJAMIN HATCHER & Mr. JOHN MILNER, 30 May 1679, deserted, & now granted by order, &c.; 103 acs. adj. for trans. of: JAMES URWIN 10 times.

Mr. ROBERT WOODSON, Mr. RICHARD FERRES (FERRIS), MR. GILES CARTER, WM. FERRIS & ROGER CUMMINS, 1780 acs. Henrico Co., Verina Par., N. side of James Riv., at the White Oak Swamp; 21 Oct. 1687, p. 601. Beg. nigh Barr hill Br; crossing Deep Run to JOHN WADSON, &c. Trans. of 36 pers: JOHN STRONG, JNO. HICKSOE, GEO. SWALLOW, EDMUND YERNSHER, MOSES REEST, PATRICK ROBERTSON, JNO. WORTH, ANTHO. GRANT, WM. NORRIS, HANAH ELLIT, HANAH DEANE, DANLL. WALKER, THO. ADCOCK, THO. CLARK, ED. DAVEHILL, ELIZA.PHIPS, JOANE WILKS, BENJA. CLARKE, JNO. MARSH, THO. ELLIOTT, MARY SMITH, JNO. MOLE, RICHD. SMITH, JNO. JACKSON, JNO. FINCH, CHA. LOCKEY, JNO. GOWER, JONATHAN COCKS, PHILL MARSHALL, MARY ALLEN, JNO. HOLMES, ELINOR BUSHELL, KATH. PRICE, CORNELIUS ORTS; FRANK & KATE, Negroes.

Mr. ROBERT WOODSON, Senr., Mr. JOHN WOODSON, Senr., WM. LEWIS & THOMAS CHARLES 470 acs., Henrico Co., Verina Par., on N. side of James Riv., 21 Oct. 1687, p. 602. Beg. neere the Colls (Colonel's) Path so called; to PHILEMON CHILDERS, on W. br. of the Deep Run; by RICHARD

FERRES' line; & along SOLOMON KNIBBS' line. Trans. of 10 pers: JAMES HAYES, ROGER INGRAM, WM. BATES, ELLINOR HARRIS, JAMES WILCOX, RICE JONES, ADAM TAYLER, SUSAN HOYLE, REBECCA DAVIS, JANE ADCOCK.

THOMAS TAYLOR, Planter, 1053 acs. Henrico Co., at Harahadocks (Harahadox); N. side of James Riv. 21 Oct. 1687, p. 633. Beg. on the river, a little below the orchard, by land now, or late, JOHN COX's along path to 4 Mi. Cr.; over the Roundabout Sw; to land now or late FRANCIS REDFORD's; to BURTON & TAYLOR's river land, to Harahadox Cr. mouth at the river, &c. 631 acs. due THOMAS TAYLOR (the uncle, late dec'd) by patt., 23 Sept. & descended to the above named THOMAS; 422 acs. lying parte within & parte contiguous to sd. 631 acs., due the nephew THOMAS for trans. of 9 pers: GEORGE DICK; THOMAS LAWRENCE; CTSAR. GUV. ABASSE; GEORGE COOKE; one child MARIA. Marginal note: "Fees & seale charged."

HENRY PEWE (PEW), 411 acs. on N. side of James Riv. bet. the brs, & maine run of 4 Mi. Cr., 23 Apr. 1688, p. 637. Beg. by a slash of LEMMAN's Br.; over BEAUCHAMP's Path, &c. Trans. of 9 pers: WM. SAUNDERS, JOHN PAINE, OTHO. HUGHES, WM. JAMES, REBECCA HUGHES, EDWARD SAUNDERS, JOHN EMETSON, WM. FLOYD, JOHN EDGER.

JOHN WOODSON, Senr., 1850 acs. Henrico Co., Verina Par., S. side of Chickahominy Riv., 23 Apr. 1688. p. 639. Trans. of 37 pers: ROBERT JARRET, THO. STEPHENS, JOSE HUGHES, EDW. PETTO(or PETTS), JAMES GOLD, ROBERT BEARGE, EDWD. COWED, JNO. GRUMBALL, JNO. TAYLER, MARTHA TAYLER, DANLL. FRIGNALE, SARAH ARNELL, JANE FARHAM, JANE COX, ELIZ. THOMPSON, JNO. COOK, WM. BININHAM (?), ROBERT JONES, JNO. COLE, RICH. CRAWLEY, JNO. BROMLEY, LEWIS HALES, HENRY LIDGOLD, JNO. BROTHERS, EDWD. MORRIS, JANE GREENE, SAVELL COVELL, ROBERT JARRET, ABRAHAM RENOLS, JANE RENOLS, JAMES BIGFORD, ADAM RANDALL, JER. GRIFFIN, JANE RELFE.

Mr. THOMAS PEREN, 140 acs. Henrico Co., in Verina Par., on N. side of James Riv., 20 Oct. 1688, p. 666. Adj. Mr. RICHARD PEREN, & ABRAHAM BAYLY; on Cornelius Creek; to WM. GILES (GYLES); & THOMAS BAYLY. Trans. of 3 pers: THOMAS MORTIN(MARTIN), JONATHAN BAYLY, WM. JESOP.

Mr. NICHOLAS MARSH, 528 acs. Henrico Co., Verina Par., on N. side of James Riv., 20 Oct. 1688, p. 666. Adj. Mr. JOHN PLEASANTS, on the head of Barrow; crossing SAMPSON's Slash; to ISAC CRESWELL; on Cornelius' Cr. to HENRY TRENT, &c. Trans. of 11 pers: EDWARD RICHARDSON, RICH. MARTIN, THO. HILL; "8 more out of Cert. RANDOLPH."

Mr. ABRAHAM BAYLY, 142 acs. Henrico Co., Verina Par., on N. side of James Riv., called Mount Peloin (or Pelom): ———, of Oct, 1688, p. 667. Beg. nigh the goeing of Cornelius' Cr., to Mr. BURTON; on head of Holly Br. Trans. of 3 pers: JNO. GOOD, MARY & FRANK ———'

Mr. THOMAS COCK, Senr., 1650 acs. Henrico Co., Verina Par., S. side of Chick-

ahominy maine Sw., adj. Mr. JNO. WOODSON; 20 Oct. 1688, p. 668. Trans. of
33 pers; JNO. SMITH, ANNE COLLINS, AVIS COLLINS, JNO. BESS, ROGER NORRIS,
EDW. RICHARDS, THO. CHARLES, HUMPHREY BRADSHAW, MARY GODFREY, THO. MITCHELL,
ROBT. GREEN, HUMPH. SMITH, LAMBERT TYE, MARTIN GARDNER, DANLL. JORDAN, EDWD.
RICHARDSON, RICHD. MARTIN, THO. HILL, ROGER DORMER, WM. LAMBORT (?), ROGER
HOLDEN, WM. BANKS, HENRY HENDERSON, DANLL. COCK, MARY CLIFFORD, SUSANNA TUR-
NER, NICHOLAS PRIOR, ROBT. COOK, WM. SOANE, JOB. ———, THO. LIBURNE, PETER
BRANT; MARIA a Negro.

ALEXANDER MACKENNY, 296 A., 3 R., 19 P., Henrico Co., N. side of James Riv.,
adj. Mr. THO. COCK, & Mr. JNO. WATSON; neer Cedar Br. falling into White Oake
Br. neer New Kent Road; along line of WALTON; Oct. 1688, p. 691. Granted
THOMAS WELLS, 3 Jan. 1677, deserted & now granted by order, &c. Trans. of 6
pers.* 6 Rts. from a certificate granted by CHILTON to LANCT. BATHURST, 7
Apr. 1687.

DANIEL JOHNSON, 391 acs. Henrico Co., in Varina Par., N. side of James Riv.,
20 Apr. 1689, p. 713. Adj. JOSHUA STAPP, crossing Shacko Cr., & Pequoucky
(or Peynoucky?) Path; ROBT. GREEN's path, &c. Trans. of 8 pers; JNO. STAN-
FORD, ROBT. ELLIOT, JNO. SAMPSON, ABRA. HOLDER, WM. RANGER, JNO. OVERTON,
SARAH OVERTON, WM. BISHOP.

THOMAS CARDWELL, Planter, 550 acs. Henrico Co., in Varina Par., N. side of
James Riv., 20 Apr. 1689, p. 716. Beg. at SAMUELL BRIDGEWATER, on N. br. of
Gilley's Cr., &c. Trans. of 11 pers.*

Patent Book No. 8

GILLEY GRUMEREN, 481 acs. Henrico Co., Verina Parish, 20 Oct. 1689, p. 1. N.
side of James Riv., nigh Chickahaminy Sw., beg. at a former survey. Importation of 10 pers.*

THOMAS COCK, Senr., 816 acs. Henrico Co., Verina Parish, (date blank), p. 1.
S. side Chickahaminy main Sw., beg. at land known as Oposum, in possession
of JNO. BAXTER; crossing a br. of Oposum, to Mr. BLAND's corner, along Mr.
RICHARD COCK, &c. Imp. of 17 pers; JANE BORAR, ROBT. BEASLEY, JNO. WITT,
JOANE WHITE, ALEX ———, PATRICK FOSTER, ROBT. POVEY, JNO. EDWARDS, GILL.
FUCKETT, THOS. MATHEWS, HEN. BALTIMORE, FRA. CLEAVELY, HUGH DAVIS, JNO. HER-
BERT, ELIZA. HARRISON; Negro NELL, BENETTA CLAME (CLAINE).

ROBERT BEVERLEY, 988 acs. Henrico Co., Verina Par., 20 Oct. 1689, p. 2. N.
side of James Riv., above the falls; beg. by a great point of rocks just
above the old Powhite feilds, &c. crossing branches falling into Chickaham-
iny Sw., on Westham Cr., nigh a great Beaver pond, &c. Imp. of 20 pers; JNO.
BUTTERFEILD, WILL. HITCHINS, JNO. DIXON, ANNE DAVIS, JANE JACKSON, JOAN
SANDERS, REECE (?) WILLIAMS, JULIUS DEEDS, vɛRA BOSWELL, AMY BOSWELL, PETER
WILLIAMS, JAMES JACKSON, ANN SWANLEY; 6 Negroes; TOM. MINGO, SAMBO, SANTO,
TONEY, BESS.

EDMUND JENNINGS, Esqr., 6513 acs. N. side of James Riv., about 12 or 14
mi. above the foot of the falls; 20 Oct. 1689, p. 2. Part of which was
taken up by one RAMSEY & GROVES; by them lapsed, for which sd. JENNINGS hath
the Governor's grant; the rest being King's land; beg. at Tuckahoe Cr.,
where it forks into the river; to the Horse Pen Br., which is supposed to be
the upper side of Westham, &c. Imp. of 131 pers: JOHN BELL, THO. RAY, GEO.
PHILLIPS, ANNE ELDER, BENJ. HAELES, JNO. START, WM. BAYTS, SARAH HUGHS, DEB-
ORAH SHORT, GEO. STONE, DARCY HUGHS, JNO. DUNCOMB, HEN. HALL, MARGART. ROE,
TIMO. BRIESS (?), MATHEW HALL, DAVID MANSFEILD, GEO. HARVEY, THO. HULL, JNO.
LACKMAN, THO. LOYD, JNO. FAIRFACE, ANNE HULETT, WM. HALCHARD, HENRY WILLIS,
FRA. EATON, THO. PAYTON, JNO. BURLEY, ISAAC HILL, ELIZA. HAMBLETON, JANE
BULL, HEN. MITCHELL, HUMP. MOODY, THO. PALL, JNO. ASHBY, GEO. MORLEY, WM.
CREEDE, WALTER WATERS, DENNIS MILLFORD, HUGH NANNY, ABELL WINDSOR, REBECCA
BREEDON, JNO. STORY, HEN. HOPKINS, JNO. PARDOE (or BARDOE), SARAH HATTEN,
OLIVER STONE, OWEN PARKER, JNO. WOODEN, ALICE ALLEN, THO. MARSTON, RICHD.
DIXON, EDWARD DOVER, SAMLL. HUNT, SUDEAVOR AUSTINE, BARTHO. SAVAGE, GEO.
SHERNE, EDWD. FOWLER, RICHD. BATTS, JOSH. HENLEY, STAPLETON UBANK, GAWEN
WILSON, THO. BROTHWAITE, JNO. KINGSTON, WM. WOODWARD, OWEN MICRAUGH, ELIZA.
HARRISON, FRA. INCH, AN. RUGGLES, SUSAN HOLLAWAY, ELIZA. VENIS, THO. MIT-
CHELL, ROBT. GREENE, HUMPHRY SMITH, LAMBERT TYE, MAITIN GARDNER, DANLL.
JORDAN, JNO. GREENE, JAMES HORMELL (or HORSNELL), JNO. AYRES, CHRISTIAN
PEIRSON, JONE ROBERTS, GRACE JONES, THO. MORRIS, RICHD. ROGERS, JNO. WELSH,
ROBERT WILLIAMSON, HONOR PEACH, WM. GRACE, JOHN WISEMAN, ROBERT OWEN, JONE
OWEN, WM. OWEN, ABRAHAM JOHNSON, WM. READE, SARA ROOKINGS, JNO. TURNER, JA.
WILSON, OWEN TUNSTALL, RICH. HEATHFEILD, JNO. BANISTER, JAMES POWELL,
WALTER THOMPSON, JONAS ROBERTS, JNO. WESTOBY, THO. WHITE, JNO. LAMBART,
HESTER LAMBERT; & 23 Negroes.

JAMES MOORE, 573 acs. Henrico Co., in Verina Par., on S. side of Chicka-
hominy Main Sw., on Uffnum brook; 21 Apr. 1690, p. 27. Adj. JAMES LISLE
(LILE); FRA. WARREN, & Mrs. IZARD. Imp. of 12 pers: MARY GODFREY, HUMPH.
SMITH, DANLL. JORDAN, THOMAS HILL, THO. MICHELL, LAMBERT TYE, EDW. RICHARD-
SON, ROBT. GREENE, MARTIN GARDNER, RICHD. MARTIN, FRA. HAYES, JOHN COLE.

JOHN WADSON, 480 acs. Henrico Co., Verina Par., on S. side of Chickahominy
Sw. adj. Mr. THOMAS COCLE 7 on a br. of Gilley's Creek; 21 Apr. 1690, p. 28.
Trans. 10 pers: JOHN NEWTON, JAMES ECHOLLS, SAMLL. NEWBY, SARAH ORTON,
ALEX RICHARDSON, JAMES RALFE, JOHN ASHTON; JONE, ROBIN & TOM, Negroes.

WILLIAM PORTER & DANIELL PRICE, 440 acs. Henrico Co., Verina Par., on N.
side of James River, Nigh Chickahominy Sw., 21 Apr. 1690, p. 29. Adj.
LIONELL MORRIS, & GILLEY GRUMMEREN; crossing a br. of Gilley's Cr., &c.
Imp. of 9 pers: JOHN BYRD, ELLEN BROWNE, ANTHO. BOURN (?), JOHN WORTH,
JAMES SANDERS, JNO. PARTRIDGE, JANE SYKES, WM. PARROTT, JANE PRICE.

ALEXANDER MEKENEY (MACKENNY), 640 acs. Henrico Co., Verina Par., on N. side
of James Riv., 21 Apr. 1690, p. 31. Beg. at SAMLL. BRIDGWATER on Gilley's
Cr., to JOSHA. STEP, & DANLL. JONSON. Imp. of 13 pers: JNO. RICHARDS,

JAMES REDMAN, ANTHO. CORNISH, THO. ANDREWS, JANE ANDREWS, WM. HUNTER, JNO.
SHORT, ROBERT PRIDEMAN; TONY, SAMBO, DIC, HECTOR, FRANCK, Negroes.

Mr. JAMES BLAIR, Mr. JEREMIAH BROWNE & Mr. NICHOLAS BULLINGTON (BULENTING),
130 acs. bounding on their plantations in Henrico Co., in Verina Par., on N.
side of James. Riv., over against Neck of Land; 21 Apr. 1690, p. 37. Beg. at
the Gleabe Land, to mouth of 2 Mi. Cr., &c. Imp. of: JAMES IRWIN (or URWIN)
3 times.

JOHN WOODSON, Senr., 1324 acs. Henrico Co., in Verina Par., on S. side of
Chickahominy Sw., 21 Apr. 1690, p. 50. Beg. at his land neare New Kent Road,
to the falls, down a br. of White Oake Sw., to Mr. Cock; down Bare Sw., &c.
Imp. of 27 pers: ROBT MARTIN, ALICE HILL, FRA. SINK, DIANE SEARES, THO. LANG-
DELL, DANLL. HORTON, RICHD. STIBALL, FRA. WHITWELL, THO. DEVIN, ROBT. HALL,
JNO. LAUTHORP, JNO. LOUTH, ELIZ. CLIFTON, ANNE SCOFEILD, SER. SOMERSCALES,
KATH.GERRULLD, THO. ELDER, WM. LEIGH, JOSH. LOWDER, THO. KEGAN, ELIZA. YOWELI
ANN KEES, ELIZA. HOTON, JNO. WADE, THO. BRISCOM (?), THO. WELCH (?), WM.
SELBE.

Mr. JOHN WOODSON, Junr., 1385 acs. Henrico Co., in Varina Par., N. side of
James Riv., 23 Oct. 1690, p. 83. Beg. at land of HENRY PUE, crossing the
main br. of 4 Mi. Cr. on Cornelius Cr. to Mr. BLEARE (?), DOWN THE MAIN ROAD,
&c. Trans. of 28 pers: CHA. SCARBURGH 2, WM. WEST, WM. BOLDRY, JNO. EVANS,
JNO. EVES (or EVER), JNO. NEWELL,BRDGET CLARE, THO. JONES, JNO. JONES, KATH.
NEWJANT, HEN. WHEELER, HUMP. JONES, SUSAN JONES, ED. MORRIS, RICHD. HAYES,
ELIZA. FRANK (or FUNK), GEO. WILSON, JONAS TERREY, SARAH JONES, her 2 child-
ren, DICK, MARY, JNO., JONE, TOM; MASUN, Negroes.

JNO. WOODSON,Junr., 735 acs. upon brs. of Chickahominy Sw., at a place called half sink, upon Stoney Point; 23 Oct. 1690, p. 84. Imp. of 15 pers.*

Mr. JOHN PLEASANTS, 2625 acs. Henrico Co., in Varina Par., N. side of James
Riv., 23 Oct. 1690, p. 85. Adj. EDWD. MATHEWS, PHILMON CHILDERS & ROBERT
WOODSON; down W. br. of Deep Run to RICHARD FERRELL, on the White Oak Sw., to
br. of 4 Mi. Cr. Imp. of 53 pers: ABRAHAM BLAGG 8; JNO. BUCKLEY 2; THO.
HILTON, ELIZA. LONG, HERBERT DUNCUMB, JNO. WRIGHT, his wife & child; WM. THO-
MAS,JNO. FEURAY, SARA AUDRY, TIMO. HAIR, JNO. BELSON, ISAC (A), french boy,
OWEN MACDARMOTT, WM. PENQUIT, JNO. CHAINEY, MARY SWILLIFANT, THO. KELLEY,
HONOR KELLEY, her son & daughter, GILBERT WRIGHT, his wife & 5 children; WM.
BROWNING, SARAH SPENCER, HONOR BERK, SENR. (?); MARY ———, JACK, a Negro,
DEBORA, an Indian.

WM. EDWARDS, 1626 acs. Henrico Co., in Varina Par., N. side of James Riv.,
23 Oct. 1690, p. 99. Beg. at HENRY WEYAT, to GILLY GRUMEREN; on br. of
Ufnam Brooke, to JAMES MORE, & JAMES LISLE, on a br. of Horse Swamp, to line
of FRANCIS WARREN, &c. Imp. of 33 pers.*

JOHN JAMESON, 89 acs. on N. side of James River, 23 Oct. 1690, p. 102.

Beg. at WM. BARTUE, up the gr. piney slash to ROBT. BARTUE, to br. of the Roundabout, to his own land, &c. Imp. of 2 pers: THOS. ROBINS, JNO. TEMPLE.

JOHN CANNON, 158 acs. Henrico Co., N. side of James River, adj. JOHN PLEDGE, on 4 Mi. Creek, 23 Oct. 1690, p. 111. Imp. 4 pers: JOHN BRODNAX 3 times, & ANTHONY BOURN.

HENRY WADKINS, 60 acs. Henrico Co., in Varina Par., N. side of James Riv., 23 Oct. 1690, p. 122. Adj. his own, THO. WALES, & land of Madam BLAND, on run of Turkey Island Cr. Imp. of 2 pers: ROBT. FELLOWS, JNO. TROTMAN.

SAMUEL JOURDAN Gent. an Ancient Planter, 450 acs. Chas. City Co., 10 Dec. 1620, p. 125. (Note: See Vol I, p. 228 for full copy).

Mr. RICHARD COCKE (COCK), 270 acs. Henrico Co., in Verina Par., 28 Apr. 1691, p. 157. Beg. at the hedgrow deviding Bremow & the patent of Curles; crossing the main cr. of Curles Swamp, down the main river, &c. Trans. of 6 pers: JOHN HAMMON, MARY SUEWELL; POMP, TOM, WILL, SUE, Negroes.

Mr. JOHN PLEASANTS, 1221 acs. Henrico Co., Verina Par., N. side of James Riv., 20 Oct. 1691, p. 173. Beg. at mouth of West Ham Creek & mouth of a br. of Tuckahow Cr., &c. Imp. of 25 pers: WM. RANDOLPH, GEORGE LYNN, WILLIAM DOD, MARY LYNN, KATH. MATHERS, MARY MADDEN, ALLANSON CLARKE, CHARLES RUMBOLD, WINEFRED CONNER, JANE SAWKINS, JOHN SAWKINS, BARTHO. FOWLER, WM. OAKE: WILL, TOM, TONY, EASTHAM, CONEY, YAMON, SCIPIO, HANIBALL, TOBO, SAMBO.

Mr. GILES WEBB, 132 acs. Henrico Co., on N. side of James Riv., bet. Ho&ble. WILLM. BYRD, Esqr., & Mr. ROBT. BEVERLEY; 29 Apr. 1692, p. 242. Beg. at a heap of Great Rocks on up side of sd. BYRD's land, &c. Imp. of 3 pers: RICHD. GRIFFIN, ROBIN & JANE, Negroes.

Same, 344 acs. same location, date & page. In Varina Parish; on the middle run bet. COLSON's & Deep bottom; on Mr. FRANCIS REEVES; HENRY TRENT; on head of Barrow-land; cor. of Mr. PLEASANTS. Imp. of 7 pers: ANNE HUGHES, JOHN ELDERKIN, EDW. TUSTIN, (or TUFFIN); ROBIN, TOM, BETTY, JENNY, Negroes.

THOMAS COCKE (COCK), Junr., 528 acs., Henrico Co., in Virina Par., on N. side of James Riv., 29 Apr. 1693, p. 260. Beg. at Mr. PLEASANTS on the head of Barrow, crossing SAMPSON's Slash, to ISAAC CRESWELL, up Cornelius' Cr, to HENRY TRENT, &c. Granted NICHOLAS MARSH 20 Oct. 1688, deserted, & now granted by order, &c. Imp. of 11 pers: JOHN JAMES, THO. WILLIAMS, WILLIAM JOHNS, JOSEPH THOMAS, JOHN THOMAS, ARTHUR ROBINS, JOHN ROBINS, THOMAS ROBERTS, WILLIAM RICHARDS, OLIVER RICHARDS.

MARTYN ELAM, 17 A., 2 R., Henrico Co., in Varina Par., S. side of James River, adj. his own land of THOMAS WELLS, & EDWARD STRATTON, 29 Apr. 1693, p. 270. Imp. of: EDWARD BANKS.

STEPHEN COCK, of Henrico Co., 1040 acs. in Jas. & Chas. City Cos. on S. W.
side of the head of Chickahominy Riv., 29 Apr. 1693, p. 300. Below the Wad-
ing place, on Strawberry Hill Run, through JAMES COLLAINE's cornefield, &c.
Granted to RICHARD WILLIAMS together with 800 (acs.) more for 750 acs., 24
Jan. 1655; for want of seating granted to sd. COCK by order, &c. Imp. of 21
pers: EDWARD ELLESTON, WM. DAVIES, JAMES WILLIS, JOHN SUILLMAN (SULLIVAN?),
JANE TUCKER, THO. MICHELL, JOSEPH BURCHER, ELIZA. SKIPS, WM. STEPHENS, RACH-
ELL BAKER, HEN. RICHARDSON, JAMES OGLEVY, RICHD. BROOKES, JOHN GORAM, JOHN
LEASAM. ROGER BOLT, JOHN BUTT; 4 Negroes.

RICHARD LIGON & JAMES EAKENS, Junr., 285 acs. Henrico Co., in Bristoll Par.
at Swift Cr., 29 Apr. 1693, p. 304. Beg. at mouth of Poplar Br. on head of
Proctor's, Mr. JOHN WORTHAM & EDWARD STRATTON, &c. Imp. of 6 pers: MARMADUKE
WOODUM, ROBERT FLYNT, SAMUEL POLLY, RICHARD COLLINS, ANTHONY FISHER, WILLIAM
THOSATT (or FOSSATT.).

SAMUEL KNIBB, 82 acs. Henrico Co., in Varina Par., in Burmoedy Hundred Neck,
20 Apr. 1694, p. 372. Part of 150 acs. granted JOHN HOWELL, 10 June 1639,
who assigned to JOHN MORGAN & his heires, 18 Oct. 1644; MORGAN died having
one only daughter Jane who intermarried with SAMUEL KNIBB, by whom she had
SAMUEL who entered sd. land; & bequeathed same to his son SAMUEL. Beg. at
the maine river next (to) Shirly Hundred, through the Sw. to Capt. ROYALL, to
a great grape vine adj. RICHARD DEWE's, Mr. ELAM's & Mr. BOWMAN's land. Imp.
of 2 pers.*

WALTER CLATWORTHY, 341 acs. Henrico Co., in Verina Par. adj. ROBERT THOMPSON,
crossing BRANCH's brook, &c., Apr. 1694, p. 379. Imp. of 7 Negroes,* by the
Friendship.

SAMUEL GOOD, 888 acs. Henrico Co., in Verina Par., S. side of James River, 20
Apr. 1694, p. 380. Beg. neare a gr. Piney Slash, adj. JOHN GOOD, S. Col.
WILLIAM BYRD. Granted to JOHN STOWERS & JOHN GOOD, deserted, & now granted
by order, &c. Imp. of 18 pers.*

EDWARD HILL, Esqr., 445 acs. Chas. City Co., Westopher Par., on N. side of
James Riv., adj. the CATTAILS & N. br. of Herin Cr., 26 Oct. 1694, p. 388.
Beg. at JOHN ROATCH, down the W. br. to Maj. STITH, &c. Imp. of 7 pers: ANN
NEWTON, MARY BLACKBEARD: 7 Negroes.

THOMAS CHRISTIAN, Senr., 193 acs. Chas. City Co., in Westopher Par., on S.
side of Chickahominy Sw., adj. land of BAXTER, on the W. br. of Oposom Maine
br., & land of WALLTALL SHIPLEY, &c., 26 Oct. 1694, p. 393. Imp. of 4 pers.

Mr. JOHN BRODNAX (BROADNAX), 435 acs. Henrico Co., in Varina Par., S. side of
James Riv., & N. side of Falling Cr., crossing GRINDALL's run, 26 Oct. 1694,
p. 394. Granted Mr. CHARLES DOUGLAS, 23 Oct. 1690, deserted, & now granted
by order, &c. Imp. of 9 pers: JNO. MORRIS, ELIZA. MORRIS, CHA. FOSTER, JNO.
TOBY, FRA. ADAMS, SARAH DILLON, JNO. CARLISLE, SARAH HIS WIFE; DICK, a Negro.

Capt. WILLIAM SOANE, 130 acs. Henrico Co., in Verina Par., N. side of James
Riv., over against Neck of Land, upon plantations of Mr. JAMES BLAIR, Mr.
JEREMIAH BROWN, & Mr. NICHOLAS BULLINGTON (BULLENTON); beg. at the Gleab Land
to mouth of 2 Mi. Cr., &c., 26 Apr. 1695, p. 404. Granted sd. BLAIR, BROWN, &
BULLENTON 20 Apr. 1690, deserted, & now granted for Imp. of 3 pers: ZARUE,
HUTCHIN, DINA.

WILLIAM RANDOLPH, Esqr., 1221 acs. Henrico Co., in Verina Par., N. side of
James Riv., above Westham Cr., 21 Apr. 1695, p. 408. Beg. at mouth of sd.
Cr. & mouth of a br. of Tuckahoe Cr., & granted Mr. JOHN PLEASANTS 20 Oct.
1691, deserted, & now granted by order, &c. Imp. 25 pers: TOM, JACK, JAMES,
ABRAM, DAVY, SCIPIO, HANIBALL, GEORGE, HARRY, JUPITER, MINGO, WILL. CONDE,
NAN, MOLL, HANNAH, WINNY, TONY, EFFY, SAM, NED, GILES. SAMBO, MOSES, MANUELL.

Patent book No. 9

Mr. BARTHOLOMEW FOWLER, 344 acs. Henrico Co., in Varina Par., on N. side of
James Riv., 29 Oct. 1696, p. 62, Beg. on the middle run, bet. COLSON's &
Deep Botton, along HENRY TRENT, to head of Barrow land, by Mr. Pleasants, &c.
Granted Mr. GILES WEBB, 29 Apr. 1692, deserted & now granted by order, &c.
Imp. of 7 Negroes.*

Mr. RICHARD COCK, 975 acs. Chas. City Co., N. side of James River, 29 Oct.
1696, p. 67. Beg. at Mr. JNO. TURNER on Chickahominy Path, to place nnown by
the name of Arrow Reedes up Fishing Run, on line supposed to be of ROBT.
PEAKE, to THO. MURRELL, &c. Imp. of 20 pers: DANLL. CARR, JNO. GOODMAN,
SUSANA & NICHOLAS LIPSCOME, WM. WHITE, & 15 Negroes.*

WILLIAM RANDOLPH, Gent. of Henrico Co., in Virginia, for diverse good causes,
&c., freely delivered up &c., for myself & my heires, &c., unto his Majestie,
King WILLIAM, the pattent granted me 25 Oct. 1695 for 2926 acs. &c. Signed:
WILLIAM RANDOLPH. In presence of: ROBT. BEVERLEY & HUGH DAVIS. P. 72.

Mr. JAMES COCK, 311 acs. Henrico Co., 28 Oct. 1697, p. 86. Adj. JOHN FOWLER,
& BATT. CHANDLER, nigh the Indian Path, along Old Towne Runn, &c. Being part
of 754 acs., 1 Rood & 3 poles, granted THOMAS WEBSTER, 28 Oct. 1673, deserted,
& now granted by order, &c. Imp. of 7 pers: ERRA, SUE, JENNY, WILL, TOM,
CIS, TONY.

Capt. FRANCIS EPS (EPES), 68 acs. Henrico Co., N. side of James River, on the
head of Long feald land, adj. his own, ROBERT & WM. BURTON, & land of JOHN
PEMSTON (?), 28 Oct. 1697, p. 105. Trans. of 2 pers: JA. JACKSON, WM. OATLEY.

Mr. GILES WEBB, 528 acs. Henrico Co., in Verina Par., on N. side of James
River, 28 Oct. 1697, p. 128. Beg. at Mr. JOHN PLEASANTS, on head of Barrow,
crossing SAMSON slash, to ISAAC CRESWELL on Cornelius' Creek to HENRY TRENT.
Granted Mr. THO. COCKE, Junr., 29 Apr. 1693, deserted, & now granted by order,
&c. Trans. of 11 pers: DICK, HARRY, MUTEA, DAVID, SAM, JOAN, SUE, NED, WILL,
TONY, CARTA.

35

Mr. THO. COCK, 49 acs. Henrico Co., N. side of James River, adj. JOHN ROBERT-
SON, to line of White Oakes land, on head line of the patent of MONGYES, 26
Apr. 1698, p. 138. Trans. of JOHN THWEAT.

WM. COCK, 256 A., 1 R., 24 P., Henrico Co., 26 Apr. 1698, p. 139. Beg. at
PERRIN's patent, over a br. of Cornelius' Run, along the Piney Slash, &c.
Granted to RICHD. PERRIN & joyned in patent of 740 A., 1 R., 20 P. 15 Mar.
1672, deserted & now granted by order, &c., Trans. of 6 pers: TONY, MINGO,
HANAH, HARRY, BESS, RACHELL.

WM. BURTON, 144 acs. Henrico Co., in Verina Par., N. side of James River, 26
Apr. 1698, p. 144. Beg. in a piney slash parting land of Capt. EPES & ROB-
ERT BURTON, 100 acs. granted (him), 22 Mar. 1665/6; 44 acs. being (the) King's
land; adj. JOHN GEMSTON. Trans. of 3 pers: TONY, MINGO, JACK.

Capt. JOSEPH ROYALL, 235 acs., Henrico Co., on Procter's branch, 15 Oct. 1698,
p. 159. Adj. JOHN CLARKE, Mr. THOMAS BRANCH, & ROBT. THOMPSON. Trans. of 5
pers.*

JOSEPH ROYALL, 50 acs. Henrico Co., 15 Oct. 1698, p. 160. Escheated from
JOHN CHAPLIN by inquisition under WM. RANDOLPH, Esch'r., &c.

FRANCIS EPES, 60 acs., Henrico Co. 15 Oct. 1698, p. 161. Escheated from ED-
WARD ELTON by inquisition under WM. RANDOLPH, Esch'r. &c.

ABRAHAM WOMECK, 200 acs. Henrico Co., 15 Oct. 1698, p. 161. Escheated from
GILBERT DEACON, by inquisition under WM. RANDOLPH, Esqr. Esch'r. &c.

ROBERT BURTON, 1300 acs. Henrico Co., on N. side of James Riv., 6 June 1699,
p. 187. Beg. at Lilly Valley, to COLE's run, nigh Cornelius Cr., over Mr.
BEAUCHAMPT's path, &c. Granted EDWARD HATCHER 6 Oct. 1675, deserted, & now
granted by order, &c. Imp. of 26 pers.*

JOHN PLEASANTS, 732 acs. on branches of Chickahominy Sw. at a place called
Half Sink, upon Stoney point, &c. 6 June 1699, p. 191. Granted Mr. JOHN
WOODSON, Junr., 23 Oct. 1690, deserted, & now granted by order, &c. Imp. of
15 pers.*

Same, 3087 A., 3 R., 24 P., Henrico Co., on N. side of James River, same date
& page. Beg. at S. side of Chickahominy Sw., adj. Mr. Beauchamp, &c. Granted Mr. THOMAS COCKE, 4 Oct. 1675, deserted & now granted by order, &c. Imp.
62 pers.*

JOSEPH PLEASANTS, 98 acs. Henrico Co., on Chickahominy Sw., & known by the
name of JOHN BOTTOM's Plantation & is King's land, adj. patent granted Capt.
COCK, Senr., known by the name of High Hills, beg. on the Queen's Cabbin Br.,
on Chickahominy Riv., &c. 26 Oct. 1699, p. 236. Trans. of 2 pers: LAWRENCE
FOX, EDWD. PETERS.

JOHN DAVIS, 200 acs. Henrico Co., 26 Oct. 1699, p. 237. Being part of patent for 500 acs. granted JOHN DAVIS, his father, 1 Oct. 1672, deserted & now granted by order, &c. Trans. of 4 pers.*

RICHARD DEARELOVE, 223 acs. Henrico Co., in Verina Par., S. side of James Riv. 24 Apr. 1700, p. 268. Adj. WALTALL CLATTWORTHY, ROBERT THOMPSON, SHEF-FELL's land, & Honble. Col. BYRD's line. Trans. of 5 pers.* Note: 5 rights paid for to WM. BYRD, Esqr., Auditor.

WILLIAM RANDOLPH, Gent., 1230 acs., Henrico Co., 7 May, 1700, p. 270. 480 acs. part thereof called Curles, formerly Long Feild, being part of patent to THOMAS HARRIS, dated 25 Feb. 1638, with the Swamp & Marsh, beg. at a Cr. over against Capt. MARTIN, N. on back of Sw., E.S.E. into the woods towards Breemo W.N.W. upon the main river, &c., 750 acs. commonly called the Slashes, lying on the poplar Brook on head of lands formerly Capt. DANIEL LEWELLIN's, E. along the heads thereof two (to) Mawborn Hills, &c. Late in the seizen & inheritance of NATHANIEL BACON, Junr., Esqr., dec'd. from whom it escheated by his attainer for high treason,                     as by inquisition under WILLIAM RANDOLPH, Esch'r., &c., 21 July 1698, who hath paid to his Majestie's Auditor & Receiver Generall, &c., the valuable consideration of 150 lbs. Sterling, &c.

EPHRAIM GARTHRIGHT, 165 acs. Henrico Co., on S. side of White Oaks Sw., 7 Nov. 1700, p. 273. Beg. at WILLIAM PORTER, on line of JOHN WADSON by the roade to sd. Sw., up Pigg Slash to THOMAS EAST, &c. Trans. of 4 pers: MARGARET MAC-ARTY, BYRAN ONEALE, ANNE BIBY, ELIZ. SANDERS.

JOHN DAVIS, 254 A., 3 R., 8 P., Henrico Co., on N. side of James Riv., adj. FRANCIS RADFORD, nigh the Roundabout Slash, 7 Nov. 1700, p. 287. Granted FRANCIS RADFORD, 5 Aug. 1669, who on 1 July 1672, joyned in patent for 629 A., 3 R., 18 P., & by him deserted, & now granted by order, &c. Trans. of 5 pers.*

ROBERT BURTON, Senr., 300 acs. Henrico Co., in Varina Par., on E. side of Carneleses Cr., by PARKER's Path, 25 Apr. 1701, p. 307. Trans. of 6 pers.* Note: 6 rights paid for to WM. BYRD, Esqr., Auditor.

JOHN BOLLING, Gent., 50 acs. Henrico Co., Verina Par., 25 Apr. 1701, p. 318. Escheated from NATHLL. BACON, Junr., by his attainer for high Treason, as by inquisition under WILLIAM RANDOLPH, Esch'r., 21 July, 1698. Consideration: 30 lbs. Sterling.

FRANCIS PERCE, 137 acs., Henrico Co., N. side of James Riv., a little below mouth of 3 Mi. Cr., to 2 Mi. Cr. 25 Apr. 1701, p. 319. Trans. of 3 pers: RICHARD FLEMING, PETER MORGAN, JACOB JOHNSON.

JOHN WOODSON, Senr., 1020 acs. Henrico Co., in Verina Par., in Rawsonsey Neck, 25 Apr. 1701, p. 321. Beg. at HENRY TURNER's, on Mrs. IZARD's line;

to Beachen Runn, down Rockey Run, on JOHN WOODSON, Junr., &c. Trans. of 21 pers: JAMES DEANE, JOHN DUFF, JOHN MAN, PETER MAY, HUMPHRY HOW, WM. BLUNT, WM. RUSSELL, JOHN DENHAM, HENRY PEIRCE, RALPH ROGERS, WM. SPILLMAN, WM. BLESSINGTON, PETER HOLLAND, RICHD. LAKELAND, THOMAS MINOR, THOMAS TWYNE, JOHN JOHNSON, SARAH DAVIS, ISABELLA TIPLADY, HELLENA PARKER, ELIZABETH SPRIGGE.

JOHN PLEASANTS, 2994 A., 2 R., 35 P., 25 Apr. 1701, p. 322.  2093 A., 1 R., 35 P¼ S. side of Chickahominy Sw., on Col. OWIN's quarter, above Pamunkey Path, over Cowtaile quarter run; 901 A., & 1 R., in Henrico Co., on N. side of James Riv., known by the name of the forkes of Cattaile run, along Mr. RICHARD COCKE, Senr., to line of Mr. GREEN,; granted JOHN BEAUCHAMP, RICHARD COCK, Senr., 21 June 1644, deserted, & by now granted by order, &c.  Trans. of 60 pers:  JOHN FRY, JOHN FOSTER, JOHN WOODY, GREGORY DAWSON, THOMAS BURKE, ALEX. MACKDANIEL, MARGT. REA, ELIZ. PERRY, SAMUEL SEAT, THOMAS ROBERTS, WM. ROGERS, FRANCIS BOCKEN, MARY STEELE, ROBERT DAVIS, THOMAS BROWNE, ROBERT HYDE, EDWARD CHAMBERLAINE, ELIZA. BLACKSHOTT, JOSEPH PEGG, JANE COME, DOROTHY LOVE, WILLIAM MARSHALL, JAMES CAMELL, MARY HUGINS, ABIGALL ADDAMS, MARGT. BURK, KATHERINE CLARE, ZACH. CLARK, WM. SPENCER, THOMAS MONTFORT, JOHN MASSEY, ANNE DOOD, ANN BELL, MARY BARROW, MARY BENNETT, WM. BARKSTEAD, EDWARD JONES, MARGT. STAPLES; 22 rights more paid for to WM. BYRD, Esqr., Auditor.

THOMAS COCK, 628 acs. Henrico Co., on N. side of James River, 24 Oct. 1701, p. 373.  Being part of patent for 1228 A., 1 R., & 26 p., granted Mr. ROWLAND PLACE, 25 Aug. 1669; deserted, & now granted by order, &c., Trans. of 13 pers:  JOHN KENT, EDWD. GEER, WM. WARREN, SARAH RICHARDSON, MARY PARTREE, ELIZA. JOHNSON, CHARLES RAWSON, JOHN BROINRAN (?), CHARLES AUGUSTIN, THOMAS WISE, WM. JOHNSON, JOHN SHORT, PHILIP LEAKE.

THOMAS FARRAR, 126 acs. Henrico Co., N. side of James River, on Cornelious' Cr., adj. MICHAEL TURPEN, the Bridge Run, RICHARD COX & ROBERT BURTON, 24 Oct. 1701, p. 390.  Trans. of 3 pers:  THOMAS NICHOLLS, JNO. JA. VALTON, JOHN PAGESTER.

Capt. THOMAS COCK, 1170 acs. Chas. City Co., in Westover Par., 24 Oct. 1701, p. 403, adj. Mr. HARRISON, sd. COCK & SHIPLEIGH, THOMAS CHRISTIAN, & Capt. BAXTER's line.  Trans. of 24 pers.*  24 rights paid for to Mr. WM. BYRD, Esqr, Auditor.

Capt. WM. SOANES, 51 acs. Henrico Co., in Verina Par., known by the name of Chinkapin Island, on N. side of Roundabout Br., adj. Mr. JOHN BOWLING, & Mr. JOHN RADFORD, 25 Apr. 1702, p. 432.  Trans. of 1 pers.*  Note: 1 right paid for to WM. BYRD, Esqr., Auditor.

NICHOLAS HUTCHINS, 230 acs. Henrico Co., on N. side of James Riv., on W. side of 4 Mi. Cr. adj. HENRY PEW, & Mr. JOHN WOODSON, 25 Apr. 1702, p. 436.  Trans. of 5 pers.*  Note: 5 rights paid for to WM. BYRD, Esqr., Auditor.

JOHN BOLLING, 350 acs. Henrico Co., N. side of James River, 25 Apr. 1702, p.

437. Beg. on N. side of Round about, to S. side of same, cor. of JOHN COX, to
4 Mi. Cr. old path, N.W. upon his own land called Harrahattocks, &c. Granted
THOMAS TAYLOR, with other lands, 23 Sept. 1667; deserted, & now granted by
order, &c. Trans. of 7 pers: JOHN BLAIR, WALTER CROMMIE, JAMES SHEILS, JAMES
MORRIS, JOHN SINCOCK, MARGT. BROWN, ISAAC WOODBURNE.

MOSES WOOD, 237 acs. Henrico Co., S. side James River, being the plantation
whereon he lives, 25 Apr. 1702, p. 443. Adj. JAMES BAUGH, JOHN GRANGER, PETER
ASHBROOK, line of the orphans of Mr. JOSEPH TANNER, JAMES ATKINS, & ROBERT
RUCELL's cor. Trans. of 5 pers: EDMD. NEWCOMB, MARY NEWCOMB, HANNAH FACY,
CHARLES PISTOR, CHRISTIAN PISTOR.

JOHN WILSON, Senr., 94 acs. Henrico Co., on the Old Towne Run, adj. Mr. PHI-
LIP JONES; 28 Oct. 1702, p. 488. Trans. of 2 pers: RICHARD GRIFFIN, RICHD.
KENNON.

PETER HARRIS, 94 acs. Henrico Co., N. side James River, adj. lands of GILEY
GREWMEREN, Mr. JOHN PLEASANTS, & MR. WADKINES, 28 Oct. 1702, p. 488. Trans.
of 2 pers: ISAAC MINNS, JOHN CANSTALL.

JAMES COCKE, 570 acs. Henrico Co., in Verina Par., N. side of James Riv., beg.
in the forke of White Oake Sw., where the N. & S. brs. meet, by the Pidgen
Land, &c., 28 Oct. 1702, p. 491. Trans. of 12 pers: THOMAS WADDS, ROBERT
BLOW, SARAH WOOD, & 9 rights more paid for to WM. BYRD, Esqr., Auditor.

HENRY BREAZEALE, Junr., 300 acs. Henrico Co., on N. side of James River, 28
Oct. 1702, p. 501. Beg. on N. side of Gilley's Cr., cor. of HENRY BREAZEALE,
Senr., on line of GILLEY, to THO. EAST, Senr. Trans. of 6 pers: THEODORIC
BLAND, JOHN LEINCH, JAMES ROBBINSON, ELIANOR REENER; & 2 rights more paid for
to WM. BYRD, Esqr., Auditor.

GILES WEBB, 1797 acs. Henrico Co., on N. side of James River, at a place
known by the name of Westham; 28 Oct. 1702, p. 502. Beg. at Mr. ROBERT BEV-
ERLEY, to Col. RANDOLPH, down Tuckahow Cr. to mouth of lower Westmam Cr. &c.
Trans. of 36 pers: THOMAS JONES, JAMES SPENSE, EDWD. FULLMOW (or FILLMORE),
ELIZ. THOMSON, EDWD. PALMER, THOMAS SMITH, ELIZA. PALMER, JOHN EARLE, JOSEPH
POTTER, JOHN BAZY, THOMAS CLASPER, ROBERT BARKER, EDWD. BAYNES, HENRY FREEMAN,
JOHN WHITE, ANNE GROSE, CATHERINE KENDALL, ELIZA. JONES, HARTHORNE DRAYTONN,
GOODLOVE SMITH, MARY STILLS (or STILES), THOMAS LEECH, RICHD. KANADAY, EMLIN
LIGHT; & 12 rights more paid for to WM. BYRD, Esqr., Auditor.

JOHN ROBINSON, 831 acs. Henrico Co., N. side of James River, at a place known
by Gilley's Creek, 24 Apr. 1703, p. 521. Beg. at JOHN BAYLY, across the
Southern Br., & crossing Gilley's main Cr., Trans of 17 pers: HUGH EDWARDS,
JAMES EVANS, MARY HORNEY, MARTHA FLOYD; & 13 rights paid for to WM. BYRD,
Esqr., Auditor.

WALTER COCKE (COCK), 350 acs. upon the main brs. of Up. Chippoakes Cr., along
land late of Mr. EDWARD BLAND; 24 Apr. 1703, p. 523. granted THOMAS Senr.

6 Apr. 1664, deserted, & now granted by order, &c.  Trans. of 7 pers.*  Note:
7 rights paid for to WM. BYRD, Esqr. Auditor.

Mr. JOHN WOODSON, 2700 acs., Henrico Co., N. side of James River, 24 Apr.
1703, p. 525.  Beg. at mouth of Gennitoe Cr., 116 pole above a large Island.
Trans. of 54 pers:  JOHN TULLETT, JOHN WHALEY, JNO. WILLIAMSON, JOHN STIBBINS,
ROBERT LANG, ROSAMOND MADEN, MARY CRABB, ROBERT POVALL, SAML. HOSIER, MARY
FISHER, MARY LYDALL, CHARLES DUDLEY, JOAN TUDER, JAMES LEACH, HANNAH TULLETT,
JOHN GLANEY, JOHN JACKSON, JOHN CRABB, DANIEL SWALEY, TAB TABITHA, MARTHA HAM-
OND, ELIZA. POVALL, JOHN MATTHEWS, GEO. BLOYD, THO. PIPER, JOHN SAWKINS, MARY
MATHY, JOHNIANE, JOHN ISBELL, JOHN NEWMAN, ROBERT WEAVER, TIMO. OMOONEY, ELIZA.
CARTER, JOHN BEST, ROBT. POVALL, Junr., CHA. DOUGLAS, MARY WEATLY, JAMES
JACKSON, ROBT. LEATHER, PHILIP SWINFEILD; & 14 rights more paid for to WM.
BYRD, Esqr., Auditor.

Mr. JOHN FARLAR, Junr., 471 acs., Henrico County, S. side of the James
River, in the forks of Procters, adj. Mr. HENRY WALTERS, S. crossing Myery Br.,
24 Apr. 1703, p. 528.  Trans. of 10 Pers:  JOHN WEBB, WM. SWIFTON, JOHN SOWARD,
RICHD. LEWIS, JOHN SLEDGE, JOHN HASTINS, MARY LEWIS, JOHN HARDIMAN, ROBERT
SMITH, WM. HODGES.  (Note: This name first written FARRAR.)

Mr. DRURY STITH, & SAMUEL EALE, 680 A., 1 R., & 19 P., Chas. City Co., on N.
side of James River, 24 Apr. 1703, p. 539.  Adj. JONAS LISCOM, WM. FEATHER-
STON, & JNO. EDWARDS' line, down E. br. of Possum runn, along THOMAS CHRIST-
IAN's line, GILLEY's Br., on the Long Br., on JOHN STOCKES' line, to E. br. of
Herring Cr.  Trans of 14 pers.*  Note: 14 rights paid for to WM BYRD, Esqr.,
Auditor.

FRANCIS REIVES, 896 acs., Henrico Co., N. side of James River, about 2 mi.
below the falls, beg. at mouth of Almond's Cr., to mouth of the Deep Bottom,
to land now or late of SNUGG on sd. Cr., 23 Oct. 1703, p. 575.  Being found
within bounds of patent for 600 acs. granted HUMPHRY LISTER, from whom by
severall conveyances it came to sd. REIVES; 296 acs. for imp. of 6 pers.*
Note: 6 rights paid for to WM. BYRD, Esqr., Auditor.

ANN PERRIN, 200 acs., Henrico Co., Varina Par., on N. side of James River, adj.
Capt. KNOWLES, & JOHN OLDEY, & Capt. WEBB, crossing SAMPSON's Slash, 23 Oct.,
1703, p. 575.  Trans. of 4 pers:  THO. WALKER, THO. DAWSON, EDW. CROWDER,
CATHERINE JOHNSON.

WILLIAM RANDOLPH, Junr., 132 acs. Henrico Co., N. side of James River, bet.
lands of Honbl. WM. BYRD, Esqr. & Mr. ROBERT BEVERLEY; beg. at a heap of great
rocks on upper side of sd. BYRD's land, 23 Oct. 1703, p. 576.  Granted GILES
WEBB, 29 Apr. 1692, deserted, & now granted by order, &c.  Trans. of 3 pers:
MARY NELSON, JOHN JONES, HANNAH JONES.

Honbl. WM. BYRD, Esqr., 344 acs. Henrico Co., on S. side of James River, "within the limits of the land laid out for the French refugees, but not by any of

40

them seated," 20 Oct. 1704, p. 612. Bounded vizt: "Beginning at a corner upon the upper Manakin Creek in the french head line thence along the same East forty Degrees South two hundred & eighty pole to a corner thence North Eight Degrees East three hundred & sixteen pole to a corner upon the creek below the Cole mine thence up the water course of the same according to the severall meanders." Trans. of 7 pers: Note Paid her majesty for 7 rights as appears by a certificate of the aforesaid WM. BYRD., being Auditor.

Same. 3664 acs. same Co., & date, p. 613. S. side of James River, on both sides of the Road to the French settlement, beg. upon water course of Powhite Cr., to cor. of Mr. THOMAS JEFFERSON & partners, up water course of Lucy's Br., above the spring, to cor. of Shamapoke, up water course of Pocoshock, &c. Trans. of 74 pers: Note: Same as second above.

CHARLES EVANS, 383 acs., Henrico Co., on N. side of gr. or main br. of Proctors (Cr.), 20 Oct. 1704, p. 621. Granted to MARY LIGON, former wife of WM. LIGON, dec'd., 26 Oct. 1699, deserted & now granted by order, &c. Trans. of 8 pers* Note: Paid WILLIAM BYRD, Esqr., Auditor, for 8 rights.

JEREMIAH BENSKIN, 324 acs. Henrico Co., on S. side of James River, 20 Oct. 1704, p. 623. Beg. at mouth of lower Westham Cr., & crossing up Westham Cr. Trans. of 7 pers.* Note: Paid WM. BYRD, Esqr., Auditor, for 7 rights.

WALTER SCOTT, 250 acs. Henrico Co., South side of James River, on the back of Warrick & Knowne by the name of Selkrig, 20 Oct. 1704, p. 624. Adj. Mr. SAMUEL GOOD, Mr. WM. BLACKMAN, & HENRY TRENT, to branch making the fork of GRINDON's (Cr.). Trans. of 6 pers: DANLL. MACKARTYHAN, RICHD. DULE, DANLL. MACKALLAM, JAMES CASUM, WM. HOCKLES.

ROBERT EASLY (EASLEY - ESELY), 315 acs. Henrico Co., on E. side of the Reedy Cr., 20 Oct. 1704, p. 624. Trans. of 7 pers.* Note: Paid WM. WYRD, Esqr., Auditor for 7 rights.

Mr. THOMAS JEFFERSON, THO. HARRIS, MATTHEW BRANCH & THO. TURPIN, 628 acs. Henrico Co., on N. side of James River, 20 Oct. 1704, p. 627. Beg. on br. of Lucy's Spring. Trans. of 13 pers: RICHD. WRIGHT, JOHN RAINS, CHARLES MACKCULLA, JOHN PLANT, THO. EDSELL, THO. STELL, EDWD. EVANS, JOHN FULKS, ROBT. HATFEILD, JOHN FERRYMAN, JONATHAN IVE (?), HENRY WALTON, JOHN HENRY.

JOHN PLEASANTS & JOSEPH PLEASANTS, 286 acs. Henrico Co., on head of the White Oake Swamp, 20 Oct. 1704, p. 627. Trans. of 6 pers.* Note paid WM. BYRD, Esqr., Auditor for 6 rights.

Mr. ROBERT WOODSON, 171 acs. Henrico Co., on N. side of Uʃnom brook, 20 Oct. 1704, p. 629. Adj. Mr. JOHN PLEASANTS. Trans. of 4 pers.* Note: Paid Mr. Auditor BYRD for 4 rights.

ROBERT BOLLING, 50 acs. Henrico Co., 2 May 1705, p. 646. Escheated from John

COOKNEY, dec'd., by inquisition under WILLIAM RANDOLPH, Gent., Esch'r. &c.

CHARLES EVANS, 140 acs. Henrico Co., in Varina Par., on N. side of James Riv. 2 May 1705, p. 665. Adj. Mr. RICHARD PERRIN, ABRAHAM BAYLY, up Cornelius' Creek; WM. GILES, & THOMAS BAYLY. Granted THOMAS PERIN, 20 Oct. 1688, deserted, & now granted by order, &c. Trans. of 3 pers: CHAS. MACKULLY, EDWD. WALTERS, WM. MOSS.

ALLESON CLARKE & CHARLES RUSSELL, 945 acs. named Windsor Forrest, Henrico Co. on N. side of James Riv., & E. side of the main br. of Tuckahoe Cr., 2 May 1705, p. 673. Trans. of 19 pers: EDWD. HALL, GEO. WALL, WILL. BALL, JOHN BRUMFEILD, JOS. SMITH, THO. CHAPMAN, JOHN ENGLISH, WM. WEST, MILL MITCHELL, MARY COLLETT, SARA HONOR, WM. SAMPSON, THOMAS BUSBY, NICHO. MARSH, JOS. PRICHARD, CONSTANT BEMBRIDGE, THO. BEMBRIDGE, WM. SAMPSON, NICHO. SUTTLE.

ABRAHAM MICHAUX, 574 acs. Henrico Co., S. side of James River & on both sides of lower Manakin Towne Cr., 2 Nov. 1705, p. 679. Imp. of 12 pers: JOHN ROBERTS, Junr., JAMES WEST, JAMES LOYD, WM. BROOKES, JOHN BOIS (?), JAMES YOUNG, WM. THROGMORTON, HENRY HEWS, ROBT. BLAW, THO. ROBERTSON, WM. ADLAN, SUSAN COBBS.

WILLIAM BYRD, 385 acs. being an island encompassed by James River, in Henrico Co., the lower end of sd. island lying opposite against the upper end of the Manakin Towne, 2 Nov. 1705, p. 688. Trans. of 8 pers: GEO. YEATS, ROBT. HENNICK, DANL. DONNEVAN, HUGH BURLEY, ROBT. BENNETT, JO. HARRIS, ROBT. WILLIAMS, JOHN DENHAM.

RICHARD HOLMES, 252 acs. Henrico Co. on Swift Cr., adj. Capt. JOHN BOWLING, 2 Nov. 1705, p. 696. Trans. of 5 pers: JOHN OSBORNE, DAVID CAROHSHAW, GEO. WALL, HENRY RATTENBURY, ROBERT CLOKE (or PLOKE).

RICHARD COCK, Junr., 570 acs. Henrico Co., in Verina Par. N. side of James River, beg. in fork of White Oake Sw. where N. & S. brs. meet, to br. of the N. br. by Pidgeon Land, 1 May 1706, p. 722. Granted JAMES COCK, 28 Oct. 1702, deserted, & now granted by order, &c. Trans. of 12 pers: THOMAS TISDALE, WM. FORD, MARY SLAH, MATHEW RESONS, ROGER CARRELL, WILL. WEST, EDWD. MITCHELL, THO. ROBINSON, SIMON LANE, LOTT DORAN, HANNAH CARRELL, JOHN FIFIELD

CHARLES EVANS, 1468 A., 1 R., 28 P., Henrico Co., on S. side of James River, 2 May 1706, p. 737. 167 A. 1 R. & 12 P. part being ½ of land granted THO. LIGGON & Maj. WM. FARRAR, 3 Oct. 1664, beg. at the river about the middle bet the bottom joyning lower side of Mount My Lady Feild & the bottom next it; to a cor. of Maj. HARRIS; 1301 A., & 16 P., beg. at the 2nd. bottom below Mount My Lady, adj. Maj. HARRIS, on the dry bottom, to the head of the red water, by br. of Ashen Sw., to old poetan Path. Granted Col. THO. LIGGON 28 Sept. 1671, deserted, and now granted by order, &c., Trans. of 30 pers.

Patent Book No. 10

ABRAHAM SALLE of Henrico Co., 232 acs. (N.L.) in sd. Co. S. side of James Riv. 19 Dec. 1711, p. 42. Beg. on bank of sd. Riv. to JOHN MARCHES' Cor., to Lower Manakin Cr., &c. 5 Shill. Imp. of 4 pers: ABRA. SALLE, OLIVER SALLE, ABRA. SALLE, Junr., JACOB SALLE. (Marginal note: 230 acs.)

TARLTON WOODSON, 102 acs. (N.L.) Henrico Co., S. side James Riv., 2 May 1713, p. 73. On W. side of Neca Land Sw. 10 Shill.

WILLIAM SHEAPARD & RICHARD BAKER, 400 acs. (N.L.) Henrico Co., S. side of the main br. of Chicahominy Sw., 2 May 1713, p. 82. Imp. of 12 pers: WM. LAWSON, JOHN ROBINSON, THOMAS HARTON, WILLIAM LATTIMORE, ROBERT AVERY, JOHN WHATLEY, JOHN MAY, JOHN ROGERS.

JOSEPH PLEASANTS, 1029 acs. (N.L.), Henrico Co., N. side of James Riv. 13 Nov. 1713, p. 93. Adj. Mr. JOHN PLEASANTS. Imp. of 21 pers: PHILIP THORNE, RICHD. WINSELL, HENRY THOMAS, EDMD. LIPTROT, JAMES NICHOLS, FRANCES NICHOLS, JOHN COSAM, THOS. PAINE, HENRY KINGLY, JOHN BRITTAINE, WM. WETHERS, JOHN WILLIAM- SON, ROGER CROSDALE, ISAAC SHEFFEILD, JOHN HARTFORD, CHARLES COAKER, MARTHA LIMBER, THOS. PINDALE, HENRY WOODCOCK, JOHN WINTER, ELIZA. WOOD.

JOHN PLEASANTS, 1385 acs. (N.L.), Henrico Co., N. side of James Riv., 13 Nov. 1713, p. 94. Adj. JOHN WOODSON, below the mouth of Beaver Dam Cr., & land of AMOS LEAD. Imp. of 28 pers: ELIZA. PENERY (or PEURY), JOHN BALYE, JNO. EDER- KIN (Or ELDERKIN), THOS. HAYWORTH, ANDREW OSWALD, THOS. POTTS, THOS. SMITHES, JOHN SHARP, JOHN WHITEBREAD, THOS. MARTIN, WM. GARRETT, ELIZA. SKIP, WM. THOMPSON, JOSEPH SMALLWOOD, JAMES WAITE, CHARLES POTTER, SAML. HODGES, MARY HILL, SARAH GARNETT, NICHOLAS HUTCHINS, WM. LEEY, JOHN ROBINSON, RICHD. JOHN- SON, WM. COLEGROVE, ROBT. CATE, MARY LEWIS, THOS. DUPREE, WM. FIDLER.

JOHN CALVERT, 100 acs. (N.L.), Henrico Co., S. side of James Riv., 30 Apr. 1714, p. 125. Beg. at upper cor. of the french lands, to JOHN PLEASANTS' line, &c. Being taken out of 258 acs. surveyed for Mr. JOHN PLEASANTS, by order of the Gov'r & Council. 10 Shill.

DAVID PATTISON, 400 acs. (N.L.), Henrico Co., N. side of James Riv. on E. side of Licking Hole Cr., adj. Capt. JOHN BOLLING, 16 June 1714, p. 128. 2 Lbs. money.

HENRY GILL, 500 acs. (N.L.), Henrico Co., N. side of James Riv. & on E. side of br. of Pamunkey Riv., adj. WM. LEAD (LAD); on E. side of the N. br. of Beaver Dam br., 16 June 1714, p. 130.
WILLIAM LEAD, 500 acs. (N.L.), Henrico Co., on N. side of James Riv., in the fork of Beaver Dam Cr; beg. at AMOS LEAD, on E. side of the N. br. of the sd. Cr., 16 June 1714, p. 132. 50 Shill.

JOHN BURTON, 341 ACS. (N.L.), Henrico Co., at a place known as Deep Cr., on the S. side of James Riv., down Elbow Branch, 16 June 1714, p. 134. Imp. of 7 pers: HENRY THOMAS, WM. BASS, JOHN BOLDING, MARY SPITS, FRANCES BRAY, ELIZA-BETH PASSIFULL, HANNAH WEBB.

JAMES CHRISTIAN, 382 acs. (N.L.), Henrico Co.,on N. side of James Riv., adj. THOMAS CHRISTIAN, on W. side of W. br. of Beaver Dam Cr., S. Mr. JOSEPH PLEAS-ANTS, 16 June 1714, p. 139. 2 Lbs. money.

STEPHEN CHASTIENE, 138 acs. (N.L.), Henrico Co., on N. side of Upper Manakin Town Cr., on Mr. STEPHEN MALLETT, & the FRENCH line, 16 June 1714, p. 142. 15 Shill.

WILLIAM CLARKE, Senr., 229 acs. (O.& N.L), Henrico Co., on S. side of James Riv., line of THOMAS SHIPEY & GILBERT ELAM, 16 June 1714, p. 148. Part of 324 acs. granted GILBERT DEKER, 18 Mar. 1662; 124 acs. granted him by deed from Mr. MARTIN ELAM, 2 Nov. 1672, & likewise by escheat patent in 1685, 105 acs. being surplus. Imp. of 3 pers: THOMAS WATTS, JANE PENTICON, ANNE BOND.

THOMAS CHRISTIAN, 400 acs. (N.L.), Henrico Co., on N. side of James Riv., on E. side of the W. br. of Beaver Dam Cr., 16 June 1714, p. 148. 40 Shill.

CHARLES FLEMING, 732 acs. (N.L.), Henrico Co., on N. side of James Riv., beg. at his own land, crossing a br. to the back river against Elk Island, &c., 16 June 1714, p. 151. 40 Shill., & Imp. of 7 pers: ROBERT BROOMLY, JAMES DOLL-ARD, EDWD. MORGAN, MARGT. Mc DANIEL, WM. GOBELL, DENNIS SHEEHORNE, MARGT. SHEPPARD.

STEPHEN CHASTEANE, 280 acs. (N.L.), Henrico Co., on W. side of the Up. Manakin Town Cr., 16 June 1714, p. 156. 30 Shill.

JOHN PLEASANTS, 541 acs. (N.L.), Henrico Co., on brs. of Upnim (Ufnum?) adj. land of JOHN WOODSON, 16 June 1714, p. 157. Imp. of 11 pers: THOMAS JONES, CHARLES EVANS, FRA. NICHOLLS, MARY LOWDER, CHARLES SUBLY, THOS. TINDALE, THOS. HEWIT, WM. STEWART, JNO. BOMBAY, JOHN HEWLET (or NEWLET), JOHN LYNES. Note: "See an order of Councill relating to this land in the 254th page of this booke."

CHARLES EVANS, 577 acs. (N.L.), Henrico Co., N. side of James Riv., on head of Mill Cr., beg. on N. side of S. br. from the Beaver Ponds of Tuckahoe Cr., along a br. of Genitoe Cr., 16 June 1714, p. 161. 3 Lbs.

Mr. CHARLES FLEMING, 670 acs. (N.L.), Henrico Co., S. side of James River, beg. on N. side of a small br., near a gr. point of Rocks opposite against the middle of Elk Island, to N. side of WILLSE's Cr., 16 June 1714, p. 164. Imp. of 14 pers: JOHN LIGHTFOOT, THOS. HARLONG, JOSEPH DAY, MARY HOLT, ELIZA. NASH, CHARLES KING, ELEANORE DEMSEY, WM. STEPHENS, WM. GENTLEMAN, THOS. GRANT, JOHN COLLINS, NICHOLAS FITCHCOMB, ANNE MEEDS, RACHEL (?) GARDNER.

JOHN WOODSON & CHARLES FLEMING, 1278 acs (N.L.), Henrico Co., on N. side of

James Riv., called Elk Island & land adjacent, 16 June 1714, p. 166. Imp. of
26 pers: JOHN PLUM, JOHN HARPER, JOHN GREEN, NATHANIEL COCK, THOS. BATES,
JOHN DAVIS, GEO. THOMPSON, WM. SOUTHALL, PETER DIXON, CHR. SCOOT, WM.HILLIARD,
THO. STOONE, NICHO. TAYLOR, JOHN THOMAS, WM. GEVERSON, NICH. MOLTMAIN (?),
WM. WALDRON, JANE CONSTABLE, HANNAH STORY, ANNE BLESSING, ANNE MILLS, ELIZA.
LEE, THOMAS RICE, MARY MITCHELL, ANNE SKEPOSON, ALE. FORD.

ANTHONY RAPPEENE, 190 acs. (N.L.), Henrico Co., S. side of James River, beg.
on S. side of up. Manakin Cr., to French line, 16 June 1714, p. 167. 20 Shill.

AMOS LADD, 1085 acs. (N.L.), Henrico Co., on N. side of James Riv., beg. at
Mr. PLEASANTS on a gr. br. of James Riv., known by the Beaver Ponds, 16 June
1714, p. 171. 5 Shill., & Imp. of 21 pers: JOHN JONES, ANDREW KING, JOHN
TOLWIN (or POLWIN), JOHN LINCH, EDWD. BOOKE, WM. PILKINGTON, THOS. FOSTER,
FRANCIS CERLEY, RICHD. BURKE, ELLEN BROWN, WILLIAM IRBY, ISAAC SWEET, GARRETT
AUGBURD, JOHN GITSHILL, BENJ. FRENCH, JOHN CLOYSON, MAIDEN MASCALL, ROBT. SILK,
ROBT. SPAIDMAN, WM. DOBYE, MARKE LIFEHOLY.

WILLIAM COX, 440 acs. (N.L.), Henrico Co., on N. side of James Riv. beg. on
line of Mr. JOHN WOODSON, over against the Manakin Town. on Mr. WM. WOMACK's
line, 16 June 1724*, p. 190. Imp. of 9 pers: JOHN TRUSTUM, THO. KING, WM.
WRIGHT, MARGT. OWEN, JOSEPH SLEEPS, THO. SHARPE, DAVID WATTALS, JOHN SICKLY-
MORE & MARTIN SLEPS. *(Henrico Co. Land Patents and Grants, p. 558 should be
1714.-L.H.F.)

THOMAS HARROD, 448 acs. (N.L.), Co. & Parish of Henrico; N. side of James Riv.,
& on Giley's Cr., adj. land of HENRY BRAZELE, JOHN ROBERTSON, EDWD. MOSEBY, &
WM. PORTER, 16 June 1714, p. 191. Imp. of 9 pers: HEZEKIAH GOBBLE, RUTH
GARFORD, WM. PILKINTON, MARY BROOKES, ELIZA. HOLMES, PETER SPENCER, GERRAUD
CANNAH, (or CAVNAH), ARTHUR CANNAH (or CAVNAH), ARCHABALL MACCARRELL.

GILLY GRUMURREN, 500 acs. (N.L.), Henrico Co., on N.W. side of the main br.
of Tuckahoe, adj. Mr. CLARK, 16 Dec. 1714, p. 210. 2 Lbs., 10 Shill.

EBENEZER ADAMS, 670 acs. (N.L.), Henrico Co., N. side of James Riv., on S.
side of the W. br. of Beaver Dam Cr., 23 Dec. 1714, p. 216. 3 Lbs., 10 Shill.

ROBERT WOODSON, Junr., 1494 acs. (N.L.), Henrico Co., N. side of James Riv.,
on brs. of Mill Cr..& Jenitoe Cr., adj. Mr. JOHN PLEASANTS' line, 23 Dec. 1714,
p. 216. 7 Lbs., 10 S.

THOMAS MIMS, 500 acs. (N.L.), Henrico Co., S. side of main br. of Tuckahoe
(Cr.), adj. WM. BURTON, BENJ. WOODSON; & MICHAEL JOHNSON, 23 Dec. 1714, p. 217.
50 Shill.

RICHARD COCKE, Junr., 2497 acs. (N.L.), Henrico Co., N. side of James Riv.,
adj. Mr. JOSEPH PLEASANTS, on S. side the W. br. of Beaver Dam Cr., Mr. JOHN
WOODSON, & PLEASANTS, 23 Dec. 1714, p. 217. 12 Lbs., 10 Shill.

ISAAC LAFEIT, 133 acs. (N.L.), Henrico Co., on S. side of James Riv., out of the upper part of the last 5,000 acs. surveyed French refugees; beg. at JOHN CALVERT & his own corner., 23 Dec. 1714, p. 229. Imp. of 3 pers: ISAAC LA-FAITE, ELIZA. LAFAITE, & ESTER LAFAITE.

Major JOHN BOLLING, 1388 acs. (N.L.), Henrico Co., on N. side of James Riv., beg. at his own & land of JOHN WOODSON, to S. side of Licking Hole Cr., now called Treasurer's Run, 23 Dec. 1714, p. 235. 4 Lbs., 15 Shill., & Imp. of 9 pers: FRANCIS RIBOT, JANE RIBOT, NICHO. RIBOT, JNO. RIBOT, SUSANNA BROWN, SUSANNA RIBOT, MARTHA RIBOT, MARIA RIBOT, WM. SMITH SINGLEMAN (Single man ?).

JOHN WOODSON, 1596 acs. (N.L.), Henrico Co., S. side of James Riv., beg. at mouth of Giney-Towe Cr., 16 Aug. 1715, p. 237. Imp. of 32 pers: CALEB WARE, SIGFRED CLEMENTSON (or CLEMETSON), JOHN PATISON, STEPHEN GILL, JOHN BANNION, ROBT. ANDERSON, JAMES GRAY, GLOUD DOGOE, GILBERT WETHERLEE, WM. HURST, CHARLES OGLEBEY, RICHD. KAKE, ROBT. CARVERSON, ROBT. POKE, JOHN MACKASSEY, JNO. WHALEY, JAMES GUNN, JOHN STINGSTON, JOHN JOHNSON, WM. RED, WALTER BULLENY, FAIRHAIR JAMES JOHNSON, ALLEN MACKLANE, DANIEL MACARTEE, JOHN RED, WM. EDWARDS, PETER BLACKETTER, BENJA. CARBIND, JOHN POTTER, WILLIAM STANDLEY, BENJA. CARAN, EDWD FARNED.

Same. 348 acs. (N.L.), same Co., date & page. On N. side of James Riv., beg. at    mouth & on E. side of a gr. creek. Imp. of 7 pers: SARAH BAREFOOT, ANNE HOLMES, JANE BRAND, ELIZA. BRAND, ELIZA. MIDDLETON, ESTHER GIBBINS, MARY QUIN-ELL.

Same. 892 acs. (N.L.), same Co. & date, p. 238. On N. side of James Riv., beg. at up. side of Genitoe Cr., crossing Mill Cr. Imp. of 18 pers: JONE KING, DANIEL DUGON, ELLIN WELSH, JOHN HEFFERNAND, JANE MURFFY, ALICE COMING, MARY BURK, MARY FLING, ALICE SULLIVAN, JONE CORBET, TIMOTHY SULLIVAN, MARGT. KELLY, WM. CHAPP, CATHERINE DENT, ANNA CUSTILLY, CATHERINE BURK, CATHERINE DUGON, MARGARET BRYAN.

JOHN PLEASANTS, 258 acs. (N.L.), Henrico Co., on S. side of James Riv., beg. at his own land, to the French Land, 16 Aug. 1715, p. 238. Imp. of 6 pers: ANTHONY PROUINSALL, JAMES BRYANT, RICHD. DICKENSON, RICHD. GOODWIN, EDWD. DAVIS, WM. CLARK.

Same. 1309 acs. (N.L.), & 2 Islands, same location & date, p. 239. Beg. 1½ mi. below mouth of Fine Cr. 6 Lbs., 15 Shill.

HENRY SHACKLEFORD, 371 A., 40 P., (N.L.), in the fork of the main run of Matta-pony Riv., beg. on the W. br. being the lower part of the Neck: 16 Aug. 1715, p. 239. Imp. of 8 pers: DANIEL FENNER, ALICE THOMAS, RICHD. BAGGERLEY, THOS. NICHOLS, GEORGE BROOKES, ABRAHAM LAMB, MARY BUGG, THOMAS DAVIS.

WILLIAM WOMACK, 950 acs., (N.L.), Henrico Co., on N. side of James Riv., Hen-rico Co.,                              adj. Mr. JOHN WOODSON, over against Mana-kin Town, & Col. WM. RANDOLPH, 16 Aug. 1715, p. 240. Imp. of 19 pers: WM. BROWN,

ANDREW CRAWFORD, ARTHUR DORGILL, JNO. ALCORNE, MORGAN FEASER, JAMES SINKLER, WM. REED, RINGIN SPENCE, JAMES MORGAN, JNO. MECLARE, WM. ROBBINSON, JAMES MORE, JAMES KING, GEO. WILSON, JNO. ROBINSON, ARTH. MEDANE, JNO. MILLER, JNO. CARE, GOLUG AGE.

THOMAS BAYLEY, 350 acs. (N.L.), Henrico Co., on N. side of Deep Run, adj. WM. COCKE (COCK); 16 Aug. 1715, p. 241. 35 Shill.

THOMAS WATKINS, 400 acs. (N.L.), Henrico Co., on N. side of the main br. of Tuckahoe (Cr.), below the Devil's Wood Yard; 16 Aug. 1715, p. 244. 25 Shill. and Imp. of 3 pers: JAMES MACKENTUSH, FRANCIS HILL, JNO. COOK.

BARTHOLOMEW STAVALL, 318 acs. (N.L.), Henrico Co., on S. side of James Riv., at a place known as Deep Creek, down Solomon's branch, 16 Aug. 1715, p. 245. 30 Shill., & Imp. of: TIMOTHY CONNER.

CHARLES CHRISTIAN, 400 acs. (N.L.), Henrico Co., on N. side of James Riv., adj. DAVIS PATTISON, crossing Licking Hole Cr., 16 Aug. 1715, p. 246. 2 Lbs. Money.

RICHARD COX, 167 acs. (N.L.), Henrico Co., on N. side of James Riv., in gr. fork of Tuckahoe Cr., adj. land of Mr. CLERK & RUSSELL; 16 Aug. 1715, p. 247. 20 Shill.

JOHN MARTIN, 180 acs. (N.L.), Henrico Co., beg. in slash parting this & land of JAMES BILBAND (or BILBAUD), 23 Mar. 1715, p. 252. Being part of the lower part of the last 5,000 acs. surveyed for the French Refugees.

Same. 444 acs. (N.L.), same Co., date & page. Adj. MOSES LIVERAN (or LIVERAU). Part of the first 5,000 acs. surveyed for the French refugees.

Capt. ABRAHAM SALLE, 133 acs. (N.L.), Henrico Co., on S. side of the James River, 23 Mar. 1715, p. 253. Part of the lower part of the 1st 5,000 acs. surveyed for the French Refugees.

JOHN WHITLOE, 155 acs. (N.L.), Henrico Co., on N. side of James Riv., beg. on E. side of 2 Mi. Cr., near the head; adj. JOHN WOODSON, HENRY PEW, NICHOLAS HUTCHINSON, ABRAHAM CHILDERS, Senr., & land of WM. WHITLOE, Senr., down Miry Run, 23 Mar. 1715, p. 253. 15 Shill.

WILLIAM WHITLOE, Junr., 400 acs. (N.L.), Henrico Co., on N. side of James Riv., adj. AMOS LEAD's survey, on a br. of Tuckahoe Cr., & CHARLES HUDSON's line, 23 Mar. 1715, p. 253. 2 Lbs., Money.

At a Council held at the Capitol the 20th of Apr. 1716. On reading at this Board the petition of JOHN WATSON of Henrico Co. setting forth that in 1713 he purchased of JOHN PLEASANTS late of sd. Co., dec'd. his right to 551 acs. surveyed for him on the N. brs. of Upham Brook, & praying that a patent for same may pass in his name, it appearing a patent has already been assigned for sd.

land in the name of JOHN PLEASANTS, the elder, & that it was unknown that sd. JOHN was dead at the time of signing, the Govr'or & Council think fit to declare that the patent was never intended for the benefit of any other person than sd. JOHN PLEASANTS, the elder, & that JOHN, the younger, who was the only person alive of that name at the time of granting sd. patent, hath not any right to the land, & it is ordered that this declaration be entered in the record, &c. Signed: WIL. ROBERTSON, Clk. Council. Marginal note: See patent in 157th page of this book.

JOSEPH PLEASANTS, 550 acs. (N.L.), Henrico Co., N. side of James Riv., on N. side of West Br. of Beaver Dam Cr., adj. Mr. JOHN & JOSEPH PLEASANTS, 16 Aug. 1715, p. 254. 25 Shill., & Imp. of 6 pers: SARAH MORRIS, ANNE YOUNG, DANIEL HAY, JOHN MIDDLETON, DARK GLASS.

PETER DUTOY, 61 A., 1 R., 31 P. (N.L.), Henrico Co., bet. Up. & Low. Manakin Creeks, adj. his own land of JOUANY; & STEPHEN CHASTAIN, down James River, 23 Mar. 1715, p. 266. Being part of the first portion of land laid out for the French Refugees.

PETER CHASTAINE, 111 acs. (N.L.), Henrico Co., on S. side of James River, adj. ANTHONY MALOONE, his own land, & the widow GORY's line, 23 Mar. 1715, p. 266. Part of the 1st 5,000 acs. surveyed for the French Refugees.

JOHN CHASTAINE, 90 acs. (N.L.), Henrico Co., on S. side of James Riv., beg. at his own land & land of JACOB AMONET, 23 Mar. 1715, p. 267. Part of the 1st 5,000 acs. surveyed for the French Refugees.

ABRAHAM SOBLET, Junr., 88 acs. (N.L.), Henrico Co., on S. side of James Riv. adj. his own & land of PETER DAVID, 23 Mar. 1715, p. 267. Part of the 1st 5,000 acs. surveyed for the French Refugees.

ABRAHAM SALLE, 57 acs. (N.L.), Henrico Co., on S. side of James Riv., adj. ABRAHAM MISSHUEX, on W. side of lower Manakin Cr., 23 Mar. 1715, p. 282. Being part of the 1st 5,000 acs. surveyed for the French Rofugees.

Same. 55 acs. (N.L.), same location, date, & page. Adj. ANTHONY GEAVODAN (or GEAVODAU), on S. side the Monakin lower Cr., by the cole pit road. Part of the 1st 5,000 acs. surveyed for the French Refugees.

JACOB AMONET, 168 acs. (N.L.), Henrico Co., on S. side of James Riv., adj. DANIEL FOUR, 23 Mar. 1715, p. 282. Being part of the lower part of the last 5,000 acs. surveyed for the French Refugees.

MATTHEW OAGE, 221 acs. (N.L.), Henrico Co., on S. side of James Riv., adj. STEPHEN BUNARD, 23 Mar. 1715, p. 282. Part of the last 5,000 acs. surveyed for the French Refugees.

STEPHEN RENNO, 133 acs. (N.L.), Henrico Co., S. side of James Riv. adj. Peter FOURE, 23 Mar. 1715, p. 283. Being part of the lower part of the last 5,000 acs. surveyed for the French Refugees.

MARYAN MALLET, 75 acs. (N.L.), Henrico Co., on S. side of James Riv., beg. at
upper corner of 1st Survey, down Jones' Cr, parting sd. MALLET & JOHN JONES;
23 Mar. 1715, p. 283. Being part of the lower part of the last 5,000 acs.
surveyed for the Franch Refugees.

JOHN LAVILLIAN, 200 acs. (N.L.), Henrico Co., S. side of James Riv., adj.
ANTHONY GEVODAN, 23 Mar. 1715, p. 284. Part of the last 5,000 acs. surveyed
for the French Refugees.

JOHN JONES, 133 acs. (N.L.), Henrico Co., S. side of James River, adj. STEPHEN
RENNO & CAPOONE, 23 Mar. 1715, p. 284. Being part of the lower part of the
last 5,000 acs. surveyed for the Franch Refugees.

ABRAHAM REMY (REMEY), 85 acs. (N.L.), Henrico Co., S. side of James River, adj.
JACOB FLORENOY, 23 Mar. 1715, p. 284. Being part of the last 5,000 acs. surveyed for the French Refugees.

ABRAHAM MISSHUEX, 230 acs. (N.L.), Henrico Co., S. side. of James River, adj.
Capt. ABRAHAM SALLE, on N. side of the lower Manakin Creek, & on line of
BARTHOLOMEW DUPEE, 23 Mar. 1715, p. 284. Being part of the lower part of the
last 5,000 acs. surveyed for the French Refugees.

ANTHONY MATOONE, 107 acs. (N.L.), Henrico Co., S. side of Ja es River, adj.
NICHOLAS SOULLIE, 23 Mar. 1715, p. 285. Part of the upper part of the 5,000
acs. surveyed for the French Refugees.

ANTHONY TRIBUE, 163 acs. (N.L.), Henrico Co., S. side of James River, adj.
ABRAHAM REMMY, 23 Mar. 1715, p. 285. Being part of the 1st 5,000 acs. & lower
part of the last 5,000 acs. for the French Refugees.

ANTHONY GEVODAN, 128 acs. (N.L.), Henrico Co., on S. side of James River, adj.
JOHN LAVILLIAN, & Capt. ABRAHAM SALLE, 23 Mar. 1715, p. 285. Part of the 1st
5,000 acs. & part of the last 5,000 acs. surveyed for the French Refugees.

DANIEL FOURE, 296 acs. (N.L.), Henrico Co. beg. the (James) River, at cor.
parting PETER MORRISET & sd. FOURE, 23 Mar. 1715, p. 285. Part of the last
5,000 acs. surveyed for the French Refugees.

JACOB FLORENOY, 133 acs. (N.L.), Henrico Co., S. side James River, adj. AN-
THONY TRIBUE, 23 Mar. 1715, p. 285. Part of the lower part of the last 5,000
acs. surveyed for the French Refugees.

ABRAHAM REMMY, 85 acs. (N.L.), beg. on the (James) River, cor. of JOHN MARTIN
& (ANTHONY) TRIBUE, 23 Mar. 1715, p. 286. Part of the 1st 5,000 acs. surveyed
for the French Refugees.

PETER DAVID, 88 acs. (N.L.), Henrico Co., S. side of James River, adj. PETER SOBLET, & ABRAHAM SOBLET, Junr., 23 Mar. 1715, p. 286. Part of the 1st 5,000 acs. surveyed for the French Refugees.

JAMES BILBAUD, 119 A., 3 R., 24 P., (N.L.)., Henrico Co., S. side of James River, adj. ISAAC PARENTAN (or PARENTAU), 23 Mar. 1715, p. 286. Part of the 1st 5,000 acs. surveyed for the French Refugees.

JOSEPH CALLIO, 75 acs. (N.L.), Henrico Co., S. side of James River, on Gleeb Line, 31 Oct. 1716, p. 291. Part of the lower part of the 5,000 acs. surveyed for the French Refugees.

JOHN FONVILLE, 168 acs. (N.L.), Henrico Co., on S. side of James River, adj. land of the Widow MINETREE, 31 Oct. 1716, p. 291. Part of the 1st 5,000 acs. surveyed for the French Refugees.

LEWIS MORRILL, 66 acs. (N.L.), Henrico Co., on S. side of James River, adj. ABRAHAM SOBLET, on French line, 31 Oct. 1716, p. 292. Being part of the 1st 5,000 acs. surveyed for the French Refugees.

MITCHELL CAMPEE (CHAMPEE), 52 acs. (N.L.), Henrico Co., on S. side of James River, 31 Oct. 1716, p. 292. Part of the 1st 5,000 acs. surveyed for the French Refugees.

JOHN MARTIN, 92 A., 2 R., 20 P., (N.L.), Henrico Co., on S. side of James River, adj. FRANCIS SASSIN, 31 Oct. 1716, p. 292. Part of the 1st 5,000 acs. surveyed for the French Refugees.

FRANCIS LORANGE (or LORAUGE), 59 acs. (N.L.), Henrico Co., on S. side of James River, adj. JOHN PANITUER, 31 Oct. 1716, p. 292. Part of the 1st 5,000 acs. surveyed for the French Refugees. Part of the 1st 5,000 acs, surveyed for the French Refugees.
GIDEON CHAMBOONE, 33 acs. (N.L.), Henrico Co., on S. side of James River, adj. ANTHONY MATTOON & CLAUDE GORY, 31 Oct. 1716, p. 293. Part of the 1st 5,000 acs, surveyed for the French Refugees.

MOSES LIVERAN, 117 acs. (N.L.), Henrico Co., on S. side of James River, adj. JACOB CAPOONE, 31 Oct. 1716, p. 293. Part of the 1st 5,000 acs. surveyed for the French Refugees.

CLAUDE GORY, 50 acs. (N.L.), Henrico Co., on S. side of James River, adj. GIDEON CHAMBOONE, & JOHN PANITEUR. 31 Oct. 1716, p. 293. Part of the 1st 5,000 acs. surveyed for the French Refugees.

STEPHEN MALLET, 125 acs. (N.L.), Henrico Co., on S. side of James River, adj. ANDREW AUBERRY & upper cor. of the 1st 5,000 acs; 31 Oct. 1716, p. 294. Being the upper part of the last 5,000 acs. surveyed for the French Refugees.

PETER SABOTTE, 88 acs. (N.L.), Henrico Co. S. side of James Riv. adj.

LAFEAVER's land, 31 Oct. 1716, p. 294. Part of 1st 5,000 acs. surveyed for the French Refugees.

FRANCIS DUPEE, 46 acs. (N.L.). Henrico Co., S. side of James River, adj. ANTHONY MATOONE, 31 Oct. 1716, p. 294. Part of the upper part of the last 5,000 acs. surveyed for the French Refugees.

ISAAC PARENTAU, 105 acs. (N.L.), Henrico Co., on S. side of James River, adj. CLAUDE GORY, 31 Oct. 1716, p. 294. The lower part of the 5,000 acs. surveyed for the French Refugees.

PETER MORISET, 129 A., 1 R., 35 P., (N.L.), Henrico Co., on S. side of James River, adj. JOHN LUNADO. 31 Oct. 1716, p. 295. Part of the lower part of the last 5,000 acs. surveyed for the French Refugees.

STEPHEN CHASTAINE, 12 acs. (N.L.), Henrico Co., on S. side of James River, adj. JAMES DIORET, on Upper Manakin Cr., 31 Oct. 1716, p. 295. Part of the 1st 5,000 acs. surveyed for the French Refugees.

JOHN FORCURAN, 170 acs. (N.L.), Henrico Co., on S. side of James River, adj. MOSES LIVERAU, 31 Oct. 1716, p. 295. Part of the 1st 5,000 acs. surveyed for the French Refugees.

JAMES BILBAUD, 43 acs. (N.L.), Henrico Co., on S. side of James River, adj. ISAAC PARENTAU, 31 Oct. 1716, p. 295. Part of 1st 5,000 acs. surveyed for the Franch Refugees.

STEPHEN BUCCARD, 93 A., 2 R., (N.L.), Henrico Co., on S. side of James River, adj. CHARLES PERAULT, 31 Oct. 1716, p. 295. Part of the upper part of the last 5,000 acs. surveyed for the French Refugees.

NICHOLAS SOULLIE, 133 acs. (N.L.), Henrico Co., on S. side James River, adj. ANTHONY RAPINE, on N. side of Jones' Creek, 31 Oct. 1716, p. 296. Part of the upper part of the last 5,000 acs. surveyed for the French Refugees.

JOHN JONES, 53 acs. (N.L.), Henrico Co., on S. side of Jamea River, adj. JAMES BULBAUD, on DILLWAIT's line, 31 Oct. 1716, p. 296. Part of the first 5,000 acs. surveyed for the French Refugees.

PETER FOURE, 107 A., 1 R., 13 P., (N.L.), Henrico Co., on S. side of James River, adj. STEPHEN CHASTAINE, 31 Oct. 1716, p. 296. Part of the upper part of the last 5,000 acs. surveyed for the French Refugees.

JOHN FARCEE, 40 acs. (N.L.), Henrico Co. on S. side of James River, adj. STE-PHEN CHASTAINE, on ABRA. ——, to back line of the French Lands, &c. on 31 Oct. 1716, p. 296. Part of the 1st 5,000 acs. surveyed for the French Refu-gees.

CHARLES PERAULT, 133 acs. (N.L.), Henrico Co., on S. side of James River, adj. ISAAC LAFEIT, 31 Oct. 1716, p. 296. Part of the upper part of the last 5,000 acs. surveyed for the French Refugees.

JOHN SOLEAGER, 275 acs. (N.L.), Henrico Co., on S. side of James River, adj. JACOB AMONET, 31 Oct. 1716, p. 294. Part of the last 5,000 acs. surveyed for the French Refugees.

JACOB AMONET, 88 acs. (N.L.), Henrico Co., on S. side of James River, adj. PETER SABOTTE, & JOHN CHASTAINE, 31 Oct. 1716, p. 297. Part of the 1st 5,000 acres surveyed for the French Refugees.

ANTHONY RAPINE, 122 acs. (N.L.), Henrico Co., on S. side of James River, adj. JACOB CAPOONE, 31 Oct. 1716, p. 297. Part of the upper part of the last 5,000 acs. surveyed for the French Refugees.

ISAAC LAFEAVOUR, 68 acs. (N.L.), on S. side of James River, adj. the Widow CHAMBOONE, & PETER SABOTTE, 31 Oct. 1716, p. 297. Part of the 1st part of 5,000 acs. surveyed for the French Refugees.

JOHN PANITEUR, 76 acs. (N.L.), on S. side of James River, adj. CLAUDE GORY, 31 Oct. 1716, p. 297. Part of 1st 5,000 acs. surveyed for the French Refugees. Henrico Co.

JACOB CAPOONE, 34 acs. (N.L.), Henrico Co., on S. side of James River, adj. FRANCIS LORANGE, 31 Oct. 1716, p. 298. Part of the 1st part of 1st 5,000 acs. surveyed for the French Refugees.

ANTHONY MATTOONE, 58 acs. (N.L.), Henrico Co., adj. PETER CHASTAINE, CLAUDE GORY & GIDEON CHAMBOONE, 31 Oct. 1716, p. 298. On James River. Part of the 1st part of 5,000 acs. surveyed for the French Refugees.

STEPHEN CHASTAIN, 95 A., 3 R., 30 P., (N.L.), Henrico Co., on S. side of James River, adj. PETER LEWIS SOBLET, 31 Oct. 1716, p. 298. Part of the upper part of the 1st 5,000 acs. surveyed for the French Refugees.

THOMAS HARDEN, 319 acs. (N.L.), N. side of James Riv., on E. side of the Main E. br. of Tuckahoe (Cr.), beg. at a Beaver Pond belonging to JOHN ELESS, 31 Oct. 1716, p. 298. 5 Shill., & Imp. of 6 pers: MOSES REATHWORTH, THOMAS BRANAN, CHRISTOPHER BELL, JOHN LYLES, SUSANNAH COBBS, ANNE BRIDGES. Henrico Co.

PHILEMON CHILDERS, Junr., 97 acs. (N.L.), Henrico Co., on N. side of James River, beg. on line of SOLOMON KNIBB, crossing GRINDOLES' run, to WILLIAM HOBSON. 31 Oct. 1716, p. 300. 10 Shill.

FRANCIS EPES, 311 acs. (Lapsed L.), Henrico Co., 31 Oct. 1716, p. 301. Granted JAMES COCK, being the added part of patent of 754 A., 1 R., & 3 P., beg. at JOHN FOWLER, to BATT. CHANDLER's line, nigh the Indian Path, on the Old Town Run, upon condition of planting, &c., which he failed to do, now granted, &c. 10 Shill. & Imp. of 5 pers: ROBT. GREEDEWELL, ANTHO. DUNEN (?), JOHN

JOHNSON, TIMOTHY HARRIS, ROBT. SMITH.

EDWARD CURD, 531 acs. (N.L.), Henrico Co., N. side of James Riv., on W. side of the N. br. of Beaver Dam Cr., 31 Oct., 1716, p. 307. 55 Shill.

JOHN BOLLING, 320 acs. (N.L.), Henrico Co., N. side of James River, on E. side of Licking Hole Cr., 1 Apr. 1717, p. 311. Imp. of 7 pers: THOMAS WOOD, JOHN BISHOP, ABRAH. DISHON, JNO. DERFEE, JOHN MORGAN, JOHN CHAMBERFORD, DOROTHY WILLIAMS.

Major JOHN BOLLING, 300 acs. (N.L.), Henrico Co., being an Island against land of CHARLES FLEMING, on on N. side of James River, 15 July, 1717, p. 321. 20 Shill. & Imp. 2 pers: THOMAS HUTCHINSON & ROBT. HUTCHINSON.

TARLTON WOODSON, 2307 acs. (N.L.), known by the name of Bear Forrest, Henrico Co., N. side of James Riv., on N. side of a br. of Pamunkey (Riv.); & N. side of Bear Br., 15 July, 1717, p. 321. 11 Lbs., 5 Shill. & Imp. of 2 pers: ROBERT REYALLS & THOMAS JONES.

ROBERT BURTON, 17 A., 3 R., (N.L.), Henrico Co., in Varina Par., N. side of James Riv., on head of Long Field patent, adj. THOMAS TAYLOR, & WILLIAM BURTON, 15 July 1717, p. 324. Imp. of ALEXANDER HATTON.

JOHN BOLLING, Gent. 1019 acs. (N.L.), Henrico Co., on N. side of James Riv., above Licking Hole Cr., beg. at land of JOHN WOODSON & JOHN PLEASANTS, up the main river to a great rock known by the name of Rock Castle, 15 July 1717. p. 324. Imp. of 21 pers: CHARLES GOODWIN, WM. LEWIS, WM. CORAM, MARY RENT, GEO. HAMEY, ABRAHAM CODDLE, THOMAS CLIFTON, LUKE PARKER, HANNAH PARKER, HENRY YOUNG, EDWARD SEED, JAMES SEED, Junr., JAMES SEED,Senr., JAMES HOWELL, ROBERT HAWKINS, JAMES BUTLER, ELIZA. STAPLE, MARY WILSON, THOMAS WHITE, MARY DYER, GEO. MASON.

DOROTHY PLEASANTS, 463 acs. (N.L.), Henrico Co., on N. side of James Riv., beg. on E. side of Woolfpit Br., adj. JOHN PLEASANTS, Mr. JOHN WOODSON & AMOS LAD's line, 15 July 1717, p. 329. Imp. of 10 pers: JOHN BELLOMY, JOHN LYES, THOMAS ALLEN, HUGH ROSE, JOHN DICKSON, NATHL. LOMESS, JOHN NUTT, MARK LIFEHOLY, WILLIAM HEWS, MATHEW MARK.

FRANCIS SASSIN, 104 acs. (N.L.), Henrico Co., on S. side of James River, 15 July 1717, p. 329. Out of the lower part of the last 5,000 acs. surveyed for the French Refugees.

MICAEL JOHNSON, 500 acs. (N.L.), Henrico Co., on S. side of the main br. of Tuckahoe (Cr.); adj. BENJA. HARRISON's survey, Mr. JOHN WOODSON's Mill Cr.,& THOS. MIMS' land, 22 Jan 1717, p. 345. 50 Shill.

AMOS LEAD (LAD), 472 acs. (N.L.), Henrico Co., N. side of James Riv., on E. side of the N. br. of Beaverdam Cr. at the mouth of Horsepen Cr., adj. his own land, 22 Jan. 1717, p. 347. 50 Shill.

BARTHOLOMEW DUPEE, 133 acs. (N.L.), Henrico Co., on S. side of James River, adj. ABRA. MISSHIUX, on Monakin Cr., where the Cole Pit Road crosses, 11 Mar. 1717, p. 364. Part of the 1st 5,000 acs. surveyed for the French Refugees.

ANTHONY TREBUE, 522 acs. (N.L.), Henrico Co., on the gr. fork of Swift Creek, 18 Mar. 1717, p. 364. Imp. of 11 pers: ANTHONY GOADTON, PETER GIPSON, CARLETON RICE, WILLM. MAY, MARTHA ALLICE, PETER KADOW, ANTHONY TRIBUE, KATH. TREBUE, PETER LEVIA, BERNARD PROVINSALL, RACHELL BARLY.

JAMES BRANCH, 31 acs. (N.L.), Henrico Co., on S. side of James River, adj. RICHARD DENNIS, Kings land, DENNIS & SEAFIELD's & Mr. THOMAS BRANCH's line, 18 Mar. 1717, p. 369. 5 Shill.

RALPH HUDSPITH, Junr., 370 acs.(N.L.), Henrico Co., on N. side of James Riv., beg. at THOMAS PLEASANTS' on Woolfpitt Br., parting sd. PLEASANTS & FRANCIS SAMPSON, 12 July 1718, p. 377. 40 Shill.

SAMUEL GARTHRITE, 143 acs. (N.L.), Henrico Co., on N. side of James Riv., at a place known by the name of Hell Garden, beg. at THO. EAST, to Piges Slash, adj. ROBT. WADSON, & ROBERT WOODSON, 12 July 1718, p. 377. 15 Shill.

JAMES LEGRAN (LEGRAND), 365 acs. (N.L.), Henrico Co., on N. side of the gr. swamp of Swift Cr., on line of RICHARD WOMACK, to land of ANTHONY TRIBUE, 12 July 1718, p. 377, Imp. of 8 pers: MOIZE LEVEREAU (or LEVEREAN), VRY (or URY), LEVEREAU (or LEVEREAN), PETER LEGRAND, Senr., PETER LEGRAND, Junr., DANIEL LEGRAND, JOHN LEGRAND & JOHN PETER LEGRAND.

JAMES AKEN, Senr., 340 acs. (N.L.), Henrico Co., in the forks of Procter's (Cr.), nigh head of the Cold Water Run, adj. his old line, 12 July 1718, p. 378. 35 Shill.

CHARLES FLEMING, 1430 acs.(N.L.), on N. side of James Riv., Henrico Co., beg. at Capt. JOHN BOLLING & AMOS LAD, above Capt. BOLLIN's ISLAND, 12 July 1718, p. 378. 3 Lbs., 10 Shill. & Imp. of 15 pers: PETER CRUTCHFIELDE, SAML. CRUTCH-FIELDE, HENRY CONASTASTINE, WILLIAM EXON, ROBT. BROOKES, EDWD, BROWMAN, WILLIAM CARPENTER, JOHN WHITE, GEORGE SMITH, WILLIAM JACKSON, JOSEPH OWEN, ELIZ. ASHLEY, FRANCIS GLENISTER, MARY HANDCOCK, RICHD. DUNKERT.

THOMAS JEFFERSON, THOMAS TURPIN, JOHN ARTCHER & ROBERT ESELEY, 1500 acs. (N. L.), Henrico Co., at a place known by the name of Fine Creek, beg. above the upper fall of the sd. creek, to br. of the up. Monakin Town Cr., to mouth of Spring Run, &c., 12 July 1718, p. 378. 3 Lbs., & Imp. of 18 pers: GEO. COLE, CHARLES PETERS, GEO. WALL, WILLIAM BALL, FRANCIS HORSE, LUKE SHAW, GEORGE ROADES, MARY ELDERS, MARTH. BRIDGERS, JANE LEWIS, ROBT. BUSILL, THOMAS HOWARTH, JOHN HATCHELL, NICH. HATCHER, JOSEPH SMITH, JOHN EVARD, THOMAS BEND-BRIDGE, CONSTANT BENDBRIDGE.

JAMES MOSS, 400 acs. (N.L.), Henrico Co., N. side of James Riv., on N. side of Broad Br. at GILLY GREWMARRIN's corner, 12 July 1718, p. 379. 15 Shill., &

Imp. of 5 pers: ABRAHAM BRAN, ELINOR THOMPSON, MARY DAINE, JOHN STEWARD, ELIZABETH CHAMPAINE.

JOHN BARNES, Junr., & WILLIAM BARNES, 365 acs. (N.L.), Henrico Co., on N. side of James Riv., in a fork of the N. br. of Tuckahoe; on Wadkins Br., 12 July 1718, p. 379. 40 Shill.

JAMES JOHNSON, 400 acs. (N.L.), Henrico Co., on N. side of James Riv., adj. CHA. EAVENS, JOHN JOHNSON, JOSEPH WOODSON, & BENJ. WOODSON, 12 July 1718, p. 380. 40 Shill.

JOHN JOHNSON, 400 acs. (N.L.), Henrico Co., on N. side of James Riv., adj. CHA. EAVENS, on N. side & near head of Tuckahoe Cr., his own, JAMES JOHNSON, & MICHAEL JOHNSON, 12 July 1718, p. 380. 40 Shill.

OWEN EAVEN, 150 acs. (N.L.), Henrico Co., on S. side of Swift Cr., adj. HENRY RANDOLPH Junr., & JAMES EAKINS' land, 12 July 1718, p. 380. 15 Shill.

AMOS LAD, 250 acs. (N.L.), Henrico Co., on N. side of James Riv., adj. HENRY GILL, on N. side of the E. br. of Beaver Dam Cr., on W. side of Turkey Cr., 12 July 1718, p. 381. 25 Shill.

JOHN BOLLING, Gent., 800 acs. (N.L.), Henrico Co., on S. side of James River, adj. ABRAHAM MISSHEUX's land, 14 July 1718, p. 393. 4 Lbs., Money.

GEORGE FREEMAN, (N.L.), Henrico Co., on E. side of Tuckahoe main branch, & down Deep run, 22 Jan. 1718, p. 408. 40 Shill. 400 acs.

MATTHEW LIGON & RICHARD LIGON, Junr., 290 acs. (N.L.), Henrico Co., on S. side of Swift Cr. crossing the 4th branch, 22 Jan. 1718, p. 409. 30 Shill.

EDWARD HATCHER, Junr., 223 acs. (N.L.), Henrico Co., on both sides of Tuckahoe main Cr., on N. side of James River, beg. in line of Mr. Clarke, to mouth of Deep Run, on line of WM. BURSTON, 22 Jan. 1718, p. 411. 25 Shill.

CHRISTOPHER CLARK, 500 acs. (N.L.), Henrico Co., on N. side of James River, beg. on E. side of BROOKES' Branch, adj. JOHN STONE, THOMAS FARRAR, & JOSEPH WATSON's lines, on N. side of a br. of Gold Mine Cr., on GEORGE ALVIS' line, & Capt. WEST's line, 22 Jan. 1718, p. 412. 50 Shill. Note: CHRISTOPHER CLARKE's patent for 500 acres of land in Henrico County or (as some would have it) in New Kent County."

JOHN STONE, 400 acs. (N.L.), Henrico Co., on N. side of James River, on Capt. NATHANIEL WEST's line, on E. side of BROOKE's Branch, 22 Jan. 1718, p. 412. 40 Shill. Note: Same as above.

JOHN MARTIN, 400 acs. (N.L.), Henrico Co., beg. in the French Line, parting his own & land of Capt. ABRAHAM SALLE, 11 July 1719, p. 419. Out of the lower part of the last 5,000 acs. surveyed for the French Refugees.

GEORGE FLOYD, 200 acs. (N.L.), Henrico Co., on N. side of James River, beg. adj. corner of ROBERT WOODSON, JOHN WOODSON & his own land, on E. side of rockey br. of Jenny Toe Cr., 11 July 1719, p. 420. 20 Shill.

BOUTH NAPIER, 497 acs. (N.L.), Henrico Co., N. side of James Riv., on N. side of Tuckahoe Cr., on THOMAS WADKINS' line, 11 July 1719, p. 420. 50 Shill.

JEAN JOUANY, 650 acs. (N.L.), Henrico Co., on S. side of James Riv., beg. on the main upper br. of the Monakin Cr., on JOHN PLEASANTS' line, to upper broad rock of Fine Cr., to mouth of a meadow br. parting this & land of Capt. JEFFERSON, 11 July, 1719, p. 421. 3 Lbs., Money, & Imp. of JOHN JONES.

TARLTON WOODSON, 3090 acs. (N.L.), Henrico Co., on N. side of James Riv., beg. at his own & land of JOSEPH PLEASANTS, to S. side of the W. br. of Beaverdam Cr., on Maj. JOHN BOLLING's line, 11 July 1719, p. 422. 6 Lbs., 15 Shill., & Imp. of 35 pers: MARTIN LAWRENCE, WILL. READ, JOHN RAY, JOHN BRUMFIELD, JOHN HUGGINS, ELIZABETH PARKER, JUNE LEWIS, DAVID COWLISHAW, JOHN JONES, GEORGE WILLIAMSON, PETER HALL, JOHN OATES, WM. SERGANT, ROBERT RUSSELL, TIMOTHY BRETT, AMBROSE FELLOWS, GEO. COLE, RICHD. WHITBY, JOHN DARBY, ROBT. DAVIS, THO. WADDY, (or WADDS), THO. ALLEN, JAMES BRYANT, DARBY KEA, TIMOTHY MURFY, RICHD. WILLIAMS, EDWD. RICHESON, JNO. MITCHELL, RALPH DENBY (or DENLY), JOHN MURRY, COLEN MCKENNY, MARY DICKERSON, DANIEL MOODEY (or MOODRY), ANGILO MARSHALL, RICHARD JONES.

WILLIAM FINNEY, 40 acs. (N.L.), Henrico Co., on N. side of James Riv., beg. at JOHN WOODALL, on W. side of the main br. of Jennytoe Cr. adj. JOS. WOODSON's line, & GEORGE FLOYD; 11 July 1719, p. 423. 40 Shill.

JAMES CHRISTIAN, 368 acs. (N.L.), Henrico Co., on N. side of James River, adj. JOSEPH PLEASANTS on E. side of the Western Br. of Beaverdam Cr., & THOMAS CHRISTIAN's line, 20 Feb. 1719, p. 457. 15 Shill. & Imp. of 5 pers: WILLIAM HAYNES, RICHARD BRYAN, JOHN EPPERSON, JOHN SIMPSON, THOMAS TINDALL.

MARGARET MARTIN, 118 acs. (N.L.), Henrico Co., on James River, adj. JOHN FORCURAN; 20 Feb. 1719, p. 458. Out of the 1st 5000 acs. surveyed for the French Refugees.

JOHN MARTIN, 182 acs. (N.L.), Henrico Co., on S. side of James River, 20 Feb. 1719, p. 458. Out of the lower part of the last 5,000 acs. surveyed for the French Refugees.

FRANCES LORANGE, 133 acs. (N.L.), Henrico Co., on James River, adj. PETER GORY; 20 Feb. 1719, p. 458. Out of the lower part of the last 5,000 acs. surveyed for the French Refugees.

Patent Book 11

JOHN GUN, 150 acs. (N.L.), Henrico Co., on N. side of James River. 17 Aug., 1720, p. 44. 15 Shill.

JOSEPH BRADLY, 378 acs. (N.L.), on N. side of James River, on land of WALTER CLAPTON; 17 Aug. 1720, p. 44. Imp. of 8 pers: MARGARET GRINWELL, JOHN WALKER, JOHN ROBERTS, WILLIAM HAYES, THOMAS NEWMAN, WILLIAM PRICE, ANDREW AUTOM, JOHN COOK. Henrico Co.

JAMES NOWELLIN, 282 acs. (N.L.), Henrico Co., on N. side of James River; 17 Aug. 1720, p. 45. 30 Shill.

AMOS LAD, 343 acs. (N.L.), Henrico Co., on N. side of James River, in the fork of a br. parting this & land of EDWD. CURD; 17 Aug. 1720, p. 45. 35 Shill.

WALTER CLAPTON, 400 acs. (N.L), Henrico Co., on N. side of James River; 17 Aug. 1720, p. 46. 40 Shill.

STEPHEN CHASTAIN, 37 acs. (N.L.), Henrico Co., within bounds of the land laid out for the French Refugees; adj. PETER DUTOI, down James River; 17 Aug. 1720, p. 46. 5 Shill.

EDMUND NEW, 400 acs. (N.L.), Henrico Co., on N. side of James Riv., on W. side of Little Horsepen Cr.; 17 Aug. 1720, p. 47. 40 Shill.

JOHN BOLLING, 4480 acs. (O.& N.L.), Henrico Co., on N. side of James Riv., 2 May, 1721, p. 60. 753 acs. beg. at his 320 acs., on E. side of the W. br. of Licking Hole, or Treasurer's Run, near WALTER CLOPTON's fence, on sd. BOLLING's line of his survey joining to Rock Castle; 1388 acs. bounded as by patent dated 23 Dec., 1713; granted sd. BOLLING; 320 acs. bounded as by his patent dated 1 Apr. 1717; 1019 acs. as by his patent dated 15 July 1717. 8 Lbs., 15 Shill.

Same. 2407 acs.(O.&N.L,) same Co., date, & page. On S. side of James Riv., opposite Licking Hole (run); 1607 acs. beg. at his own land, on MICHAUX's line crossing br. of MAHOOK Cr., near JOHN STEPHENS' fence; 800 acs. bounded as by his patent dated 14 July 1718. 8 Lbs. 5 Shill.

JOHN THORNTON, of New Kent Co., 3600 acs. (N.L.), Henrico Co., on N. side of James Riv., 6 Nov. 1721, p. 64. Beg. at mouth of Byrd (Cr.) which runs into sd. river, on his own line, to the mouth of the Rivanna Riv. 18 Lbs. Money.

AMOS LAD, 300 acs. (N.L.), Henrico Co., on N. side of James River; cor. of EDWARD CURD, in a fork of a br. of Beaverdam Cr., on Capt. RICHARD COCK; & down Cattail Br.; 13 Nov. 1721, p. 71. 30 Shill.

THOMAS FARRAR, 400 acs. (N.L.), Henrico Co., on N. side of James Riv., adj. THOMAS WADKINS, on E. side of WADKINS' br., & JOHN BARNS' line; 21 Apr. 1722, p. 87. 40 Shill.

THOMAS RANDOLPH, 670 acs. (Lapsed L.), Henrico Co., on S. side of James Riv., 3 June 1722, p. 89. Granted CHARLES FLEMING; 16 June 1714, upon condition of cultivating, &c., on N. side of a small br. near a great point of rocks on sd. river opposite against the middle of Elk Island; S. on N. side of WILLIS' Cr. 3 Lbs., 10 Shill.

Same. 1000 acs. (N.L.), same Co., & date, p. 91. S. side of James Riv., on Fine Creek, on line of THOMAS TURPIN of the land he in company with JEFFERSON EASLY & ARCHER surveyed & patented.

DANIEL GROOM, 400 acs. (N.L.), Henrico Co., on S. side of James Riv., on a Br. of JONES' Cr. near head of a br. a small distance from a broad rock, called Magnum Lapis; 22 June 1722, p. 107. 40 Shill.

JOHN JONES, 52 acs. (N.L.), Henrico Co. on S. side of James Riv., adj. MARTIN MALLETT, on N. side of JONES' Cr., 22 June 1722, p. 108. Being part of the 1st 5,000 acs. surveyed for the French Refugees.

BENJAMIN WATKINS, 500 acs. (N.L.), Henrico Co., S. side of James River; 22 June 1722, p. 109. 50 Shill.

DAVID PATTISON, 337 acs. (N.L.), Henrico Co., on N. side of James Riv., adj. CHARLES CHRISTIAN; 22 June 1722, p. 110. 35 Shill.

BENJAMIN WOODSON, 178 acs. (N.L.), Henrico Co., N. side of James Riv., on Rockey Run, on line of Mr. JOHN WOODSON; 22 June 1722, p. 110. 20 Shill.

ANTHONY RAPEEN, 400 acs. (N.L.), Henrico Co., on S. side of James Riv., cor. of his French land, on Jones' Cr; 22 June 1722, p. 111. 40 Shill.

JOHN GUN, 250 acs. (N.L.), Henrico Co., on Horse Pen Cr. of Beaver Dam, on N. side of James Riv., adj. his own, JOSEPH WOODSON, & land of WM. LADD; 18 Feb. 1722, p. 157. 2 Shill.

EDWARD SCOTT, 400 acs. (N.L.), Henrico Co., on N. side of James River, adj. THOMAS & JOHN WOOD, on N. side of Tuckahoe Cr., AMOS LAD, & CONSTANT PERKINS; 18 Feb. 1722, p. 158. 40 Shill.

ROBERT BLAWS, JOSEPH WOODSON, JOHN WOODSON, & JOHN WOODSON, Junr., 400 acs. (N.L.), Henrico Co., S. side of James Riv., & on W. side of Fine Cr., on PLEASANTS' line; 18 Feb. 1722, p. 158. 40 Shill.

JAMES HOLEMAN, 400 acs. (N.L.), Henrico Co., N. side of James Riv., on E. side of Dear Pen Br., along EVANS' line & RUSSELL & CLARK's line; 18 Feb. 1722, p. 159. 40 Shill.

MATTHEW COX, 400 acs. (N.L.), Henrico Co., S. side of James Riv., on Fine Cr., down EASLEY's line; 18 Feb. 1722, p. 159. 40 Shill.

CHARLES EVANS, 788 acs. (N.L.), Henrico Co., N. side of James River, known by the name of Hicary Points, on Col. BIRD's line, to Mr. JOHN PLEASANTS, crossing N. br. of UFNAM Brook, to E. side of the gr. Branch, adj. ROBERT BEVERLEY & Capt. GILES WEBB, crossing Pyconockney Path; 13 Aug 1723, p. 199. 4 Lbs. Money.

VALENTINE WARE, 262 acs. (N.L.), Henrico Co., in the fork of Tuckahoe Cr., on N. side of James Riv., adj. FRANCIS CHUMLEY; 5 Sept. 1723, p. 203. 30 Shill.

MATTHEW LIGON, 300 acs. (N.L.), Henrico Co., S. side of James Riv., on E. side of Fine Cr., 5 Sept. 1723, p. 240. 30 Shill.

JOHN WOODALL, 300 acs. (N.L.), Henrico Co., N. side of James River, on W. side of Jennestoe Cr., 5 Sept. 1723, p. 240. 30 Shill.

WILLIAM LEWIS, 400 acs. (N.L.), Henrico Co., S. side of James Riv., on S. side of the Up. Manakin Cr.; 5 Sept. 1723, p. 241. 40 Shill.

JOSEPH WATSON & JOHN WATSON, 400 acs. (N.L.), Henrico Co., on N. side of James River, on THOMAS FARRAR's line; 5 Sept. 1723, p. 243. 40 Shill.

EDWARD RIVIS & THOMAS ALLY, 400 acs. (N.L.), Henrico Co., on S. side of James River, on WILLIAM COCKE's land, crossing Stony Run; 5 Sept. 1723, p. 244. 30 Shill., & Imp. of 2 pers: SARAH MULLINAX & JAMES GRIGG.

WILLIAM BROWN, 268 acs. (N.L.), Henrico Co., N. side of James River, on S. side of the main Cr. of Tuckahoe, parting sd. COX & ROBERT ADAMS, to GILLY GREW MARRAIN's line; 5 Sept. 1723, p. 244. 30 Shill.

GEORGE SMITH, 367½ acs. (N.L.), Henrico Co., S. side of James River, on br. of JONES' Cr., known by the name of CHASTAIN's Br. on CHASTAIN's land. 5 Sept. 1723, p. 245. 40 Shill.

DANIEL HIX, 225 acs. (N.L.), Henrico Co., N. side of James Riv., adj. his own survey, on RUSSEL's & CLERK's lines, JAMES HOLEMAN & THOMAS EVANS' lines; 5 Sept. 1723, p. 245. 30 Shill.

Same. 370 acs. (N.L.), same Co., date, & page. On N. side of James River, near Tuckahoe Cr., adj. THOMAS EVANS, Maj. THOMAS RANDOLPH, the main Road, hard by BUCK branch, HATCHER's line, RUSSEL's & CLERK's line. 40 Shill.

EBENEZER ADAMS, 400 acs. (N.L.), Henrico Co., on N. side of James River, on THOMAS TINDALL's line, on W. side of Little Horse Pen Cr.; 5 Sept. 1723, p. 246. 40 Shill.

HUTCHINS BURTON, 400 acs. (N.L.), Henrico Co., N. side of James River, on Westham Cr., on land of Col.WILLIAM RANDOLPH; 5 Sept. 1723, p. 246. 40 Shill.

THOMAS RANDOLPH, 734 acs. (N.L.), Henrico Co., on N. side of James River & W. side of Tuckahoe Cr. adj. survey whereon he lives, WOODSON's lines, on Buck branch, down the main road to land of EDMUND JENINGS, Esqr., sold to sd.

RANDOLPH; 5 Sept. 1723, p. 247. 3 Lbs., 15 Shill.

STEPHEN SUNTER, 400 acs. (N.L.), Henrico Co., on S. side of the main br. of Chiccahomony Sw., adj. JOHN WOODSON's survey; 18 Mar. 1717, p. 365. 40 Shill.

ELIZABETH BOWMAN, 50 acs. (N.L.), Henrico Co., on S. side of James River, on Fox Slash, adj. WILLIAM CLARKE & WILLIAM SOANE's/; 9 Feb 1718, p. 416. 5 Shill.

STEPHEN CHASTAIN, 219 acs. (N.L.), Henrico Co., on S. side of James River, adj. land whereon he lives, on the French Line; 5 Sept. 1723, p. 247. 25 Shill.

THOMAS EAVINS, 400 acs. (N.L.), Henrico Co., on N. side of James River, 31 Oct. 1723, p. 292. 15 Shill. & Imp. of 5 pers: WILLIAM BANBURY, ELIZABETH YOUNG, JONE LITTLEWORTH, GEORGE RANER, SARAH HONOUR.

THOMAS RANDOLPH, Gent. 2870 acs. (O.& N.L.), Henrico Co., on S. side of James Riv., at a place known by name of WILLIS' Creek; 16 Dec. 1723, p. 302. 11 Lbs. Money. 670 acs. granted him 2 June 1722.

RENA LA FORCE, 1000 acs. (N.L.), on N. side of James Riv., adj. cor. parting THOMAS WADKINS, Mr. THOMAS FARRAR, & Sd. LA FORCE; 20 Feb. 1723, p. 307. 5 Lbs. Money.

FRANCIS FLOURNOY, 400 acs. (N.L.), Henrico Co., on N. side of Swift Cr.,beg. adj. his own, & land of ANTHONY TRIBUE; 20 Feb. 1723, p. 307. 40 Shill.

RICHARD WADE, 400 acs. (N.L.), Henrico Co., on N. side of James River, on land of THOMAS & WILLIAM HARDIN; 20 Feb. 1723, p. 309. Imp. of 8 pers: FRANCES NICHOLS, PHILLIP LAKE, WILLIAM STEWART, WILLIAM CLERK, ELIZABETH TAYLOR, KATHERINE FRENCH, WILLIAM BROWNE, MILLER HARRIS.

JAMES SKELTON, 1200 acs. (N.L.), Henrico Co., on N. side of S. fork of James River, down same below the point of a Rocky Island, & crossing HARDWARS Cr.; 20 Feb. 1723, p. 338. 6 Lbs. money.

Same, 400 acs. (N.L.), same Co., date & page. S. side the James River, ½ mi. below a gr. creek known by the name of the Second Fork. 40 Shill.

Same, 400 acs. (N.L.), same Co., & date, p. 339. S. side of James River, at a 2nd Fork, adj. his 400 acs., surveyed the same day. 40 Shill.

Same. 400 acs. (N.L.), same Co., date & page. On S. side of James River, near the 2nd Fork, on an Island. 40 Shill.

JOHN WOODSON, Gent., of Henrico Co., 400 acs. (N.L.), on N. side of James River, adj. his own land & WILLIAM & BENJAMIN WOODSON; 16 Mar. 1723, p. 340. 40 Shill.

PETER BLAZE, 400 acs. (N.L.), Henrico Co., on N. side of James River, on line of THOMAS CHRISTIAN, & on a br. of Beaverdam Cr.; 16 Mar. 1723, p. 340. 40 Shill.

NICHOLAS COX, 400 acs. (N.L.), Henrico Co., on N. side of James River, on PETERS.' br. of Tuckahoe (Cr.), adj. JOHN ELLIS, & CHUMLEY's line; 16 Mar. 1723, p. 341.

Same. 400 acs. (N.L.), same Co., date & page. N. side of James River, on br. of Tuckahoe Cr., on COTREL's line, to br. of Chicohominy, on MARTIN's line. 40 Shill.

Same. 400 acs. (N.L.), same Co., & date, p. 342. On N. side of James River. 40 Shill.

### Patent Book No. 12

Maj. THOMAS RANDOLPH, Gent., 363 acs. (N.L.), Henrico Co., on N. side of Flue Anna (Riv.), adj. land of Mr. THOMAS CROOKE, dec'd.; 9 July 1724, p. 3. 40 Shill.

CONSTANTINE PERKINS, 347 A., 3 R., & 20 P., (N.L.), Henrico Co., beg. on his own line, & crossing br. of Beaverdam Cr.; 9 July 1724, p. 3. 35 Shill.

JOHN PRIDE, 400 acs. (N.L.), Henrico Co., on the main br. of Swift Cr., above the Beaver Ponds, crossing Genetoe Br.; 9 July 1724, p. 6. 40 Shill.

CONSTANTINE PERKINS, 250 acs. (N.L.), Henrico Co., N. side of James Riv., beg. on W. side of the main Br. of Beaverdam Cr.; 9 July, 1724, p. 6. 25 Shill.

JOHN LAGRAN (or LAGRAU), 50 A., 2 R., 30 P., (N.L.), Henrico Co., S. side of James Riv., beg. at his own land, adj. MITCHEL CAMPE, on the French line, &c.; 9 July 1724, p. 11. Being part of the first 5000 acs. surveyed for the French Refugees.

JOHN PRICE, 390 acs. (N.L.), Henrico Co., N. side of James Riv., on br. of Tuckahoe Cr., to Mr. CHARLES HUDSON; 9 July 1724, p. 13. 40 Shill.

Capt. JOHN BEAVILL, 300 acs. (N.L.), Henrico Co., on N. side of YOULE Br., on S. side of the Locust Br., on SAPPONY Path, in LAR. HOBBY's line; 9 July 1724, p. 13. Imp. of 6 pers: THOMAS BOTT, EDWARD LEWEAS, ROBERT SNUGGS, JOHN BUL-LOCK, JOHN BULLOCK, JOHN SHARPE, WILLIAM WATTS.

WILLIAM GORDING, 400 acs. (N.L.), Henrico Co., N. side of James Riv., near head of a br. of Westham (Cr.), down br. of UFNAM Brook, 9 July 1724; p. 14. 15 Shill., & Imp. of 3 pers: THOMAS BREANT, ANNA BREANT, RACHELL BREANT.

ARTHUR MOSELEY, 400 acs. (N.L.), Henrico Co., N. side of Swift Cr., beg. at ANTHONY TRIBUE, on E. side of Tomahawke Br., to Mr. JOHN TULLITS'line; 9 July 1724, p. 14. 30 Shill., & Imp. of 2 pers: GLOWD DODGE & WALTER SCOTT.

MARTHA BLANKENSHIP, 250 acs. (N.L.), Henrico Co., S. side of James Riv., beg. in Mr. HENRY WALTHALL's lines to E. side of the main road; 9 July 1724, p. 15. 20 Shill., & Imp. of FRANCIS CLAPPE.

THOMAS RANDOLPH, Gent., 400 acs. (N.L.), on S. side of James Riv.,; 9 July 1724, p. 15. 40 Shill.

Capt. PETER CHASTAINE, 379 A., 1 R., 10 P., (N.L.), Henrico Co., W. side of JONES' Cr., on S. side of James Riv., beg. at PETER FORD's cor. on JONES & PLEASANTS line; 9 July 1724, p. 15. 20 Shill. & Imp. of 4 pers: MARY CHAS-TAIN, JANE CHASTAIN, PETER CHASTAIN, Junr., & WALTER BEATLE.

FRANCIS FLOURNOY, Gent., 400 acs. (N.L.), Henrico Co., N. side of Swift Cr., beg. on W. side of TRIBUE's branch; to E. side of the main br. of Tomahake Br. 9 July 1724, p. 17. 40 Shill.

Same. 400 acs. (N.L.), same location, date & page. Beg. on N. side of Nutt tree Br., parting this & land of JOHN BOWMAN, on SAMUEL SOANE's LINE. 40 Shill.

Same. 400 acs. (N.L.), same location & date, p. 18. Beg. on W. side of TRI-BUE's Br., down br. of Tomahake Br. 40 Shill.

MICHAEL HOLLAND, 400 acs. (N.L.), Henrico Co., adj. his own land on S. side of Chickahominy Sw.; 9 July 1724, p. 18. 40 Shill.

Same. 400 acs. (N.L.), same location & date, p. 19. 40 Shill. Marginal note: This land petitioned for by WALKER.

THOMAS FARRAR, 400 acs. (N.L.), Henrico Co., on N. side of James Riv., & on S. side of the main br. of Chiccohominy Sw.; 9 July 1724, p. 19. 40 Shill.

THOMAS MEREDITH, 400 acs. (N.L.), Henrico Co., on Chickahominy Sw., beg. at land of SAMUEL SENTER (or SEUTER), down MEREDITH's Br.; 9 July 1724, p. 20. 40 Shill.

JAMES HOLEMAN, 400 acs. (N.L.), Henrico Co., N. side of James Riv., beg. at his own land, to broad branch of Tuckaho (Cr.), to JAMES MOSS, up the Drinking Hole Br.; 9 July 1724, p. 21. 40 Shill.

JAMES CHRISTIAN, 400 acs. (N.L.), N. side of James Riv., beg. at cor. of EDWARD BAYS & Mr. TARLTON WOODSON, to W. side of Little Cr.; 9 July 1724, p. 22. 5 Shill., & Imp. of 7 pers: GEORGE LAWSON, JOHN NICHOLSON, JOHN STRONG, WILLIAM SMITH, ROGER ROBERTS, JOHN MECLARY, CORNELIUS BRYAN.

GEORGE FREEMAN, 320 acs. (N.L.), Henrico Co., N. side of James Riv., adj. Mr. CHARLES RUSSEL, WILLIAM BURTON, & JOHN ELLIS' line; 9 July 1724, p. 23. 35 Shill.

DANIEL HIX, 400 acs. (N.L.), on N. side of James River, & on brs. of Tuckaho Cr., adj. JOHN WILLIAMS' line, on Leeding Branch, MOSES' line, & Mr. HOLEMAN, on Drinking Br., 9 July 1724, p. 24. 20 Shill., & Imp. of 4 pers: JOHN WILLIAMS, WILLIAM MOORE, RICHARD LANE, BENJAMIN WICKER.

VALENTINE WARE, of K. & Q. Co., 167 acs. (Lapsed L.), Henrico Co., on N. side of James Riv., in a gr. fork of Tuckahoe Cr., adj. land of Mr. CLERK & RUSSELL; 10 Dec. 1724, p. 122. Granted RICHARD COX, 16 Aug. 1715, upon condition of seating & planting, which he failed to do; now granted, &c. 20 Shill.

WILLIAM WOODSON & BENJAMIN WOODSON, Junr., 400 acs. (N.L), Henrico Co., N. side of James Riv., adj. JOHN PLEASANTS' line, on S. side of Jinnetoe Cr., & JOHN WOODSON's line. 9 Feb. 1724, p. 126. 40 Shill.

JOHN BOLLING, Gent., 343 acs. (Lapsed L.), Henrico Co., N. side of James Riv., in a fork of a branch parting AMOS LAD & EDWARD CURD, &c.; 22 Feb. 1724, p. 128. 35 Shill. Granted AMOS LAD, 17 Aug. 1720, upon condition of seating & planting, which he failed to do, &c.

EDWARD SCOTT, 350 acs. (N.L.), Henrico Co., on E. side of Licking Hole Cr.; 22 Feb. 1724, p. 129. 35 Shill.

EDWARD CURD, 1200 acs. (N.L.), Henrico Co., on Castle branch, adj. COCK's line; 22 Feb. 1724, p. 130. 6 Lbs. Money.

Same. 341 A., 2 R., 39 Po., (N.L.), same Co., & date, p. 13. On N. side of James Riv., on the Horsepen Cr. of Beaver Dam, adj. land of JOHN BURKE. 35 Shill.

SAMUEL BURK, 400 acs. (N.L.), Henrico Co., on N. side of James Riv., beg. at Licking Hole Cr., on EDWARD SCOTT's line; Feb. 1724, p. 131. 40 Shill.

ROBERT ADDAMS (ADAMS), 400 acs. (N.L.), Henrico Co., N. side of James Riv., adj. SAMUEL BURK's corner, on a br. of Licking Hole Cr., 22 Feb. 1724, p. 132. 40 Shill.

JOHN WATSON, 400 acs. (N.L.), Henrico Co., N. side of James River, on a br. of Chickahominy Sw. called Long and Hungry; 22 Feb. 1724, p. 135. 5 Shill., & Imp. of 7 pers: ANN POWLE, MARY BUD, ELIZABETH GATEN( or GALEN), JOHN POL-WEN, MARY WHITLAW, JAMES YOUNG, SARAH CHANLER.

THOMAS WILLIAMSON, of Henrico Co., 200 acs. (N.L.), on N. side of James River, beg. on JORDAN's Br. of UFNAM Brook; 22 Feb. 1724, p. 136. 5 Shill., & Imp. of 3 pers: JOHN BUMBAY, JOHN GREEN, DENIS MECARTY.

ADAM LAVEAN (or LAVEAU), 262 acs. (N.L.), Henrico Co., in the Manakin Town, being part of King's donation to the French Refugees; 22 Feb. 1724, p. 136.

JAMES NEVIL, 400 acs. (N.L.), Henrico Co., on E. side of a br. of James Riv., called the Great Creek; 27 Apr. 1725, p. 200. 40 Shill.

HENRY CHILES, of King Wm. Co., 400 acs. (N.L.), Henrico Co., on E. side of Licking Hole Cr., adj. Mr. JOSEPH SCOTT's line; 6 May 1725, p. 209. 40 Shill.

TARLETON WOODSON, Gent. 3000 acs. (N.L.), Henrico Co., beg. at ROGER POWEL's cor. near br. of Beaverdam Creek, adj. JOHN WOODSON's land, on Jenetoe Creek; 17 Aug. 1725, p. 230. 30 Shill.

RICHARD COCKE, Junr., & BENJAMIN COCKE, 191 acs. (N.L.), on N. side of James River, beg. against a gr. open Beaver Pond of Beaver Dam Cr., on line of Mr. RICHARD COCKE, dec'd; 17 Aug. 1725, p. 236. 20 Shill. Henrico Co.

Same. 374 acs. (N.L.), same Co., date & page. On S. side of Flueanna or the S. main br. of James River, &c. 40 Shill.

Same. 384 acs. (N.L.), same Co. & date, p. 237. On S. side of S. br. of James River, beg. at mouth of Bear Garden Creek, &c. 40 Shill.

Same. 400 acs. (N.L.), same Co., date & page. On both sides of James River, beg. at cor. of THORNTON's land sold to Capt. MARTIN, down Mount Misery Branch to the mouth, &c. 40 Shill.

EDWARD CURD, 400 acs. (N.L.), Henrico Co., on N. side of James River, on brs. of Beaverdam Cr., beg. in the Castle Branch; 17 Aug. 1725, p. 238. 40 Shill.

Same. 200 acs. (N.L.), same location, date & page. Adj. Mr. ADDAM & Mr. TARLTON WOODSON's line. 20 Shill.

JOHN RADFORD, 400 acs. (N.L.), Henrico Co., on S. side of James Riv., on JONES' Cr.; 17 Aug. 1725, p. 240. 40 Shill.

JOHN CANNON, 50 acs. (N.L.), Henrico Co., on N. side of James River, adj. OBEDIAH SMITH's line, Col. BIRD's line, & GILLY's corner; 17 Aug. 1725, p. 283. 5 Shill.

THOMAS DAWSON, 400 acs. (N.L.), Henrico Co., on N. side of the W. br. of Licking Hole Cr.; 17 Aug 1725, p. 283. 40 Shill.

JOHN PRICE, 375 acs. (N.L.), Henrico Co., on Deep Run, a br. of Tuckahoe (Cr.) falling into James River.; 17 Aug. 1725, p. 284. 40 Shill.

ROGER POWEL, 400 acs. (N.L.), Henrico Co., on N. side of James River, adj. JOHN PLEASANTS' land on Wolf Br., RALPH HUDSPITH's line, & BENJAMIN JOHNSON's corner; 17 Aug. 1725, p. 284. 40 Shill.

ROBERT HUGHES, 400 acs. (N.L.), Henrico Co., on S. side of James River, crossing Muddy Creek, near HUDDLECEY's fence; 17 Aug. 1725, p. 285.  40 Shill.

GILES CARTER, 48 acs., (N.L.), Henrico Co., on N. side of James River adj. Mr. JAMES POWELL COCKE, in MACHAM's line, parting sd. COCKE & JOHN COCKE, on E. side of Deep Run, to WILLIAM SEWELL, to small island of sd. Run; 17 Aug. 1725, p. 103.  5 Shill.

JOHN MARTIN, Senr., of New Kent Co., 400 acs. (N.L.), Henrico Co., on N. side of the N. br. of James Riv., or the Rivanna at mouth of Dog Cr.; 17 Aug. 1725, p. 302.  40 Shill.

THOMAS FRANKING, 200 acs. (N.L.), Henrico Co., on S. side of the Swift Cr., adj. WILLIAM JACKSON, & on N. side of Licking Cr.; 17 Aug. 1725, p. 303.  20 Shill.

WILLIAM BARNETT, 341 acs. (N.L.), Henrico Co., N. side of James Riv., adj. JOHN BRADLEY, Mr. JOHN WOODSON, & on N. side of Br. of ALLEN's Cr.; 17 Aug. 1725, p. 305.  35 Shill.

ROBERT WILLIS, 350 acs. (N.L.), Henrico Co., on N. side of James Riv., adj. RICHARD WADE, on N. side of HARDIN's Branch; 17 Aug. 1725, p. 310.  35 Shill.

WILLIAM MAY, 400 acs. (N.L.), Henrico Co., N. side of James Riv., & E. side of Beaver Dam Cr., adj. Mr. RICHARD COCK's line, WOODSON & Company, EDWARD BAYS, & Mr. ADDAMS; 17 Aug. 1725, p. 313.  40 Shill.

ROBERT WILLIS, 400 acs. (N.L.), Henrico Co., on N. side of James Riv., adj. RICHARD WADE; 17 Aug. 1725, p. 320.  40 Shill.

JOHN PRIDE, 247 acs. (N.L.), Henrico Co., N. side of James Riv., on N. side of Deep Cr., & on N. side of Horsepen Br. of sd. Cr.; 17 Aug. 1725, p. 321.  25 Shill.

MARY BLAIR, 1600 acs. (N.L.), Henrico Co., on both sides of N. branch of James Riv., opposite CARY's Creek; 26 Oct. 1725, p. 330.  5 Lbs., 10 Shill.; & Imp. of 10 pers: ALICE CUSTILLY, TIMOTHY CUNEGEN, MARGARET CARROL, WILLIAM KILLY, MARY CAINE, MARGARET MCLAWNY, MARY MCKLAMAR, ELIZABETH BURNE, MARY ROCK, JOHN REGEN.

EBENEZER ADAMS, Gent., of New Kent Co., 400 acs. (N.L.), in the fork of James River, on the Rivanna, adj. Mr. COCKE; 26 Oct. 1725, p. 330.  40 Shill.

RICHARD COCKE & BENJAMIN COCKE, 600 acs. (N.L.), Henrico Co.,  on N. side of the S. br. of James River, down New Bremo Creek to the mouth; 15 Dec. 1725, p. 333.  30 Lbs.  Money.

PETER FORD, 400 acs. (N.L.), Henrico Co., on S. side of James River, beg. at DANIEL GROOM's corner of MATTHEWS' Branch; 13 Jan. 1725, p.336.  40 Shill.

MATTHEW OGE, 400 acs. (N.L.), Henrico Co., S. side of James Riv., on MATTHEWS' Branch, a br. of JONES' Cr., adj. JOHN PETER BONDURANT's land; 13 Jan. 1725, p. 337. 40 Shill.

Same. 400 acs. (N.L.), same Co., date & page. 40 Shill.

RICHARD DEAN, 350 acs. (N.L.), Henrico Co., on S. side of James River, adj. JOHN STEPHENS, & JOHN SANDERS line; 10 Feb. 1725, p. 339. 35 Shill.

RICHARD MOSBY, 300 acs. (N.L.), Henrico Co., on W. side of UFNAM Brook; 19 Feb. 1725, p. 339. 30 Shill.

JOHN WOODSON, 400 acs. (N.L.), Henrico Co., on N. side of James River, adj. JOHN GUN, JOHN WOODALL, NOWELL BURTON & BENJAMIN WOODSON, on JOSEPH WOODSON's line, &c.; 18 Mar. 1725, p. 344. 40 Shill.

JOHN MAN, 395 acs. (N.L.), Henrico Co., on N. side of James River, & on brs. of Licking Hole Creek; 24 Mar. 1725, p. 365. 40 Shill.

ROBERT MAN, 433 acs. (N.L.), Henrico Co., on S. side of Swift Creek on S. side of 2nd branch; beg. at HENRY VADEN's line, on a small branch being an elboe of PARISH LINE; 24 Mar. 1725, p. 371. Imp. of 9 pers: MARTIN BURK, THOMAS ROCK, MICHAEL NASH, MICHAEL WHITE, MARY RUARKE, ELLIN GIBBINS, JOHN MUGEDEN, JAMES SANDERS, ELIZABETH FITZJARRELL.

GILBERT GEE & JOHN TRENT, 400 acs. (N.L.), Henrico Co., on S. side of James River in the French Line; 24 Mar. 1725, p. 371. 40 Shill.

Maj. JOHN BOLLING, Gent., 4830 acs. (O.& N.L.), Henrico Co., on N. side of James River on Licking Hole Creek; 27 May 1726, p. 373. 350 acs. part beg. at THOMAS DAWSON's land on low side of sd. Cr., crossing same, to THOMAS BALLOW's land, on his own line, to ALEXANDER LOGEN's line, &c.; 4480 acs. bounded as in patent granted him.

JOHN WOODSON, Gent., 300 acs. (N.L.), Henrico Co., S. side of James River & E. side of STOVALL's Cr., near the main road; 24 Mar. 1725, p. 392. 30 Shill

Same. 400 acs., same county, date & page. N. side of James Riv., on head brs. against Elk Island & heads of brs. of AMOSES' Branch, beg. on S. side of the main road, hard by a place known as the Locust Thickett, on THORTON's line. 40 Shill.

FRANCIS SAMSON, 250 acs. (N.L.), on N. side of James River, beg. at Mr. JOHN PLEASANTS, on Woolfpitt Br., to E. side of Buffilow Br., on AMOS LAD's line; 24 Mar. 1725, p. 394. 25 Shill. Henrico Co.

THOMAS SANDERS, 400 acs. (N.L.), Henrico Co., N. side of James River adj. lines of AMOS LAD, CONSTANT PERKINS & WILLIAM BURTON; 24 Mar. 1725, p. 396. 40 Shill.

MARTIN MARTIN, 358 acs. (N.L.), Henrico Co., S. side of James River & on W. side of Fine Cr., on JOSEPH WOODSON's land; 24 Mar. 1725, p. 398. 40 Shill.

THOMAS BAYLEY, 229 acs. (N.L.), Henrico Co., on N. side of James River corner of EDWARD NEW,near head of a br. of Little Licking Hole Creek; 24 Mar. 1725, p. 399. 25 Shill.

JOHN PETER BONDURANT, 400 acs. (N.L.), Henrico Co., on S. side of James River on JONES' Hole Cr., on MATHEW's branch; 24 Mar. 1725, p. 399. 40 Shill.

JOHN SANDERS, 400 acs. (N.L.), Henrico Co., on S. side of James River, beg. at STOVALL's branch, on BARTHOLOMEW STOVALL's line, to STOVALL's Creek; 24 Mar. 1725, p.404. 40 Shill.

Same. 400 acs. (N.L.), same Co., date & page. 40 Shill.

JACOB MICHAUX, 350 acs. (N.L.), Henrico Co., S. side of James River on MAHOOK Creek, adj. BOLLING's line, & land of MICHAUX, dec'd. &c.; 24 Mar. 1725. p. 405. 35 Shill.

FRANCIS DEPUY of Henrico Co., 200 acs. (N.L.), on S. side of James River at a fork of SHASTAIN's (CHASTAIN's) & DITWAY's branches; 24 Mar. 1725, p. 405. 20 Shill.

HUTCHINS BURTON, 400 acs. (N.L.), Henrico Co., N. side of James River, on Westham Creek, cor. of Col. RANDOLPH; 24 Mar. 1725, p. 406. 40 Shill.

JOHN UTLEY, 400 acs. (N.L.), Henrico Co., on N. side of James River on Tuckaho Cr., near the ridge bet. James & Pomonkey Rivers, adj. ALVIS' & COTTRIL's lands; 24 Mar. 1725, p. 407. 40 Shill.

EDWARD HATHCER, 200 acs. (N.L.), Henrico Co., adj. JOHN ELLIS' land; 24 Mar. 1725, p. 407. 20 Shill.

WILLIAM WELDY, 390 acs. (N.L.), Henrico Co., N. side of James River & on Licking Hole Creek, adj. DAVID PETERSON's line; 24 Mar. 1725, p. 408. 40 Shill.

LEONARD BALLOW & THOMAS BALLOW, 384 acs. (N.L.), Henrico Co., on heads of FLEMING's Park Creek, crossing the main road to Ridge between head of sd. Cr. & AMOSES' Branch; 24 Mar. 1725, p. 408. 40 Shill.

JOHN UTLEY, 400 acs. (N.L.), Henrico Co., on Little Tuckahoe (Cr.), on RENE LAFORCE's line, &c.; 24 Mar. 1725, p. 409. 40 Shill.

JOHN WALTERS, 400 acs. (N.L.), Henrico Co., on E. br. of Deep Run, a br. of Tuckahoe Creek, on JOHN SPEARS' line; 24 Mar. 1725, p. 409. 40 Shill.

JOHN ELLIS, 400 acs. (N.L.), Henrico Co., on PETER's Br., of Tuckahoe Creek; 24 Mar. 1725, p. 410. 40 Shill.

ANTHONY JEVODAN, 200 acs. (N.L.), Henrico Co., S. side of James River, on
JONES' Creek, adj. MATHEW OGE; 24 Mar. 1725, p. 410. 20 Shill.

ANDREW MOOREMAN, 400 acs. (N.L.), Henrico Co., N. side of James River on E.
side of BYRD Creek;, 24 Mar. 1725, p. 411. 40 Shill.

HENRY WEBB, 400 acs. (N.L.), Henrico Co., on S. side of James River at the
Cross Swamp, a br. of Deep Creek; 24 Mar. 1725, p. 411. 40 Shill.

ANDREW MOOREMAN, 400 acs. (N.L.), Henrico Co., N. side of James River on E.
side of BYRD Creek, beg. on the BYRD, at the mouth of a gutt which makes a
small island; 24 Mar. 1725, p. 411. 40 Shill.

JOHN SPEARS, 400 acs. (N.L.), Henrico Co., N. side of James River on Deep Run;
24 Mar. 1725, p. 412. 40 Shill.

THOMAS BALLOW, 370 acs. (N.L.), Henrico Co., N. side of James River, on brs.
of Licking Hole Creek, beg. on Major JOHN BOLLING's line, to head of SACONY's
(?) branch, on THOMAS DAWSON's line, 24 Mar. 1725, p. 412. 40 Shill.

RALFE JACKSON, 275 acs. (N.L.), Henrico Co., on W. side of Swift Cr., beg.
at Maj. PETER FIELD, at mouth of the W. br. of Licking Hole Cr., crossing
older (Elder) branch; 24 Mar. 1725, p. 427. 40 Shill. & Imp. of 4 pers:
THOMAS SMART, ROBERT GILCREST, WILLIAM GOLDING, RICHARD JOHNSON.

Patent Book N. 13

DAVID MIMS, 358 acs. (N.L.), Henrico Co., N. side of James Riv., on Licking
Hole Cr., 31 Oct. 1726, p. 9. 40 Shill.

Same. 358 acs. (N.L.), same location, date & page. 40 Shill.

JOHN BOLLING, Gent. 800 acs. (N.L.), Henrico Co., on N. side of James River or
back of Mr. FLEMING's Rock Castle tract, on the path below FLEMING's Park
Creek; 6 May 1725, p. 73. 4 Lbs., money.

Col. WILLIAM COLE, of Warwick Co., 2000acs, (N.L.), Henrico Co., on JOHN BOS-
TICK's land, to a branch of BYRD (Cr.), &c.; 6 May 1727, p. 74. 10 Lbs. money

Capt. BOWLER COCKE, Gent., 800 acs. (N.L.), Henrico Co., on S. side of James
River, on E. side of GEORGE STOVALL's Horsepen Br., & on W. side of the main
Deep Cr.; 16 June 1727, p. 77. 4 Lbs., money.

JOHN TABOR, 400 acs. (N.L.), on S. side of James River adj. his own land on
Deep Creek; 16 June 1727, p. 78. 40 Shill.

LEONARD BALLOW, 300 acs.(N.L.) Henrico Co., N. side of James River on BOLLING'
Creek; 16 June, 1727, p. 78. 30 Shill.

JOHN BURK, 300 acs. (N.L.), Henrico Co., adj. WOODALL's line, & ROBERT WOODSON;
16 June 1727, p. 79. 30 Shill.

ROBERT ADDAMS, 400 acs. (N.L.), Henrico Co., on Licking Hole Cr., below the
fork, adj. his own land; 16 June 1727, p. 79, 40 Shill.

THOMAS TUNDAL, 400 acs. (N.L.), Henrico Co., on N. side of James River adj.
JONAS LAWSON; 16 June 1727, p. 79. 40 Shill.

WILLIAM HODGES, 380 acs. (N.L.), N. side of James River, on Deep Creek of
Licking Hole (Cr.), 16 June 1727, p. 80. 40 Shill. Henrico Co.

JOHN LEWIS, 250 acs. (N.L.), Henrico Co., on N. side of James River, adj.
WILLIAM COX's land, on a br. of Stony Creek; 16 June 1727, p. 81. 25 Shill.

DANIEL THOMAS, 300 acs. (N.L.), Henrico Co., on S. side of James River on
JONES' Creek, adj. JOHN RADFORD's land; 16 June 1727, p. 81. 30 Shill.

GEORGE FREEMAN, 350 acs. (N.L.), Henrico Co., on N. side of James River, adj.
EDWARD HATCHER's land, on E. side of Flatt Branch, a br. of Tuckahoe Creek, &
JENINGS' line; 16 June 1727, p. 82. 35 Shill.

THOMAS BALLOW & LEONARD BALLOW, 400 acs. (N.L.), Henrico Co., on N. side of
James River, bet. brs. of FLEMING's Park Cr. & Licking Hole Cr., on S. side
of the Main Road about 100 yards therefrom; 16 June 1727, p. 82. 40 Shill.

ROBERT ADDAMS,, 400 acs. (N.L.), Henrico Co., on the fork of Licking Hole Cr.;
16 June 1727. p. 83. 40 Shill.

JONAS LAWSON, 400 acs. (N.L.), Henrico Co., on N. side of James River, on
BYRD Creek, adj. ANDREW MOOREMAN's; 16 June 1727, p. 83. 40 Shill.

WILLIAM TOWNS, 400 acs. (N.L.), Henrico Co., on N. side of James River, adj.
AMOS LEAD's survey on a br. Tuckahoe Cr., & CHARLES HUDSON's line; 16 June
1727, p. 84. Granted WILLIAM WHITLOE, Junr., 27 Mar. 1715, on condition of
seating, &c. 35 Shill. & Imp. of ELIZABETH SCUTT.

MICHAEL HOLLAND, 400 acs. (N.L.), Henrico Co., on S. side of Chickahominy
Swamp, & down MEREDITH's Branch; 16 June 1727, p. 85. 40 Shill.

HENRY RUNNALS, 328 acs. (N.L.), Henrico Co., on N. side of James River, in
the lower fork of the Byrd Cr.; 16 June 1727, p. 85. 35 Shill.

THOMAS BALLOW & LEONARD BALLOW, 400 acs. (N.L.), Henrico Co. on N. side of
James River, on AMOS' Branch, adj. JOHN WOODSON's land, the old road to Elk
Island, & WILLIAM HODGES' corner; 16 June 1727, p. 86. 40 Shill.

MICHAEL HOLLAND, 400 acs. (N.L.), Henrico Co. near head of a br. of the W. fork
of Licking Hole Creek; 16 June 1727, p. 86. 40 Shill.

MICHAEL HOLLAND, 400 acs. (N.L.), Henrico Co., on W. side of the E. fork of Licking Hole Cr., at SCOTT's corner; 16 June 1727, p. 87. 40 Shill.

MICHAEL HOLLAND, 400 acs. (N.L.), Henrico Co., adj. SAMUEL BURK's land on W. side of the E. fork of Licking Hole Cr., cor of Col. SCOTT; 16 June 1727, p. 87. 40 Shill.

Same. 400 acs. (N.L.), same location & date, p. 88. 40 Shill.

SAME. 125 acs. (N.L.), same location, date & page. N. side of James River, on W. side of HARDIN's Br., adj. THOMAS & JOHN WOODS, & THOMAS HARDIN's line. 15 Shill.

GEORGE STOVALL, 400 acs. (N.L.), on S. side of James River, on BARTHOLOMEW STOVALL's line, & crossing brs. of STOVALL's Branch; 16 June 1727, p. 89. 40 Shill.

THOMAS CHRISTIAN of Chas. City Co., 400 acs. (N.L.), Henrico Co., on N. side of James River, adj. PETER BAISE's (BAIZE's) line, MOREMAN's land & JAMES CHRISTIAN, crossing br. of Beaverdam Cr.; 16 July 1727, p. 152. 40 Shill.

Capt. JOHN MARTIN, 6186 acs. (O.&N.L.), Henrico Co., beg. at a gutt parting said MARTIN's land & Capt. CHARLES LEWIS', by the old path, up the BYRD (Cr.), & crossing Dog Creek; 13 Oct. 1727, p. 164. 2109 acs. part formerly granted to JOHN THORNTON, & sold to said MARTIN. 20 Lbs., 10 Shill.

Capt. BOWLER COCKE, 400 acs., (N.L.), Henrico Co., S. side of James River, on Muddy Cr., beg. at mouth of Buok Br. of sd. Creek; 13 Oct. 1727, p. 194.

JOHN WOODSON, 4934 acs. (O.& N.L.), Henrico Co., on N. side of James River, on Jenitoe Cr.; 13 Oct. 1727, p. 196. 2700 acs. part granted sd. WOODSON 24 Apr. 1723, residue being surplus within the bounds. 11 (?) Lbs. 5 Shill.

HENRY HARPER, 400 acs. (N.L.), Henrico Co., on brs. of Licking Hole Cr., on ridge near JOHN MAN's branch, crossing THOMAS MIMS' Mill Run; 9 Feb. 1727, p. 201. 40 Shill.

HENRY HARPER, 400 acs. (N.L.), Henrico Co., on brs. of Licking Hole Creek, on a ridge near JOHN MAN's branch, crossing THOMAS MIMS' Mill Run; Feb. 9. 1727, p. 201. 4 Shill.

FRANCIS EPES, Gent., 300 acs. (Lapsed L.), Henrico Co., S. side of James River on E. side of Fine Creek; 13 Oct. 1727, p. 202. Granted MATTHEW LIGON; 5 Sept. 1723, upon condition of seating, &c., which he failed to do. 30 Shill.

DANIEL GROOM, 400 acs. (N.L.), Henrico Co., beg. at a cor. of Major RANDOLPH's land at TABOR, to N. side of Muddy Cr., 13 Oct. 1727, p. 217. 40 Shill.

GEORGE MARCHBANKS, 350 acs. (N.L.), Henrico Co., adj. French Line, on back of

Manakin Town, 13 Oct. 1727, p. 218.  35 Shill.

WARHAM EASELY, 400 acs. (N.L.), Henrico Co., on S. side of James River, on E. side of the main Deep Cr.; 13 Oct. 1727, p. 218.  40 Shill.

Same.  400 acs. (N.L.), same location & date, p. 219.  Beg. at Capt. BOWLER COCK, on E. side of GEORGE STOVALL's Horsepen Br. of Deep Cr., to E. side of Maple Br.  40 Shill.

Same.  400 acs. (N.L.), same location & date, p. 220.  Beg. at his own land, on W. side of TABOR's Horsepen Br. of Deep Cr.  40 Shill.

Same.  400 acs. (N.L.), same location, date & page.  Beg. on W. side of Beaver Ponds of TABOR's Horsepen Br. of Deep. Cr.  40 Shill.

Same.  400 acs. (N.L.), same location & date, p. 221.  40 Shill.

MICHELL HOLLAND, 346 acs. (N.L.), Henrico Co., on N. br. of UFNAM Brooke; 13 Oct. 1727, p. 221.  35 Shill.

JOHN PRIER & THOMAS CHRISTIAN, 400 acs. (N.L.), Henrico Co., on N. side of James River, on EDMUND NEW's line; 13 Oct. 1727, p. 222.  40 Shill.

THOMAS CHRISTIAN, 400 acs. (N.L.), Henrico Co., N. side of James River, on broad branch of Beaver Dam Cr., adj. CURD's line, JAMES CHRISTIAN & THOMAS CHRISTIAN; 13 Oct. 1727, p. 222.  40 Shill.

PETER GERANT, Gent., of Henrico Co., 400 acs. (N.L.), on S. side of James River on the lower Manakin Creek; 13 Oct. 1727, p. 223.  40 Shill.

SAMUEL ARRINGTON, 200 acs. (N.L.), Henrico Co., S. side of James River, on S. side of Deep Cr.; 13 Oct. 1727, p. 223.  20 Shill.

CHARLES CHRISTIAN, 400 acs. (N.L.), Henrico Co., on N. side of James River at his own land on W. side of Wild Boare Cr.; 13 Oct. 1727, p. 224.  40 Shill.

JOEL CHANDLER, 400 acs. (N.L.), Henrico Co., on S. side of James River, beg. adj. BARTHOLOMEW's & JOHN STOVALL's land, on W. side of STOVALL's main Creek, & on E. side of CHANDLER's path on Swift Cr., & MATHEW's Licking Br.; 13 Oct. 1727, p. 225.  40 Shill.

GEORGE STOVALL, 400 acs. (N.L.), Henrico Co., on S. side of James River, on W. side of the main Deep Cr.; 13 Oct. 1727, p. 226.  40 Shill.

BENJAMIN JOHNSON, 326 acs. (N.L.), Henrico Co., on N. side of James River, adj. ROBERT WOODSON, in the low ground of Genitoe Cr., Mr. ADDAMS & BENJAMIN WOODSON; 13 Oct. 1727, p. 227.  35 Shill.

THOMAS RANDOLPH, Gent. 400 acs. (N.L.), Henrico Co., on S. side of James

River, adj. THOMAS ATTKINSON's or JOHN RIGHT's cor., opposite Major BOLLING's plantation in his island, THOMAS MOSS, & GROOM's land, in a valley of Muddy Creek; 9 Feb. 1727, p. 228. 35 Shill.

JOHN BACON of New Kent Co., 1600 acs. (O.& N.L.), Henrico Co., beg. on UFNAM Brooke, parting his own, & land of JOHN WATSON, down sd. brook to the mouth of where it falls into the Chickahominy Riv. or Sw., adj. THOMAS OWEN; 13 Oct, 1727, p. 282. 1036 A., 5 P., part thereof granted in name of FRANCIS IZARD, 23 Apr. 1681; 563 A., 155p., being surplus within sd. patent. 3 Lbs. Money.

PHILLIP WEBBER, 1050 acs. (N.L.), Henrico Co., N. side of James Riv., on brs. of Tuckaho Cr., adj. GILLY GRUMARTIN's land, on W. side of sd. Creek; 28 Sept. 1728, p. 357. 5 Lbs., 5 Shill.

JOHN PARISH, of James City Co., 400 acs. (N.L.), Henrico Co., on N. side of James River & on each side of Ready Br. (?) of a br. of Tuckaho Cr., adj. BENJAMIN WOODSON, SCOTT's line, & land of WOODSON, & THORNHILL; 28 Sept. 1728, p. 362. 25 Shill. & Imp. of 3 pers: JOSEPH SHECKLETON , JOHN LEE & MARY JENNINGS.

WILLIAM MOSS, of New Kent Co., 400 acs. (N.L.), Henrico Co., on S. side of James Riv. adj. Capt. BOWLER COCK, on W. side of main Deep Cr.,on E.side of GEORGE STOVALL's Horsepen Branch; 28 Sept. 1728, p. 364. 40 Shill.

JOHN MARTIN, 400 acs. (N.L.), Henrico Co., N. side of James River on Drinking Hole Br., a br. of Tuckaho Cr., 28 Sept. 1728, p. 381. 40 Shill.

WILLIAM SPURLOCK, 325 acs. (N.L.), Henrico Co., on W. side of Licking Hole Cr. on CHARLES CHRISTIAN's land; 28 Sept. 1728, p. 383. 35 Shill.

CHARLES MASSIE of New Kent Co., 400 acs. (N.L.), Henrico Co., on Little BYRD (Cr), adj. Capt. MASSIE & VALENTINE AMOS' line; 27 Sept. 1729, p. 401. 40 Shil

Same. 400 acs. (N.L.), same location, date & page. 40 Shill.

ROBERT HUGHES, 400 acs. (N.L.), Henrico Co., S. side of James Riv., on HUGHES Cr. & Right Hand Branch, adj. NOLAND's line, MICHEAUX's land & JOUEY's (?) land; 27 Sept. 1729, p. 714. 40 Shill.

ANTHONY HOGGATT, 50 acs.(N.L.), Henrico Co., on N. side of Tuckahoe Cr., adj. LAFORCE's land, near HOGGATT's Mill, & HUTCHINSON's line; 28 Sept. 1728, p. 439. 5 Shill.

## Patent Book No. 14

JOHN WATSON, 400 acs. (N.L.), Henrico Co., N. side of James Riv., on a br. of Rockey Br., tO OBADIAH SMITH, to N. side of Hungry Br., parting sd. SMITH & WATSON; 26 June 1731, p. 186. 40 Shill.

JOHN WATSON, 400 acs. (N.L.), Henrico Co., on N. side of James Riv., adj. his own & land of ROBERT MOSEBY; 26 June 1731, p. 190.  40 Shill.

CHARLES CHRISTIAN, 200 acs. (N.L.), Henrico Co., on brs. of Tuckaho Cr., adj. EDWARD REVIS; 17 Sept. 1731, p. 336.  20 Shill.

JOHN WATSON, 400 acs. (N.L.), Henrico Co., on UFFNAM Brook, a br. of Chicca-homony Sw.; 17 Sept. 1731, p. 336.  40 Shill.

JOHN PHELPS, 800 acs. (N.L.), Henrico Co., S. side of James Riv. on W. side of WATSON's Br. 17 Sept. 1731, p. 340.  4 Lbs.  Money.

OBEDIAH SMITH, 400 acs. (N.L.), Henrico Co., N. side of James Riv., on N. side of JOHN WADSON's path; 17 Sept 1731, p. 355.  40 Shill.

SAME.  400 acs. (N.L.), same location, date & page, adj. his own & land of THOMAS CONWEY.  40 Shill.

THOMAS CONWAY, 400 acs. (N.L), Henrico Co., N. side of James Riv., adj. JAMES SPEARS, on S. side of Drinking Run, a br. of Deep Run, to head of a br. of Chiccahomany, to head of a br. of MERIDITH's Br., on JOHN WALLER's line; 17 Sept. 1731, p. 356.  40 Shill.

JOHN LANGFORD, 300 acs. (Lapsed L.), Henrico Co., on W. side of UFFNAM Brook; 22 Feb. 1731, p. 363.  Granted RICHARD MOSBY, 10 Feb. 1725, on condition of seating, &c.  JOHN BACON, Gent., of New Kent Co., obtained grant for same, which he made over to sd. LANGFORD, now granted, &c.  30 Shill.

WARHAM EASLY, 400 acs. (N.L.), Henrico Co., S. side of James Riv., on brs. of Deep Cr., on his own land, on WATSON's Br.; 17 Sept. 1731, p. 369.  40 Shill.

THOMAS OWEN, 400 acs. (N.L.), Henrico Co., on N. side of James Riv., adj. ROBERT MOSEBY, & ROBERT ADAMS; 7 Mar. 1731, p. 375.  40 Shill.

JAMES HAMBLETON, Gent., 18 acs. (N.L.), Henrico Co. on N. side of James Riv., adj. his own & land of WILLIAM FORD; 7 Mar. 1731, p. 376.  5 Shill.

JOHN PETER PERNE(PERUE), 122 A., 2 R., 24 P., Henrico Co., on S. side of James Riv. adj. ANDREW AWBERY, 28 Sept. 1732, p. 534.  Part of the lower part of the last 5,000 acs. surveyed for the French Refugees.

WILLIAM BRITTON, 300 acs. (N.L.), Henrico Co., on N. side of James Riv. adj. RALPH HUNT & ROBERT MOSBY, on W. side of a br. of Chickahominy Sw., THOMAS OWEN & his own land; 28 Sept. 1732, p. 536.  30 Shill.

Goochland County

Separated from western Henrico County - 1728

Patent Bok No. 13

EDWARD SCOTT, Gent., 250 acs. (N.L.), Goochland CO., on N. side of James Riv., & on W'most br. of Little Licking Hole, on TARLTON WOODSON's line, on Little Cr. at land mark of EDMUND NEW; 11 Oct. 1728, p. 317. 25 Shill.

AMOS LAD, 400 acs. (N.L.), Goochland Co., on S. side the Fluanna (Riv.) opposite to the Totero Town; 28 Sept. 1728, p. 324. 40 Shill.

Same. 400 acs. (N.L.), same location & date, page 325. 40 Shill.

ANDREW SCOTT, JOHN SCOTT & STEPHEN HUGHES, 4,000 acs. (N.L.), Goochland Co., on S. side of James Riv., on lower side of Muddy Cr., & brs. of Deep Cr., adj. BOWLER COCKE, THOMAS RAYLEY, & MAYO & COCKE's lines; 11 Oct. 1728, p. 325. 20 Lbs., Money.

JAMES HOLMAN, 400 acs. (N.L.), Goochland Co., on S. side the Flueanna (RIV.), adj. his own land; 21 Oct. 1728, p. 330. 40 Shill.

Same. 400 acs. (N.L.), same location, date & page. At mouth of NEVILS' Cr. 40 Shill.

PATRICK MULLIN, 350 acs. (N.L.), Goochland Co., on up. side of Byrd Cr., adj. line of THORNTON; 28 Sept. 1728, p. 340. 35 Shill.

RICHARD WADE, 400 acs. (N.L.), Goochland Co., in the fork of Tuckaho Cr., adj. ROBERT WILLIS, LAFORCE's line, & WOOD's or WARE's corner; 28 Sept. 1728, p. 374. 40 Shill.

JOHN MACON, 400 acs. (N.L.), Goochland Co., in BOLLING's Quarter Branch, adj. MATMADUKE HIX, & JAMES TAYLOR's land; 12 Sept. 1729, p. 381. 40 Shill.

BARTHOLOMEW STOVALL & THOMAS WALKER, 400 acs. (N.L.), Goochland Co., S. side of Riv., on W. side of Dispute Br., on E. side of JOHN TABOUR's Horsepen Br.; 27 Sept. 1729, p. 385. 40 Shill. (James River.)

NICHOLAS COX, 400 acs. N.L.), Goochland Co., on S. side of James Riv., beg. at BENJAMIN WOODSON's line, on N. side of a br. of Deep Cr., to within one chain of BOLLING's Quarter Br.; 27 Sept. 1729, p. 386. 40 Shill.

MARMADUKE HIX & WILLIAM MOSS, 400 acs. (N.L.), Goochland Co., on S. side of James Riv., on E. side of the main Deep Cr.; 27 Sept. 1729, p. 387. 40 Shill.

ASHFORD HUGHES & DANIEL PRICE, 400 acs. (N.L.), Goochland Co., on both (sides) the main forke of Deep Cr., adj. JOHN TAYLOR, JOHN WOODSON, MOSBY's line, & TABOR's land; 27 Sept. 1729, p. 387. 40 Shill.

DANIEL STONER, Gent., 3800 acs. (O.& N.L.), Goochland Co., on S. side of James River & on both sides of Fine Cr., adj. VANDERHOOD's land, WATKINS line on HUGHES' Cr., BARTHOLOMEW COX's line, the main Road, the Old Road, LAXES' line, near head of a br. of STOVAL's Cr., 27 Sept. 1729, p. 393. 2600 acs. part granted to Major THOMAS RANDOLPH; 1200 acs. part being (the) King's land adjoining. 6 Lbs., Money.

THOMAS RANDOLPH, Gent., 800 acs. (N.L.), Goochland Co., on N. side the Rivanna above JOSEPH BARINGER's land, &c., 27 Sept. 1729, p. 398. 4 Lbs., Money.

JAMES NEVIL, 400 acs. (N.L.), Goochland Co., on S. side of Fluvanna (Riv.), below the Rocky Islands; 27 Sept. 1729, p. 406. 40 Shill.

NOWELL BURTON, 400 acs. (N.L.), Goochland Co., on Beech Cr., a br. of the Little Byrd (Cr.); 27 Sept. 1729, p. 407. 40 Shill.

GEORGE PAYNE, 400 acs. (N.L.), Goochland Co., N. side of James Riv., on head brs. of Lickinghole Cr., adj. ROBERT ADAMS; 27 Sept. 1729, p. 407. 40 Shill.

JOHN MARTIN of New Kent Co., 400 acs. (N.L.), Goochland Co., on N. side the Rivanna (Riv.), on his own land; 27 Sept. 1729, p. 407. 40 Shill.

JAMES NEVIL, 400 acs. (N.L.), Goochland Co., on N. side the Flueanna (River), on HARDWAR Cr. or Pohattan River; 27 Sept. 1729, p. 407. 40 Shill.

ASHFORD HUGHES & JOSEPH THOMAS, 400 acs. (N.L.), Goochland Co., in the W. main fork of Muddy Cr., near head of MAXEY's branch, adj. their own land; 27 Sept. 1729, p. 408. 40 Shill.

Same. 400 acs. (N.L.), same location and date, p. 409. 40 Shill.

ANTHONY MORGAN, 50 acs. Goochland Co., S. side of James River; 27 Sept. 1729, p. 410. Being surplus within 850 acs. granted ABRAHAM MICHEAUX; 27 Jan. 1713. 5 Shill.

DANIEL WILMORE, of New Kent Co., 400 acs. (N.L.), Goochland Co., on BOLLING's Quarter Br., & Brs. of Deep. Cr., adj. JAMES TAYLER, WILLIAM MOSS, ASHFORD HUGHES, & JOHN MACON; 27 Sept. 1729, p. 420. 40 Shill.

JAMES HOLMAN, 100 acs. (N.L.), Goochland Co., on S. side of James Riv., adj. ISAAC LAFET, on br. of Up. Manacan Cr., & STEPHEN & WILLIAM CALVET; 30 June 1730, p. 427. Part of the 1st 5000 acs. surveyed for the Franch Refugees.

JOSEPH WOODSON & STEPHEN WOODSON, 110 acs. (N.L.), Goochland Co., on N. side of James River, bet. land of JOHN WOODSON & Major LIGHTFOOT; 24 Feb. 1729, p. 433. 15 Shill.

CHARLES CHRISTIAN, 400 acs.(N.L.), GOOCHLAND Co.,N. side of James Riv., & Deep Cr. of Licking Hole Cr. 28 Sept. 1728, p. 443. 40 Shill.

JOHN HAILES, of Chas. City Co., 400 acs. (N.L.), Goochland Co., on N. side of Appamattock Riv., adj. Capt. RICHARD RANDOLPH, on E. side of gr. br. of Fiting Cr., & Col. WILLIAM RANDOLPH; 2 June 1730, p. 444. 40 Shill.

HENRY ANDERSON, Gent., 1500 acs. (N.L.), Goochland Co., on N. side of Appamattock Riv., on HENRY CLAY's land; 27 May 1730, p. 446. 7 Lbs., 10 Shill.

ARTHUR MOSELEY, Jr., 1200 acs.(O.&N.L),Goochland Co., on N. side of Appamattock River, corner of HENRY CLAY & Capt. RICHARD RANDOLPH; 6 June 1730, p. 452. 400 acs. part granted sd. MOSELLEY, 17 Aug. 1725. 4 Lbs., Money.

JOHN OWEN, 400 acs. (N.L.), Goochland Co., on N. side of Appamattock Riv., on FREDERICK COX's land; 30 June 1730, p. 463. 40 Shill.

PHILLIP THOMAS, 400 acs. (N.L.), Goochland Co., on N. side of Appomattox Riv. adj. JOHN OWEN's line; 30 June 1730, p. 464. 40 Shill.

STEPHEN CHASTAIN, 400 acs. (N.L.), Goochland Co., on S. side of James Riv., adj. Mr. DITWAY's land, on DITWAY's Br.; 2 July 1730, p. 464. 40 Shill.

Same. 400 acs. (N.L.), same location & date, p. 465. On br. of Jones' Cr. 40 Shill.

GEORGE HUDSPITH, 400 acs. (N.L.), Goochland Co., on N. side of Appamattox Riv. adj. Col. WILLIAM RANDOLPH & NATHANIEL MANE (?),down a br. of Deep Cr., to land of BARTHOLOMEW STOVALL, THOMAS WALKER, PETER LEGRAN, ABRAHAM MISSHEUX & NATHANIEL MAXE's line; 30 June 1730, p. 465, 40 Shill.

BARTHOTOMEW DEPUY of Henrico Co., 33 acs. (N.L.), Goochland Co., in the Manakin Town, on S. side of James River adj. his own land, & PETER SOBLET; 28 Sept. 1728, p. 474. Being part of a donation of King William to the French Refugees.

Honorable JOHN CARTER, Esqr., 9350 acs. (N.L.), Goochland Co., in the fork of the James Riv., adj. CHARLES HUDSON, on W. side of a gr. mountain, crossing a cr. of the Fluvanna (Riv.); 28 Sept. 1730, p. 478. 46 Lbs., 15 Shill.

EDWARD SCOT, 400 acs. (N.L.), Goochland Co., S. side of James Riv., on both sides of Horsepen Br., of Deep Cr., adj. WARRAN EASLEY & GEORGE STOVALL's land; 28 Sept. 1730, p. 479. 40 Shill.

RALPH HUDSPITH, 400 acs. (N.L.), Goochland Co., on N. side of Appamattocks Riv. on Col. WILLIAM RANDOLPH's line, on E. side of PHILLIPS' Br., of Fiting Cr. . 28 Sept. 1730; p. 482. 40 Shill.

FRANCIS EPES, Gent. of Henrico Co., 2400 acs. (N.L.), Goochland Co., N. side of Appamattock Riv., W. side of the main Twogate Horsepen Br., being a br. of the main Deep Cr., on the main ridge parting James & Appamattock Rivers, & on Capt. HENRY ANDERSON's line; 28 Sept. 1730, p. 482. 12 Lbs., Money.

Col. FRANCIS EPES,(N.L.), Goochland Co., on brs. of Hardwar River, Rock Fish
Riv. & other brs. of Fluvanna (Riv.), adj. Capt. CHARLES HUDSON; 28 Sept.
1730, p. 486, 32 Lbs., 10 Shill.

Capt. RICHARD RANDOLPH, 400 acs. (N.L.), on N. side of James Riv., on brs. of
Tuckaho Cr., adj. EDWARD HATCHER, on W. side of the Rockey Br. of sd. Creek,
&JOHN ELLIS' land, on PETERS' Branch, to head of a Br. of Gravilly Run of Deep
Cr; 28 Sept. 1730, p. 491. 40 Shill.

GEORGE SOUTHERLAND, of Henrico Co., 400 acs. (N.L.), Goochland Co., on the
Long Br. of Licking Hole Cr., on WATERS' line; 28 Sept. 1730, p. 493. 40 Shill.

GIDEON JAMBOU (or JAMBON), 40½ acs. (N.L.), Goochland Co., bet. the 2 Manacan Creeks, on S. side of James River, adj. PETER DUPEA, & GEORGE MARSHBANK's
lines; 28 Sept. 1730, p. 493. Being part of land laid out for French Refugees.

HENRY VANDERHOOD, 400 acs. (N.L.), Goochland Co., on S. side of James Riv.,
near Mr. STOANER's land, near Fine Cr., adj. MARTIN MARTIN & WATKINS' land;
28 Sept. 1730, p. 494. 40 Shill.

HOLEMAN JAMES, 183 acs. (N.L.), Goochland Co., N. side of James Riv., on brs.
of Tuckahoe Cr., on line of WILLIAM WOMACK, in Bear Br. of the Dearpen Br. of
sd. creek, to head of the Fort Br.; 28 Sept. 1730, 494. 20 Shill.

STEPHEN CHASTAIN, 400 acs. (N.L.), Goochland Co., on S. side of James Riv. between the 2 Manacan Creeks, adj. FRANCIS FARSY, & his own land; 28 Sept. 1730,
p. 494. 40 Shill.

PETER JEFFERSON, 322 acs. (N.L.), Goochland Co., on S. side of James Riv. beg.
adj. PETER FORD, on MATTHEW AGEE's branch; 28 Sept. 1730, p. 495. 35 Shill.
Marginal note:  Vacated by order of the General Court, 23 Apr. 1746. Benj.
Waller, Cl.

WILLIAM BARNES, 400 acs. (N.L.), Goochland Co., on N. side of Appamattock Riv.
adj. EDWARD MAX, WILLIAM BLACKBURN, JOHN MAX, WILLIAM WOODSON, & MATTHEW Ligon;
28 Sept. 1730, p. 495. 40 Shill.

PETER LEGRAN, 400 acs. (N.L.), Goochland Co., N. side of James Riv., on W.
side of Dispute Branch, parting his own, land of BARTHOLOMEW STOVALL & THOMAS
WALKER, to W. side of TABOR's Horsepen Br.; 28 Sept. 1730, p. 496. 40 Shill.

THOMAS TURPIN, 283 acs. (N.L.), Goochland Co., on lower side of the upper
Manacan Cr., on S. side of James Riv., adj. JOHN PETER BONDURANT, JOSEPH
TANNER, NATHANIEL MAXEY, & JAMES COCKE; 28 Sept. 1730, p. 496. 10 Shill. &
Imp. of 4 pers: ANTHONY MATTOON, MATHEU GALLIER, JOHN GALLIER, Senr., & JOHN
GALLIER, Junr.

HENRY WOOD, Gent., of Goochland Co., 200 acs. (N.L.), Hanover Co., between
lines of WATSON & ALVES; 28 Sept. 1730, p. 502. 20 Shill.

Hon. WILLIAM RANDOLPH, Esqr., 577 acs. (Lapsed L.), in Goochland & Hanover Counties (formerly Henrico Co.), N. side of James River on head of Mill Cr. on N. side of the S. br. from the Beaverponds of Tuckahoe Cr. & a br. of Genitoe Creek; 28 Sept. 1730, p. 504. Granted CHARLES EVANS 16 June 1714, on condit- ion of seating, &c. 3 Lbs., Money.

DUDLEY DIGGS, Gent., of Henrico Co., 3650 acs. (N.L.), Goochland Co, S. side of James Riv., on brs. of WILLIS' Cr., on E. side of RANDOLPH's Creek, corner POWER & CARY, down PHELPS' Creek, to head of POWER's Creek; 28 Sept. 1730, p. 505. 18 Lbs., 5 Shill.

PETER DEP, 400 acs. (N.L.), Goochland Co., S. side of James River, on W. side of the low. Manakin Cr, 28 Sept. 1730, p. 507. 40 Shill.

HENRY WOOD, Gent., 110 acs. (N.L.), Goochland Co. on each side of Tuckahoe Cr. on N. side of James Riv., beg. at his own land, 'twix the Swamp & PETER WARE's land, on WILLIAM BROWN's line; 28 Sept. 1730, p. 512. 15 Shill.

Mr. MICHAEL HOLLAND, 400 acs. (N.L.), on S. side of the Rivanna (Riv.) on E. side of CUNNINGHAM's Creek; 28 Sept. 1730, p. 512. 40 Shill.

Same. 400 acs. (N.L.), Goochland Co., 28 Sept. 1730, p. 513. Adj. his own land, near MULKEY's path near the Ridge between the E. & W. brs. of Licking Hole Cr. 40 Shill.

WILLIAM KENT, 270 acs. (N.L.), Goochland Co., N. side of James River on brs. of Tuckaho Cr., adj. THOMAS EVANS, JOHN WILLIAMS & WILLIAM WOMACK's line; 28 Sept. 1730. p. 514. 30 Shill.

HUTCHINSON BURTON, 400 acs. (N.L.), Goochland Co., N. side of Appamattock River, adj. JOHN OWEN & his own land; 28 Sept. 1730, p. 537. 40 Shill.

AGNES NOLAND, 400 acs.(N.L.), on S. side of James River on MAHOOK Creek, adj. QUIN's line, BARTHOLOMEW COX & MICHAUX's line; 28 Sept. 1730, p. 537. 40 Shill.

BENJAMIN WOODSON, 400 acs. (N.L.), Goochland Co., on Wildboar Br. of Licking- hole Cr.; 28 Sept. 1730, p. 538. 40 Shill.

JOHN WOODSON, 1250 acs. (N.L.), Goochland Co., on N. side James River, adj. JOSEPH PAIN, on the Broad Br. of Tuckahoe , & land of RICHARD WOODSON, dec'd, on a br. of Mill Cr.; 28 Sept. 1730, p. 538. 6 Lbs., 5 Shill.

JOHN LAVILLIAN, 170 acs. (N.L.), Goochland Co., on S. side of James River adj. JUDITH VALLOW's line, & crossing lower Man: 1 Cr.; 28 Sept. 1730, p. 539. Being part of land laid out for the French Refugees.

WILLIAM ALLEN of Chas. City Co., 400 acs. (N.L.), Goochland Co., on S. side of James Riv., on Fine Cr.,adj. MATTHEW COX & MATTHEW LIGON; 28 Sept. 1728, p. 7. 40 Shill.

ANTHONY RAPEAN, 274 acs. Goochland Co., on S. side of Jones' Cr., beg. adj. CHASTAINE's land, GEORGE SMITH's, his own, & NICHOLAS SULIE's land; 28 Sept. 1730, p. 42. 30 Shill. (N.L.)

NATHANIEL MAXE, 400 acs. (N.L.), Goochland Co., on S. side of James Riv., adj. JAMES COCKE, Junr., his own, EDWARD MAXE, Junr., MATTHEW OAGE, & JOSEPH TANNER, Junr.; 28 Sept. 1730, p. 43. 40 Shill.

AMOS LAD, 400 acs. (N.L.), Goochland Co., N. side of Fluvanna (Riv.), at mouth of New Bremo Cr.; 28 Sept. 1730, p. 44. 40 Shill.

WILLIAM MAXE, 400 acs. (N.L.), Goochland Co., S. side of James Riv., adj. NATHANIEL MAXE in EDWARD MAXE's line, & land of PETER BOCCARD, on S. side of br. of MATTHEWS' Licking & on S. side of Woolf Trap Br.; 11 Dec. 1730, p. 44. 40 Shill.

NATHANIEL MAXE, 400 acs. (N.L.), Goochland Co., N. side of Appamattock Riv.; 11 Dec. 1730, p. 45. Adj. PHILLIP THOMAS, on E. side of Old Licking Hole Br., parting THOMAS & RICHARD WILLIAMSON, JOHN OWENS, RICHARD PARKER & Col.WILLIAM RANDOLPH's line. 40 Shill.

JOHN GUN, 300 acs.(N.L.), Goochland Co., on N. side of James Riv., on E. side of the Horsepen Br. of Beaverdam Cr., in line of JOSEPH WOODSON, & on line dividing Goochland & Hanover Counties; 28 Sept. 1730, p. 46. 30 Shill.

THOMAS LOCKETT, 400 acs. (N.L.), Goochland Co., N. side of Appamattock Riv. on N. side of the main Butterwood Cr., on JOHN PRIDE's line; 28 Sept. 1730, p. 48. 40 Shill.

HENRY COX, 400 acs. (N.L.), Goochland Co., N. side of Appomattocks Riv., beg. on the river just below THOMAS TURPIN's old Horsepen, alias Sandy Lick; 28 Sept. 1730, p. 48. 5 Shill., & Imp. of 7 pers; GASPARD SOBRICHE, ANN SOBRICHE, MARY SOBRICHE, JACOB SOBRICHE, ANNA SOBRICHE, SUSANNA SOBRICHE & GASPARD SOBRICHE, Junr.

GEORGE COX, 400 acs. (N.L.), Goochland Co., on N. side of Appamattox Riv., adj. HENRY COX; 28 Sept. 1730, p. 49. 40 Shill.

HUTCHINSON BURTON, 400 acs., (N.L.), Goochland Co., on N. side of Appamattox Riv., adj. FREDERICK COX, JOHN OWEN & RICHARD PARKER; 28 Sept. 1730, p. 49. 40 Shill.

WILLIAM CANNON, 300 acs. (N.L.), Goochland Co., on N. side of Fluvanna Riv., on Hardwar Cr., down Rockfish Cr., to the James or Fluvanna River; 28 Sept. 1730, p. 50. 30 Shill.

FREDRICK COX, 400 acs. (N.L.), on N. side of Appamattock Riv., adj. GEORGE COX: 28 Sept. 1730, p. 50. 40 Shill. Goochland Co.

JOSIAS PAINE, 400 acs. (N.L.), Goochland Co., on W. side of Licking Hole Cr., adj. ROBERT ADDAMS, opposite HENRY WEBB; 28 Sept. 1730, p. 51. 40 Shill.

ALLEN HOWARD Gent., 400 acs. (N.L.), Goochland Co., on N. side of Flueanna Riv., & on each side of Rockfish Riv.; 11 Jan. 1730, p. 56. 40 Shill.

ALEXANDER MARSHALL, 3000 acs. (O.& N.L.), Goochland Co., on N. side of Appamattock Riv., adj. Mr. ARTHUR MOSELEY, on E. side of Butterwood Cr., Mr. ED-WARD HASKINS, on S. side of Jennytoe Cr., Col. WILLIAM RANDOLPH, Capt. RICHARD RANDOLPH, HENRY CLAY, on the old Hunting Path, JAMES AKIN, ARTHUR MOSELEY, Junr., HALCOAT PRIDE, JOHN PRIDE, & THOMAS LOCKET: 28 Sept. 1730, p. 59. 5 Lbs., Money. 2000 acs. part granted him 7 Jan. 1725.

THOMAS RICH, 400 acs. (N.L.), on head of Beaverdam Cr., adj. Capt. JOHN SYMES, on the County Line, on head of Little Cr., & CONSTANTINE PERKIN's line; 28 Sept. 1730, p. 60. 40 Shill. Goochland Co.

THOMAS LOCKET, 900 acs. (O.& N.L.), Goochland Co., on N. side of Appamattock Riv., adj. HALCOAT PRIDE, on S. side the main Butterwood Cr., SAMUEL HANCOCK, & ARTHUR MOSELEY, 28 Sept. 1730, p. 6. 100 acs. granted SAMUEL HANCOCK & AR-THUR MOSELEY, Junr.; 22 Feb. 1724, & conveyed to sd. LOCKET by deeds ack'd.in Henrico Co.
SETH WARD, 220 acs. (N.L.), Goochland Co., on N. side of Appamatock Riv., 28 Sept. 1730, p. 115. 25 Shill.

Same. 800 acs. (N.L.), same Co. & date, p. 116. N. side of Appamatock Riv., a small distance from & below Angelo Cr. 4 Lbs., 10 Shill.

HENRY BREAZEALE, 400 acs. (N.L.), Goochland Co., at Appamatox Riv. adj. PHILIP THOMAS, RALPH HUDSPEATH, & WILLIAM RANDOLPH, Esqr.; 28 Sept. 1730, p. 129. 40

DAVID PATTERSON, 400 acs. (N.L.), Goochland Co., on W. side the lower main br., of Licking Hole Cr., adj. EDWARDS' line, JOHN MAN, & his own land; 28 Sept. 1730, p. 133. 40 Shill.

JOHN LANE, 400 acs. (N.L.), Goochland Co., adj. CHARLES CHRISTIAN, EDMON NEWS, on W. side of a br. of Licking Hole Cr., & land of WILLIAM WILDY; 28 Sept. 1730, p. 133. 40 Shill.

CHARLES CHRISTIAN, of Chas. City Co., 400 acs. (N.L.), Goochland Co., adj. THOMAS CHRISTIAN & JOHN PRIER, up Wild Boar Cr.; 28 Sept. 1730, p. 134. 40 Shill.

MARMADUKE HIX, 400 acs. (N.L.), Goochland Co., on S. side of James Riv., on W. side of Little Deep Cr., adj. SAMUEL ARRINGTON, DAVID LIKES, & EASLY's land; 28 Sept. 1730, p. 134. 40 Shill.

DAVID PATTERSON of New Kent Co., 400 acs. (N.L.), Goochland Co., on N. side of James Riv., bet. Gr. & Little Licking Hole (Creeks), adj. Mr. EDMOND NEWS, & CHARLES CHRISTIAN; 28 Sept. 1730, p. 135. 40 Shill.

HENRY ATKINSON of Hanover Co., 400 acs. (N.L.), Goochland Co., N. side of James Riv., on brs. of Licking Hole Cr., adj. his own & HOGGATT's line; 28 Sept. 1730, p. 135. 40 Shill.

JOHN MERRYMAN, 400 acs. (N.L.), on Muddy Cr., on S. side of James Riv.; 28 Sept. 1730, p. 136. 40 Shill.

STEPHEN WOODSON, 358 acs. (Lapsed L.), Goochland Co., on S. side of James Riv., on W. side of Fine Cr., adj. JOSEPH WOODSON; 28 Sept. 1730, p. 137. Granted to MARTIN MARTIN; 24 Mar. 1725, on condition of seating, &c. 40 Shill.

WILLIAM MAYO, 9350 acs. (O.& N.L.) Goochland Co., on S. side of James Riv., from upper Manacan Cr. to Deep Cr.; 28 Sept. 1730, p. 138. Beg. on N. side of sd. Creek, adj. lands of THOMAS JEFFERSON, Gent., & Company, DANIEL THOMAS, WILLIAM ALLEN, MATHEW LYGON, WILLIAM RANDOLPH, Esqr., ABRAHAM MICHEAUX, JOHN SAUNDERS, WILLIAM LAX, JOHN WOODSON, Gent., BARTHOLOMEW STOVAL, on MATHEW's Licking Br., DANIEL STONER, Gent., on N. side of Fine Cr. 1000 acs. part granted THOMAS RANDOLPH, Gent.; 2 June 1722; 400 acs. granted MATHEW COX; 18 Feb. 1722; 7950 acs. being waste land adj. 39 Lbs., 15 Shill.

HUTCHINSON BURTON, 400 acs. (N.L.), Goochland Co., on N. side of Appamatox Riv., at the mouth of Letalone Cr., on br. parting his own & land of HENRY CLAY, on S. side of a br. of CLAY's Br.; 28 Sept. 1730, p. 141. 40 Shill.

THOMAS WATKINS, 300 acs. (N.L.), Goochland Co., N. side of James Riv., on N. side of Swift Cr. on his own line; 28 Sept. 1730, p. 142. 30 Shill.

DAVID PATTERSON, 342 acs. (N.L.), Goochland Co., N. side of James River on brs. of Licking Hole Cr., on E. side of CHARLES CHRISTIAN's land; 28 Sept. 1730, p. 142. 35 Shill.

WILLIAM SALLE, 64 acs. (O.L.) Goochland Co., on S. side of James Riv., adj. JOHN LEGRAND, GEORGE MARSHBANKS & line of ——— TIMSON, Widow; 28 Sept. 1730, p. 143. Part of land laid out for the French Refugees.

ANTHONY HOGGATT, 107 acs. (N.L.), N. side of James Riv. on Tuckahoe Cr. adj. lines of SCOTT, THORNILL & BOOTH NAPIER; 28 Sept. 1730, p. 143. 15 Shill. Goochland Co.

THOMAS CARTER, Junr., 200 acs. (N.L.), Goochland Co., N. side of James Riv. adj. LEONARD BALLOW, near brs. of FLEMING's Park Cr., on brs. of sd. river falling into Rock Castle low-grounds; 28 Sept. 1730, p. 144. 20 Shill.

Capt. DANIEL STONER, 500 acs. (N.L.), Goochland Co., N. side of Appamatocks Riv. on E. side of a br. of Angoler Cr., & br. of Great Guinea Cr.; 28 Sept. 1730, p. 145. 50 Shill.

JOHN SANDERS, 400 acs. (N.L.), Goochland Co., S. side of James Riv., on E. side of a br. of Angoler Cr., & br. of Great Guinea Cr.; 28 Sept. 1730, p. 145. 50 Shill.

FRANCIS COLEY, 400 acs. (N.L.), Goochland Co., on brs. of Licking Hole Cr., adj. ROBERT ADDAMS; 28 Sept. 1730, p. 146. 40 Shill.

THOMAS MURRELL, 400 acs. (N.L.), Goochland Co., on the Little Byrd Cr., adj. JONAS LAWSON & GEORGE PAYNE; 28 Sept. 1730, p. 146. 40 Shill.

RICHARD KIRBY, 400 acs. (N.L.), Goochland Co., N. side of James Riv., on brs. of Licking Hole Cr., adj. HENRY ATKINSON, PHILIP HOGGATT & JOSEPH SCOTT; 28 Sept. 1730, p. 147. 40 Shill.

RICHARD BAKER, 350 acs. (N.L.), Goochland Co., N. side of Appamatocks Riv., adj. JOHN OWENS, on mouth of Letalone Cr., & Col. WILLIAM RANDOLPH's line; 28 Sept. 1730, p. 148. 35 Shill.

RICHARD OGLESBY, 600 acs. (O.L.), Goochland Co., on brs. of Beaverdam Cr., adj. THOMAS CHRISTIAN; 28 Sept. 1730, p. 149. 200 acs. formerly patented. 40 Shill.

MICHAEL HOLLAND, 400 acs. (N.L.), Goochland Co., on S. side & adjacent to Fluvanna Riv., on W. side of CUNNINGHAM's Cr.; 5 May 1731, p. 151. 40 Shill.

STEPHEN LACY, of Hanover Co., 400 acs. (N.L.) Goochland Co., on brs. of OWEN's Cr., beg. at his own land surveyed the same day as this, on the line bet. Goochland & Hanover Cos.; adj. HENRY ATKINSON; 26 June 1731, p. 159. 40 Shill.

THOMAS EDWARDS, 400 acs. (N.L.), Goochland Co., at Treasurer's Run on N. side of Riv. adj. DAVID PATERSON, land of Major JOHN BOLLING, dec'd,,ALEXANDER LOGAN, THOMAS DAWSON, RICHARD DEAN & JOHN MAN; 26 June 1731, p. 165. 40 Shill. (James Riv.)

MATTHEW COX, 400 acs. (N.L.), Goochland Co., bet. Deep Cr. & Muddy Cr., on S. side of James Riv., adj. WILLIAM RANDOLPH, BENJAMIN MOSEBY, WILLIAM BRADLY & THOMAS MORSE; 26 June 1731, p. 172. 40 Shill.

MARTIN KING, 400 acs. (N.L.), Goochland Co, N. side of Rivanna Riv., above mouth of HORSLEY,s Cr., on ROBERT HORSLEY's line; 26 June 1731, p. 173. 40 Shill.

THOMAS WALTON , 400 acs. (N.L.), Goochland Co., on Muddy Cr., on S. side of James Riv., adj. WILLIAM WALTON & ASHFORD HUGHES; 26 June 1731, p. 174. 40 Shill.

JOHN MERRYMAN, 400 acs. (N.L.), Goochland Co., S. side of Muddy Cr., on S.

side of James Riv., adj. his own, STEPHEN HUGHES & JACOB WINFREE's land; 26 June 1731, p. 176. 40 Shill.

ROBERT HUGHES, 1200 acs. (O.& N.L.), Goochland Co., S. side of James Riv., on Muddy Cr., adj. THOMAS ATKINSON, & COL. THOMAS RANDOLPH; 26 June 1731, p. 179. 40 Shill. 800 acs. part granted him by former patent.

THOMAS PROSSER, 400 acs. (N.L.), Goochland Co., bet. 2 Manacan Creeks, on S. side of James Riv., adj. GEORGE SMITH, on S. side of CHASTAIN's Br., FRANCIS FARSY, STEPHEN CHASTAIN, NICHOLAS SOULLIE & HENRY BAYLY; 26 June 1731, p. 181. 40 Shill.

ROBERT SPEAR, 400 acs. (N.L.), above Deep. Cr., on S. side of James Riv., adj. JOHN SPEAR, BOWLER COCK & SAMUEL SCOT; 26 June 1731, p. 185. 40 Shill. Goochland Co.

BOWLER COCKE, Gent., 2400 acs. (N.L.), Goochland Co., on S. side of James Riv. on Muddy Cr. adj. land he bought of LILES, on SCOTT's line; 26 June 1731, p. 187. 12 Lbs., Money.

JAMES AKIN, 1000 acs. (N.L.), Goochland Co., N. side of Appamattock Riv., adj. HALCOATE PRIDE & THOMAS LOCKET, on E. side of a br. of Butterwood Cr., ARTHUR MOSELY, on S. side of a br. of Swift Cr. & JOHN PRIDE's line; 26 June 1731, p. 195. 5 Lbs., Money.

ASHFORD HUGHS, 400 acs. (N.L.), Goochland Co., S. side of James Riv., on BOLLING's Quarter Br. & brs. of Muddy Cr., adj. WAMACK's line & GROOM's corner; 25 Aug. 1731, p. 256. 40 Shill.

CHARLES HUDSON, Gent., 540 acs. (N.L.), Goochland Co., on W. side of the 1st ridge of Mts. in the fork of the James River; 25 Aug. 1731, p. 157. 55 Shill.

BENJAMIN HARRIS, 400 acs. (N.L.), Goochland Co., bet. the 2 Manacan Creeks on S. side of James Riv., on N. side of Dittoes Branch, on JOHN BARRETT's line, &c. 25 Aug. 1731, p. 258. 40 Shill.

ADAM BUTRY, 120 acs. (N.L.), on S. side the Rivanna Riv., opposite land of Col. THOMAS RANDOLPH, dec'd. called Dogg Point, about $\frac{1}{4}$ of a mi. above a small island; 25 Aug. 1731, p. 259. 15 Shill. Goochland Co.

STEPHEN LACY, 400 acs. (N.L.), Goochland Co., on brs. of OWEN's Cr. on the line bet. Goochland & Hanover Counties; 25 Aug. 1731, p. 260. 40 Shill.

BENJAMIN WOODSON, 200 acs. (N.L.), Goochland Co., S. side of James Riv., near MILES CARY's land; 25 Aug. 1731, p. 261. 20 Sh 11.

CHARLES RALEY (RAYLEY), 394 acs. (N.L.), Goochland Co., S. side of James Riv., on Old JOHN's Cr., adj. WILLIAM RUNALDS' land, on the Old Road; 25 Aug. 1731, p. 261. 40 Shill.

JAMES CUNNINGHAM, 400 acs. (N.L.), Goochland Co., on WILLIS River, alias WILLIS' Cr., on S. side of James Riv., crossing GROOM's Quarter Br.; 25 Aug. 1731, p. 262. 40 Shill.

ALEXANDER LOGAN, 400 acs. (N.L.), Goochland Co., N. side of James Riv., on N. side of the W. main br. of Treasurers Run, adj. THOMAS DENSON; 25 Aug. 1731, p. 263. 40 Shill.

ROBERT ADAMS, 400 acs. (N.L.), Goochland Co., on br. of Licking Hole Cr. adj. his own, & HOLLON's land; 25 Aug. 1731, p. 264. 40 Shill.

RICHARD MOSEBY, 400 acs. (N.L.), Goochland Co., above Deep. Cr., on S. side of James Riv., on his old line crossing the Cross Sw., adj. SAMUEL ARRINGTON & JOHN PLEASANTS; 25 Aug. 1731, p. 265. 40 Shill.

HENRY BAILY, 400 acs. (N.L.), Goochland Co., S. side of James Riv., on CHAS-TAIN's Branch; 25 Aug. 1731, p. 267. 40 Shill.

ABRAHAM WAMACK, Junr., 400 acs. (N.L.), Goochland Co., S. side of James Riv., on brs. of Deep Cr., adj. THOMAS MOSS & DANIEL GROOM, on a br. of BOLLING's Quarter Br.; 25 Aug. 1731, p. 267. 40 Shill.

Capt. THAMAS FRIEND, 400 acs. (N.L.), Goochland Co., on brs. of Licking Hole Cr. adj. LEONARD BALLOW, THOMAS BALLOW, DAWSON's line & RICHARD DEAN; 25 Aug. 1731, p. 268. 40 Shill.

SAMUEL NUCKLES, 400 acs. (N.L.), Goochland Co., on Muddy Cr., on S. side of James Riv., adj. JOHN MERRYMAN & JACOB WINFREE; 25 Aug. 1731, p. 269. 40 Shill.

MICHAEL HOLLAND, 400 acs. (N.L.), on S. side & adjacent to Rivanna River; on W. side of CUNNINGHAM's Cr.; 25 Aug. 1731, p. 271. 40 Shill.

HENRY WOOD, 268 acs. (Lapsed L.) Goochland Co.; 25 Aug. 1731, p. 271. Granted to WILLIAM BROWN 5 Sept. 1723, on N. side of James Riv., in Henrico Co., beg. on S. side of the main Cr. of Tuckahoe, parting said COX & ROBERT ADAMS, to GILLY GREW MARRAIN's line, upon condition of seating, &c. 30 Shill.

NATHANIEL BASSETT, 400 acs. (Lapsed L.), Goochland Co., S. side of James Riv., on W. side of Fine Cr.; 25 Aug. 1731, p. 273. Granted ROBERT BLAWS, JOSEPH WOODSON, JOHN WOODSON, & JOHN WOODSON, Junr.; 18 Feb. 1722, then in Henrico Co., adj. PLEASANTS' line upon condition of seating, &c. 40 Shill.

WILLIAM MAYO, Gent., 2850 acs. (N.L.), Goochland Co., on both sides of WILLIS Riv., alias WILLIS' Cr., on S. side of James Riv., adj. Col. BENJAMIN HARRISON, by the Long Falls, on MERRY WEBB's line, crossing the Cattail Br.; 25 Aug. 1731, p. 274. 14 Lbs., 5 Shill.

JOHN BERNARD, 154 acs. Goochland Co., on S. side of James Riv. adj. THOMAS

JEVEDON (?), & PETER DUPEA's line, on the bounds of Henrico Co.; 25 Aug. 1731, p. 275. Being surplus of the land layed off for the French Refugees.

WILLIAM CHAMBERLAYN, 400 acs. (N.L.), Goochland Co., on N. side the Fluvanna River; 25 Aug. 1731, p. 316. 40 Shill.

ROBERT HORSLEY, 400 acs. (N.L.), Goochland Co., on N. side the Rivanna Riv., above the mouth of HORSLEY's Cr.; 17 Sept. 1731, p. 329. 40 Shill.

Rev. WILLIAM SMITH, Gent., of Hanover Co., 400 acs. (N.L.), Goochland Co., on N. side of James Riv., on brs. of Deep Cr., of Licking Hole, adj. WILLIAM WATERS & JOHN HODGES' lines; 17 Sept. 1731, p. 329. 40 Shill.

WILLIAM WALTON, 400 acs. (N.L.), Goochland Co., on Muddy Cr., on S. side of James Riv., adj. JOHN MERRYMAN; 17 Sept. 1731, p. 330. 40 Shill.

MERRY WEBB, 800 acs. (N.L.), Goochland Co., on WILLIS River, alias WILLIS' Cr., on S. side of James Riv.; 17 Sept. 1731, p. 330. 10 Lbs., Money.

JOHN TAYLER, 400 acs. (N.L.), Goochland Co., S. side of James Riv., adj. JOHN TABOR, GEORGE STOVAL, ASHFORD HUGHES, & WILLIAM MAYO; 17 Sept. 1731, p. 331. 40 Shill.

ROBERT HORSLEY of Hanover Co., 400 acs. (N.L.), Goochland Co., on up. side of Little Byrd Cr.; 17 Sept. 1731, p. 331. 40 Shill.

JOHN MAX, 250 acs. (N.L.), Goochland Co., S. side of James Riv., adj. JOHN HAILE, on head of a br. of Fiting Cr., adj. Capt. RICHARD RANDOLPH, WILLIAM BLACKBURN, EDWARD MAX, & MATTHEW LIGON; 17 Sept. 1731, p. 332. Imp. of 5 pers: ELIZABETH BANFARD, HENRY BANFARD, MATTHEW BANFARD, ELIZA. BANFARD the younger, & JOHN BANFARD.

JOSIAH PAYNE, 400 acs. (N.L.), Goochland Co., N. side of James Riv., & on lower side of Little Byrd Cr.; 17 Sept. 1731, p. 333. 40 Shill.

JOHN WIT, Junr. 400 acs. (N.L.), Goochland Co., bet. the 2 Manacan Creeks, on S. side of James Riv., on NICHOLAS SOULLIE's line, crossing DITTNOY's (or DITT-WOY's) Br. to STEPHEN CHASTAIN, & crossing Dry Br.; 17 Sept. 1731, p. 333. 40 Shill.

HENRY TURNER, 300 acs. (N.L.), Goochland Co., N. side of James Riv., on Jennitoe & Mill Creeks, beg. on Geneto Cr. on ROBERT WOODSON's line, on JOHNSON's land, up Mill Cr. to GEORGE FLOYD: 17 Sept. 1731, p. 334. 30 Shill.

GEORGE PAYNE, 400 acs. (N.L.), Goochland Co., N. side of James Riv., on Wild Boar Cr., a br. of Licking Hole Cr., adj. MICHAEL HOLLAND, & JOHN HAWKINS, on S. side of Stonehorse Br.; 17 Sept. 1731, p. 334. 40 Shill.

MATTHEW LIGON, 1000 acs. (O.& N.L.), Goochland Co., on S. side of James Riv., adj. his own, Capt. JOHN WOODSON, Col. WILLIAM RANDOLPH, & land of JOHN HAILE, at head of a br. of Fiting Cr., on WILLIAM ALLEN's line; 17 Sept. 1731, p. 340. 300 acs. granted him 15 Sept. 1723; 800 acs. never before patented. 4 Lbs., Money.

JOHN SIMKINS, 300 acs. (N.L.), Goochland Co., N. side of Appamattock Riv., on the head of a br. of Little Guinia; 17 Sept. 1731, p. 366. 30 Shill.

JOSEPH JACKSON, 400 acs. (N.L.), Goochland Co., side of James Riv. on BOLL-ING's Cr. adj. LEONARD BALLOW; 17 Sept. 1731, p. 367. 40 Shill.

THOMAS TANNER, Junr., 200 acs. Goochland Co., on S. side of James Riv., adj. MATTHEW OAGE, JOHN PETER BONDURANT, & his own land; 17 Sept. 1731, p. 367. 20 Shill. (N.L.).

JOEL CHANDLER, 400 acs. (N.L.), Goochland Co., S. side of James Riv., on brs. of STOVALL's Cr., & Fine Cr., adj. his own, BARTHOLOMEW STOVALL, & land DANIEL STONER bought of THOMAS RANDOLPH; 17 Sept. 1731, p. 368. 40 Shill.

JOSEPH BAUGH, 400 acs. (N.L.), Goochland Co., on S. side of Swift Cr., adj. JOHN PRIDE & THOMAS BAUGH; 17 Sept. 1731, p. 369. 40 Shill.

CHARLES LEWIS, Gent., 1200 acs. (N.L.), Goochland Co., on both sides of Rivanna Riv., at mouth of Buck Island Cr.; 15 Jan. 1731, p. 374. 6 Lbs., Money.

THOMAS GOOLSBY, 400 acs. (N.L.), Goochland Co., on N. side of James Riv., the Fluvanna, on his own land; 11 Apr. 1732, p. 389. 40 Shill.

Same. 400 acs. (N.L.), same Co. & date, page 390. On N. side the S. fork of James River, alias Fluvanna Riv., adj. his own land. 40 Shill.

Same. 400 acs. (N.L.), same Co. & date, page 391. On N. side the Fluvanna Riv. 40 Shill.

FRANCIS JAMES, 250 acs. (N.L.), Goochland Co., S. side of James Riv., adj. Capt. RENE LAFONE, near head of a br. of Swift Cr.; 11 Apr. 1732, p. 392. 25 Shill.

WILLIAM CHAMBERLAYNE, 1400 acs. (O.& N.L.), Goochland Co., S. side the Rivanna Riv., or N. br. of James Riv., at a mouth of CARY's Cr., adj. Mr. COCKE; 11 Apr. 1732, p. 393. 400 acs. part granted EBENEZER ADAMS. 5 Lbs., Money.

NATHANIEL MAXEY, 200 acs. (N.L.), Goochland Co., on Swift Cr., on S. side of James Riv., adj. THOMAS WATKINS, MICHAEL GARTHWRIGHT & JOHN MAXEY; 11 Apr. 1732, p. 394. 20 Shill.

ROBERT ADAMS, 400 acs. (N.L.), Goochland Co., on both sides of MICHUNCK (MACHUNCK) Cr., adjacent to the bounds of Hanover Co.; 11 Apr. 1732, p. 396. 40 Shill.

BENJAMIN JOHNSON, 400 acs. (N.L.), Goochland Co., on brs. of Byrd Cr., on Horsepen Br. of said Cr.; 11 Apr. 1732, p. 398. 40 Shill.

ASHFORD HUGHES & DANIEL PRICE, 400 acs. (N.L.), Goochland Co., S. side James Riv., bet. Muddy Cr. & WILLIS Riv., alias WILLIS Cr., adj. JOHN BOLLING in BENJAMIN HARRISON's line & ROBERT CARTER; 11 Apr. 1732, p. 403. 40 Shill.

JACOB WINFREE, 400 acs. (N.L.), Goochland Co. on S. side of James Riv., on Muddy Cr., adj. JOHN MERRYMAN, 11 Apr. 1732, p. 404. 40 Shill.

ROBERT ADAMS, 400 acs. (N.L.), on both sides of MICHUNE (or MICHUM) Cr. adjacent.to N. side of Rivanna Riv.; 11 Apr. 1732, p. 406. 40 Shill. Goochland Co.

WILLIAM MILLS, 400 acs. (N.L.), Goochland Co., on brs. of Licking Hole Cr., adj. SAMUEL COLEMAN & HENRY CHILES, & line of SCOT, & KERBY; 11 Apr. 1732, p. 407. 40 Shill.

JACOB WINFREE, 400 acs. (N.L.), on head brs. of Muddy Cr., on S. side of James Riv.; 11 Apr. 1732, p. 408. 40 Shill. Goochland Co.

STEPHEN COX, 800 acs. (N.L.), Goochland Co., on N. side of Appomattox Riv., at mouth of Rocky Br.; 11 Apr. 1732, p. 420. 4 Lbs., Money.

HENRY WEBB, 400 acs. (N.L.), Goochland Co., N. side of James Riv., on brs. of same & those of Licking Hole Cr., adj. THOMAS BALLOW; 11 Apr. 1732, p. 421. 40 Shill.

DANIEL FERO, 200 acs. (N.L.), Goochland Co., bet. the 2 Manakin Creeks, on S. side of James Riv., adj. PETER BRUCE, PETER SALLE, JOHN HARRIS, GEORGE SMITH, & FRANCIS DUPRA, crossing CHASTAIN's Br. to HENRY BAYLEY's line; 11 Apr. 1732, p. 422. 20 Shill.

JOHN WOODSON, Gent., 1000 acs. (N.L.), Goochland Co., S. side of James Riv., on Deep Cr., up MATTHEWS' Licking Br. on MAYO's line; 11 Apr. 1732, p. 423. 5 Lbs., Money.

SAME. 1500 acs. (N.L.), same Co., date & page. On brs. of Deep Cr. of James Riv. & brs. of Appamattox Riv. & on WATSON's br. of sd. Cr. adj. Col. WILLIAM RANDOLPH, on Let Alone Cr., HUTCHINS BURTON, HENRY CLAY & Capt. HENRY ANDERSON. 7 Lbs., 10 Shill.

HENRY WEBB, 400 acs. (N.L.), N. side of James Riv., on Licking Hole Cr., adj. CHARLES CHRISTIAN & line of HOLLAND's; 11 Apr. 1732, p. 424. 40 Shill.

HENRY RUNALDS, 400 acs. (N.L.), Goochland Co., on N. side the Rivanna, adj. Capt. CHARLES LEWIS; 11 Apr. 1732, p. 427. 40 Shill.

DANIEL GURRANT, 400 acs. (N.L.), Goochland Co., bet. the 2 Manacan Creeks, on

S. side of James Riv. adj. STEPHEN CHASTAIN & BARBARA DITNO's lines; 11 Apr. 1732, p. 428. 40 Shill.

MARY ANN DITWAY, 400 acs. (N.L.), Goochland Co., S. side of James Riv., on JONES Cr., adj. CHASTAIN's land, & MALLET's line; 11 Apr. 1732, p. 429. 40 Shill.

BENJAMIN MOSBY of Henrico Co., 200 acs. (N.L.), Goochland Co., on S. side of James Riv., near JOHN PLEASANTS' cor. on his Deep Cr. land; 11 Apr. 1732, p. 431. 20 Shill.

THOMAS TINDAL, 173 acs. (N.L.), Goochland Co., on Fluvanna (Riv.) beg. near point of one of the Seven Islands crossing the South Riv.; 11 Apr. 1732, p. 435. 20 Shill.

THOMAS WILLIAMSON, 400 acs. (N.L.), Goochland Co., near Appomattox Riv. adj. HENRY BREAZEAL, RICHARD WILLIAMSON, WILLIAM RANDOLPH, Esqr. & RALPH HUDSPEATH'S line; 11 Apr. 1732, p. 436.

MICHAEL HOLLAND, 400 acs. (N.L.), Goochland Co., on both sides of CUNNINGHAM Cr.; 11 Apr. 1732, p. 437. 40 Shill.

JOHN JOHNSON, 400 acs. (N.L.), Goochland Co., N. side of James Riv., on brs. of Deep. Cr. of Licking Hole Cr. & those of the E'most main br. of Byrd (Cr.), adj. GEORGE SOUTHERLAND's land, crossing DUNCAN's Br. to TINDAL's land; 11 Apr. 1732, p. 439. 40 Shill.

WILLIAM WOODSON, BENJAMIN WOODSON, Junr., JOHN WOODSON, Junr. & ROBERT WOODSON, Junr., 1500 acs. (N.L.), Goochland Co., on brs. of Deep Cr., on WATSON's Br., adj. Capt. HENRY ANDERSON, WARHAM (WARRAM) EASLY, JOHN PHELPS & JOHN WOODSON; 11 Apr. 1732, p. 440. 7 Lbs., 10 Shill.

JOHN PLEASANTS, 400 acs. (N.L.), Goochland Co., S. side of James Riv., above Deep Cr., adj. his old land, ASHFORD HUGHES & RICHARD MOSBY; 11 Apr. 1732, p. 441. 40 Shill.

THOMAS WOOLDRIDGE & EDWARD WOOLDRIDGE, 400 acs. (N.L.), Goochland Co., bet. the 2 Manakin Creeks, on S. side of James Riv., adj. FRANCIS JAMES & NICHOLAS SOULLIE, crossong DITTOES Br.; 11 Apr. 1732, p. 442. 40 Shill.

ARTHUR HOPKINS, Gent., 400 acs. (N.L.), Goochland Co., on S. side Rivanna Riv., at mouth of LEWIS Cr., below the Red Bank falls; 20 Apr. 1732, p. 443. 40 Shill.

WILLIAM SWIFT, Clerk, of Hanover Co., 400 acs. (N.L.), Goochland Co., on brs. of Deep Cr., of Licking Hole, adj. land of WILLIAM HODGES, dec'd., on N. side of a br. of AMOS' Br., LEONARD BALLOW, & WILLIAM SPURLOCK; 13 May 1732, p. 444. 40 Shill.

GIDEON CHAMBOON, 59 acs. (Escheat L.), Goochland Co., S. side of James Riv., adj. EDWARD SCOTT, & CLAUDE GORY; 9 May 1732, p. 446. Escheated from JACOB MATTOON, dec'd., for 165 acs. by inquisition under WILLIAM BYRD, Esqr.,Eschr, survey returned by WILLIAM MAYO. 2 Lbs. Tobacco, &c.

AGNES NOLAND, 350 acs. (ESCHEATED L.),    on S. side of James Riv. on MAHOOK Cr., adj. BOLLING's line & land of MICHAUX, dec'd.; 5 May, 1732, p. 447. Es- cheated from THOMAS NOLAND, dec'd. by inquisition under HENRY HARRISON, Esqr., Esch'r.; 2 Oct. 1730; survey returned by JOHN WOODSON, Deputy Surveyor. 2 Lbs. Tobacco, &c. (Marginal notation: 354 acres.) Goochland Co.

EDWARD SCOTT, 619 acs. (O.& N.L.), Goochland Co., adj. EDMUND NEWS, crossing the little cr. of Licking Hole Cr. to JOHN FLEMING; 15 June 1732, p. 448. 250 acs. part formerly patented by sd. SCOTT, & 150 acs. part by EDMOND NEWS.

ARTHUR HOPKINS, 400 acs. (N.L.), on the main Byrd Cr., of James Riv.; 24 Aug. 1732, p. 461. 40 Shill. Goochland Co.

GILES ALLEGRE (ALLEGREE), 328 acs. (N.L.), Goochland Co., S. side of James Riv. above Deep Cr., on BOLLING's quarter Br., adj. ABRAHAM WAMACK, THOMAS MORSE, WILLIAM BRADLY, RICHARD MOSBY & NICHOLAS COX; 24 Aug. 1732, p. 461, 35 Shill.

JOHN SPEAR, 200 acs. (N.L.), Goochland Co., on S. side of James Riv., adj. DANIEL WILMORE, WILLIAM MORSE, & BOWLER COCKE; 28 Sept. 1732, p. 462. 20 Shill.

JAMES NEVEL, 700 acs. (N.L.), Goochland Co., on S. side of Fluvanna Riv.; 28 Sept. 1732, p. 463. 3 Lbs., 10 Shill.

HENRY HATCHER, 400 acs.(N.L.), Goochland Co., on N. side of Appomatock Riv., adj. RICHARD PARKER & BURGANY's land, on br. of Deep Cr.; 28 Sept. 1732, p. 463. 40 Shill.

BARTHOLOMEW STOVAL, 250 acs. (N.L.), Goochland Co., S. side of James Riv., on STOVAL's Cr., adj. JOHN SANDERS, GEORGE STOVAL, & MAYO's land; 28 Sept. 1732, p. 463. 25 Shill.

JOHN BOLLING, Gent. Henrico Co., 400 acs. (N.L.), Goochland Co., S. side of James Riv. above Seven Islands, adj. WILLIAM CANNON; 28 Sept. 1732, p. 464. 40 Shill.

BARTHOLOMEW STOVAL & JOHN STOVAL, 200 acs. (N.L.), Goochland Co., on STOVAL's Cr. & Br.; 28 Sept. 1732, p. 464. 20 Shill.

DAVID LILES, 800 acs. (N.L.), Goochland Co., on Deep Cr., adj. WARRAM EASLY, on WATSON's Br., up ARRINGTON's Br. to JOHN MICHAUX; 28 Sept. 1732, p. 465. 4 Lbs., Money.

EDWARD SCOTT, 67 acs. (N.L.), Goochland Co., being an island in the River

Fluvanna, next below Rock Island, being in circuit according to its meanders. 550 poles; 28 Sept. 1732, p. 465. 10 Shill.

ABRAHAM MICHAUX, 400 acs. (N.L.), Goochland Co., S. side of James Riv., on brs. of Little Deep Cr., adj. JOHN SANDERS & PETER LE GRAND; 28 Sept. 1732, p. 466. 40 Shill.

CHARLES JOHNSON, 77 acs. (N.L.), Goochland Co., on Mill Cr. & Jenetoe Cr. on N. side of James Riv., adj. DANIEL JOHNSON, HENRY TURNER, GEORGE FLOYD, Mrs. FINNY, JAMES JOHNSON, JOHN JOHNSON & DANIEL JOHNSON; 28 Sept. 1732, p. 466. 10 Shill.

JOSEPH CHANDLER, 400 acs. (N.L.), Goochland Co., S. side of James Riv., on MATTHEWS' Licking Br., a br. of Deep Cr., adj. WILLIAM MAYES' line; 28 Sept. 1732, p. 467. 40 Shill.

JOHN ROBINSON, 200 acs. (N.L.), Goochland Co., on N. side the Rivanna Riv. crossing the Great Cr.; 28 Sept. 1732, p. 467. 20 Shill.

JACOB MICHAUX, 150 acs. (N.L.), Goochland Co., S. side of James Riv., on MA-HOOK Cr. adj. Major BOLLING, RICHARD DEAN, BARTHOLOMEW COX, & land QUIN sold to NOLAND; 28 Sept. 1732, p. 468. 15 Shill.

EDWARD SCOTT, 200 acs. (N.L.), Goochland Co., N. side Fluvanna Riv., at a place called Totier; 28 Sept. 1732, p. 468. 20 Shill.

JOHN SCLATER, of New Kent Co., 400 acs. (Lapsed L.), Goochland Co.; 28 Sept. 1732, p. 468. Granted WILLIAM TOWNES; 16 June 1727, on N. side of James Riv., then in Henrico Co., adj. AMOS LEAD, on a br. of Tuckahoe Cr., & land of CHARLES HUDSON, on condition of seating, &c. 40 Shill.

CHARLES JOHNSON, 400 acs. (N.L.), Goochland Co., on brs. of Tuckahoe Cr., adj. PHILIP WEBBER, GILLY GRUMARINE, & PARISH line; 28 Sept. 1732, p. 481. 40 Shill.

EDWARD SCOTT, 100 acs. (N.L.), Goochland Co., on N. side of Fluvanna Riv., adj. WM. CHAMBERLAYNE; 28 Sept. 1732, p. 481. 10 Shill.

SAMUEL BURK, 200 acs. (N.L.), Goochland Co., on N. side Rivanna Riv., adj. land of Col THOMAS RANDOLPH, dec'd.; 28 Sept. 1732, p.483. 20 Shill.

JOHN BOLLING, Gent., of Henrico Co., 400 acs. (N.L.), Goochland Co., S. side side of James Riv. a little below the Seven Islands; 28 Sept. 1732. p. 483. 40 Shill.

JACOB TREBUE, 117 Acs. (N.L.), Goochland Co., bet. the 2 Manacan Creeks, adj. JOHN SMITH, EDWARD MAXY, WM. MAXY & NATHANIEL MAXY; 28 Sept. 1732, p. 484. 15 Shill.

THOMAS PORTER, 384 acs. (N.L.), Goochland Co., on both sides the up. Manacan

Cr. adj. STEPHEN MALLET, STEPHEN CHASTAIN, JOHN LUQUEDOE & WILLIAM BYRD, Esqr,; 28 Sept. 1732, p. 516, 40 Shill.

WILLIAM CREASY, 400 acs. (N.L.), Goochland Co., adjacent to the S. side of Rivanna Riv. adj. MICHAEL HOLLAND, crossing Raccon Cr.: 28 Sept. 1732, p. 520. 40 Shill.

CHARLES ALLEN, 1000 acs. (N.L.), Goochland Co., on Licking Hole Cr., at mouth of Stone Horse Br., adj. JOHN HAUKIN's (or HAUKINS') line, GEORGE PAYNE, DAVID PATTERSON & land of WILLIAM WELDY; 17 Jan, 1732, p. 536. 5 Lbs. Money.
JAMES NEVIL, 700 acs. (N.L.), Goochland Co., S. side of Fluvanna Riv.; 17 Jan. 1732, p. 537. 3 Lbs., 10 Shill.

---

## ADDITIONAL LAND PATENTS

### Patent Book No. 1-Part I

THOMAS BAILIE (BAYLIE), 150 acs. Chas. Citty Co., 9 July 1635, p. 215. On the S. & near the mouth of BAYLYS Cr., beg. at a small swamp with a little brooke running in the "middest" of it & extending S. into the woods. 50 acs. due unto him as heire of his father WILLIAM BAYLIE who dyed possessed thereof & 100 acs. for trans. of 2 pers: MARY WELSH & MARV ————.

WILLIAM CLARKE, 1100 acs. Henrico Co., 29 Sept. 1636, p. 393. Beg. at a little Cr. & lying N. thereupon, E. upon the maine Riv. & W. into the woods; 100 acs. to be allowed for the marshes & swamps thereunto belonging. Due in right of his now wife DOROTHY GARNER, late widdowe to EDWARD GARNER, to whom it was due for trans. of 22 pers: ELIZ. WILLIS, EDMUND PULLUM, THOMAS LAWLEY, THOMAS SOMERSALE, JOHN HUMPHRY, BARR. FARTHING, JOHN MELDER, WILLIAM EVEREDGE, JOHN WALL, NICH. PLEDGE, ROBERT CURRANT, THOMAS COOPER, CHARLES MAXNEY, RICHARD JENINGS, OLIVER DENNINGTON, NICH. OLIVER, WILLIAM & TEAGE Irishmen, JOANE BULLOCK, ELIZ. CURTIS, IZABELL STUBBS, HESTER PARTRIDGE.

### Patent Book No. 1-Part II

THOMAS OSBORNE, Junr., 500 acs., Henrico Co., 16 June 1637, p. 512. Sly. upon fearing & Nly. into the woods, the whole tract of land to bee called by the name of Batchelers bancke. Due for his per. adv. & trans. of 9 pers: HENRY KILBYE, JOHN FINCH, WM. BURFORD, SAMLL. THORNEFORD, EDWARD WILLIAMS, JERIMIAH HOVELLER, AGNES SHERLY, JON. WEYAN, RICHARD PERRIN.

THOMAS OSBORNE, 400 acs., Henrico Co., at the head of Coxendale, Aug. 20, 1 42, Page 836. Bounded W.N.W. upon CHRISTOPHER BRANCH's land, N.N.E. upon

Mr. OSBORNE's land called Fearing, & S.S.W. into the woods. Being 200 po. in breadth from the head of Proctors Cr. towards the land called Mount my Lady, and a full mile into the woods. Trans. of 8 pers: RICH. COCK, WM. DIXON, CHRIS. PACK, JON. BAGLY, ROBT. STANTON, THO. WALDROM, JON. RUSH, FRANCIS QUASH.

---

## NOTES and MEMORANDA

# Index to Land Patents

## A

Abasse, Ctaar. Guv. 29
Abbott, Samll. 3
Abraham, Geo. 11
Adams, Anne 24; Ben. 25; Ebenezer 45, 59,65,86; Fra. 34; Robert 59, 63, 73, 75, 84 (2), 86, 87
Adcock, Tho. 28; Jane 29
Addams 64, 65, 71; Abigall 38; Robert 63, 69 (2), 80, 82
Adkins, Michaell, 22
Adlan,Wm. 42
Age, Colug. 47
Agee, Matthew 77
Aheren, Morris 25
Aken, James 54
Aketon, Morris 25
Akin, James 80, 83
Alaman, Wm. 23
Alcock, Jos. 19
Alcorne, Jno. 47
Alder, Jane 23
Alees, Geo. 26
Alford, Henry 26
Allegre (Allegree), Giles 89 (2)
Allen, Abraham 21; Alice 31; Charles 91; Fra. 19; Kath. 12; Mary 3, 28; Mathew 23; Oliver 3, 5; Teague 19; Thomas 53; Tho. 56; Timothy 27; Walter 28; William 79,81,86
Allerton, Peter 21
Allice, Martha 54
Ally, Thomas 59
Allmond, Samuell 8, 10
Almand, Jno. 23
Almond 11; Samuell 8 (2), 10 (2), 11
Alpott, Janoe 12
Alves 77
Alvis 67; George 55
Amonet, Jacob 48 (2), 52 (2)
Amos 67, 88; Valentine 72 (2); Nicholas 26
Amoss, Nicholas 26
Amys, Jno. 21
Anderson, Henry 76; Capt. Henry 76, 87, 88; Robt. 46; Samll. 25
Andrews, Jane 32; John 10, Jon. 5,

Tho. 32; Wm. 16
Anwell, Luke 13
Archer 58; Alice 13; Eliz. 24; John 54
Ardell, Tho. 24
Armestrong, Ann 16
Arnell, Eliz. 15; Sarah 29
Arrington 89; Samuel 71, 81, 84
Arrow Reedes 35
Arrye, Daniell 9
Arton, Wm. 21
Ascott, Wm. 23
Arundell, Richard 12
Ashbrook, Peter 39
Ashbrooke Geo. 24; Joane 23
Ashby, Jno. 31
Ashley, Eliz. 54
Aston (Ashton) 11, 12; Mrs. 14 (2); John 31; Walter 2, 9, 12 (2), 14, 18, 19, 22, Warbowe 9, 12
Atkenson, Wm. 19
Atkins, James 39
Atkinson, Alice 19; Henry 81, 82 (2); Thomas 72, 83
Attaway, William 7
Auberry, Andrew 50
Audry, Sara 32
Augburd, Garrett 45
Augustin, Charles 38
Austin, Ferd. (Firdinando) 19 (2)
Austine, Sudeavor 31
Auston, (Aston) Walter 12
Autom, Andrew 57
Avery, Robert 43
Awbery, Andrew 73
Ayres, Jno. 31

## B

Bacon, Nathaniel (Nathll.), Jr. 37 (2); John 72, 73
Baggerley, Richd. 46
Bagshaw, Wm. 21
Baily (see Baly, Balye, Baylie, Bayley,Bayly) 25; Henry 84; John 19
Baise (Baize) 70 (2)
Baker 28; Dorothy 14; Edward 12;

Herc. 23; John 3, 5, 6(2), 11, 14,
  20; Margery 16; Rachell 34; Rich-
  ard 43, 82; Wm. (William) 6, 8, 23
Baldwin (Baldwyn), John 3(2), Wm. 16
Balhash (see Ballhash) 10; Elizabeth
  9
Ball, Robt. 24; Will. 42; William 54
Ballard 21(2)
Ballhash (see Balhash), Edward 14;
  Elizabeth 4
Ballington (See Bullington) Nicholas
  4
Ballow, Leonard 66, 67, 68, 69(2),
  81, 84, 86, 88; Thomas 67, 68, 69
  (3), 84, 87
Balms, Symon 19
Balono, Symon 19
Baltimore, Hen. 30
Baly (see Baily, Balye, Baylie, Bay-
  ley, Bayly), Arthur 8; Richard 3
Balye (see above), John 43
Banbury, William 60
Banfard, Elizabeth (Eliza.) 85(2);
  Henry 85; John 85; Matthew 85
Banister, Jno. 31
Banks, Edward 33; Fra. 25; Henry 16;
  Richard 16; Wm. 30
Bannion, John 46
Bardoe, Jno. 31
Bardy, Nich. 26
Barefoot, Sarah 46
Barfeild, Ester 16
Barfoote, Ann 5
Baringer, Joseph 75
Barker, Robert 39; William (Wm.)8, 10
Barkstead, Wm. 38
Barlow, Stafford 11
Barly, Rachell 54
Barnard, Hen. 24
Barnes, John 57; John, Junr. 55; Wil-
  liam 55, 77
Barnett, William 65
Barrett, John 83
Barrow 20, 29, 33(2), 35(2), Mary 38
Barton, Tho. 14; William 4
Bartue, Robt. 33; Wm. 33
Barwood, Robert 11
Bass, Geo. 26; Wm. 44

Bassett, Nathaniel 84
Bates, Isa. 24; Tho. 45; Wm. 29
Bathurst, Lanct. 30
Battersee, Wm. 23
Batts, Richd. 31
Baugh 22; James 39; John 7(2), Jos-
  eph 86; Thomas 86; Wm. 23
Baxter 34; Capt. 38; Jno. 30
Bay, Obed. 24
Bayley (see Baily, Baly, Balye, Bay-
  lie, Bayly), Temp. 13; Henry 87;
  Thomas 47, 67
Baylie (see above) 20, 91
Bayliff (see above) 2
Bayly (see above) 3, 6; Abraham 29
  (2), 42; Arthur 8(3), 11, 14, 15,
  19; Clemt. 16; Godfry 23; Henry
  83; Jno. 23; John 27, 39; Johna-
  thon 29; Thomas 29, 42; Wm. 20
Baynes, Edwd. 39
Bays, Edward 62, 65
Bayts, Wm. 31
Bazy, John 39
Beachamp (see Beauchamp) Jno. 16
Beadell, John 5
Beake, Rich. 23
Beale, And. 20
Bean, Ben. 24
Bear, Forrest 53
Beare, Christ. 7
Bearge, Robert 29
Beasley, Robt. 30
Beatle, Walter 62
Beauchamp (see Beachamp) 21, 23, 25, 28
  29, 36; John 14, 15, 20, 21
  38
Beauchampe (see above), John 20
Beauchampt (see above) 24, 36
Beaver Dam 58, 63
Beaver Pond 30, 52, 64
Beaver Ponds 44, 45, 61, 71(2)
Beaverponds 78
Beavill, John 61
Bechamp (see Beachamp, Beauchamp) 25
Beck, Ja. 24; Jno. 24
Beffen, Tho. 19
Beldam, Jon. 8
Bell, Ann 38; Christopher 52; Jno. 19;

94

John 31
Bellomy, John 53
Belson, Jno. 32
Bembridge, Constant 42; Tho. 42
Bendbridge (see above), Constant 54;
    Thomas 54
Benford, Symon 21
Bennett, Abr. 21; Jon. 8; John 10;
    Mary 38; Robt. 42
Benskin, Jeremiah 41
Bently, Hen. 9
Berk, Honor, Senr. 32
Berkeley (see Burckley), hundred 8
Berkley, Wm. 19
Bermuda(see Burmoedy, Burmody)Hundred
    14
Bernard, John 84
Berry, Danll. 13; Hugh 14
Besle, Jno. 27
Bess, Jno. 30
Bessen 19
Best, John 40
Bethone, John 5
Beverley, Robert 30, 33(2), 35, 39.
    40, 59
Biby, Anne 37
Bicking, Capt. 11
Bigford, James 29
Bilbaud, James 47(2), 50, 51(2)
Billan, Mary 9
Bininham, Wm. 29
Bird (See Byrd), Col. 58, 64; Rich-
    ard 4, 11; Wm. 24(2)
Bishop, John 53; Wm. 30
Blackbeard, Mary 34
Blackburn, William 77, 85
Blacketter, Peter 46
Blackman, Jeremiah 4; Wm. 15, 23, 41
Blackshott, Eliza. 38
Blackston, Thomas 11
Blagg, Abraham 32
Blair, James 32, 35; John 39; Mary 65
Blaire (see above), James 28
Blancks, Thomas 7
Bland 30; Madam 26, 33; Edward 39;
    Theodoric 39
Blankenship, Martha 62
Blankes, Henry 16; Richard 16

Blanshard, Jonathan 20
Blaw, Robt. 42
Blaws, Robert 58, 84
Blaze, Peter 60
Bleare 32
Bleize, Mill. 25
Blessing, Anne 45
Blessington, Wm. 38
Blow, Robert 39
Bloyd, Geo. 40
Blunt, Wm. 38
Boane, Robert 13
Boate, Georg 4, 9
Boates (see above), George 4
Bobblett, Xper. 23
Boccard, Peter 79
Bocken, Francis 38
Bodyes, Anthony 11
Boeman, Thos. 26
Bois, John 42
Bolding, John 44
Boldry, Wm. 32
Bollin (see Bolling), Capt. 54
Bolling 67, 72, 86, 89, 90, John 37,
    38, 42, 43, 46, 53 (3), 54, 55,
    56, 57(2), 63, 66, 68(2), 82, 87,
    89, 90; Robert 41
Boloe, Leon 3
Bolt, Roger 34
Bolton, Mary 21
Bombay, Jno. 44
Bond, Anne 44
Bondurant, John Peter 66, 67, 77, 86
Booden, Bra. 24
Booke, Edwd. 45
Boomer, Ed. 26
Borar, Jane 30
Bostick, John 68
Boswell, Amy; Vera 30
Bott, Thomas 61
Bottom, John 36
Bough, Rebecka 47
Bourn, Antho. 31; Anthony 33
Bourne, Mary 15; Robert 12
Bowers, Jonas 8(2)
Bowman 34; Elizabeth 60; John 62;
    Robt. 21
Boyce (see Boyes, Boyse), Hannah 7

Brazele, (see Breazeal, Breazeale),
    Henry 45
Breant, Anna 61; Rachell 61; Thomas
    61
Breazeal (Breazeale; see Brazeale),
    Henry 80, 88; Henry, Junr. 39;
    Henry, Senr. 39
Breedon, Rebecca 31
Breman, Sarah 6; Wm. 12
Bremo 8, 9(2), 10, 13, 37,
Bremoes (see above) 2, 6
Bremow (see above) 33
Brett, Timothy 56
Brewer, Jeffery 2; Jno. 21; Robert 5
Bridger, Wm. 22
Bridgers, Marth. 54
Bridges, Anne 52; Eliz. 16; Rich. 21
Bridgewater (see Bridgwater), Samuell
    30
Bridgman, Anthony 14
Bridgwater (see Bridgewater), Samuel
    26, 27(2), 28, 31
Briess, Timo. 31
Brine of Channell 16
Briscom, Tho. 32
Bristoll, Jone 19
Bristoll Parish 34
Brittaine, John 43
Britton, William 73
Broadnax (see Brodnax), John 34
Broadrib, Eliz. 25, Wm. 14
Brock, Eliz. 26
Brodnax (see Broadnax), John 33, 34
Brodsha, Henry 27
Broinran, John 38
Bromley, Jno. 29
Brone, Mary 23
Brooke, Rich. 26; Thomas 2; William
    13
Brookes 55; George 46; Mary 45; Richd.
    34; Robt. 54; Thomas 6; Wm. 42
Broomly, Robert 44
Brothers, Jno. 29
Brothwaite, Tho. 31
Browman, Edwd. 54
Brown, Ellen 45; Jeremiah 35; Margt.
    39; Robert 12; Susanna 46; Will-
    iam 19, 46, 59, 78, 84

Browne, Ellen 31; Jeffery 6; Jere-
    miah 32; John 5(2), 17, 20, 22,
    23; Mary 23; Robert 16; Sara 24,
    Tho. 24; Thomas 38; William 60
Browning, George (Geo.) 2, 25, 27;
Browning, Marg. 24; Wm. 32
Brownridge, Math. 6
Bruce, Peter 87
Brumfeild (Brumfield), John 42, 56
Brutons, Hen. 21
Bryan (See Bryant), Cornelius 62;
    Margaret 46; Richard 56
Bryant (see above), Arthur 26; James
    46, 56
Buccard, Stephen 51
Buckingham, Edward 12
Buckins, Hugh 24
Buckland 10(2)
Buckley, Jno. 32
Bud, Mary 63
Bugg, Mary 46
Bugge, Smll. 26
Bulenting (See Bullenton, Bullington),
    32
Bull, Jane 31; Jno. 24; John 12, 19
Bullenton (see Bulenting, Bullington),
    Nicholas 35
Bulleny, Walter 46
Bullington (see Bullenting, Bullen-
    ton), Geo. 15; Nicholas 32, 35;
    Robert (Robt.) 20, 21, 25
Bullock, John 61(2)
Bullocke, Henry 16
Bumbay, John 63
Bumpass, Richard 3
Bunard, Stephen 48
Burch, Marg. 21
Burcher, Humphrey (Humphry) 5, 10
Burcher, Joseph 34
Burckley hundred (see Berkeley) 4
Burfoote (see Barefoot), Ann 10
Burgany 89
Burk, Catherine 46,; John 69; Margt.
    38; Martin 66; Mary 46; Samuel 63,
    70(2), 90
Burke (see above), John 63; Richd.
    45; Samuel 63, 70; Thomas 38
Burley, Hugh 42; Jno. 31

Burmoedy (see Bermuda, Burmody Hundred 34
Burmody (see above) Hundred 18
Burne, Elizabeth 65
Burr, Jeremiah 8
Burroughs, Tho. 21
Burtlett, Thomas 5
Burton 29(2); Hutchins 59, 67, 87;
   Hutchinson 78, 79, 81; Jno. 18
   (2); John 22(2), 43; Nowell 66,
   75; Ralph 13; Robert 27, 35, 36
   (2), 37, 38, 53; William 53, 55,
   62, 66; Wm. 35, 36, 45
Busby, Thomas (Tho.) 8, 42
Bushell, Elinor 28
Busill, Robt. 54
Butler, Elinore 25; James 53; Wm. 23
Butry, Adam 83
Butt, John 34
Butterfeild, Jno. 30
Buxton, Jon. 5
Byrd (see Bird) 27, 37; John 31;
   William (Wm.) 26, 27(2), 33(2),
   34, 37(2), 38(4), 39(4), 40(6),
   41(5), 42, 89, 91

C

Cable, Thomas (Tho.) 17(2)
Caddy, Jno. 23, 27
Caine, Mary 65
Calfe, Wm. 8
Callio, Joseph 50
Calvert, John 43, 46;
Calvet, Stephen 75; William 75
Camell, James 38
Campe (Campee), Mitchel (Mitchell)
   50, 61
Canadia (see Canida), Cornel. 13
Cane, Patrick 11
Canida (see Canadia), Corn. 15
Cannah, Arthur 45; Gerraud 45
Cannon, John (Jno.) 18, 19, 33, 64;
   William 79, 89
Canstall, John 39
Cantrell 12
Capoone 49; Jacob 50, 52(2)
Caran, Benja. 46
Carbind, Benja. 46

Cardwell, Thomas 30
Care, Jno. 47
Carey (see Cary), Dorothy 23; Tho. 27
Carles, Alice 26
Carlisle, Jno. 34; Sarah 34
Carmell, Tho. 25
Carohshaw, David 42
Carpenter, Jno. 21; Richard (Rich.),
   7(3), 8; William 54
Carr, Danll. 35
Carrall, Benjamine 3
Carrell, Hannah 42; Roger 42
Carrill, Benj. 7
Carrol, Margaret 65
Carter, Bridgett 23; Eliza. 40; Francis 27; Giles 13, 28, 65; Jno. 19;
   John 76; Jon. 13; Marke 20; Mary
   24; Robert 87; Sara (Sarah) 22,
   23(2), 27; Thomas 81
Carverson, Robt. 46
Cary (see Carey) 78, 86; Fran. 21;
   Miles 83; Robt. 20; Tho. 23, 27
Case, Jane 25
Cassell, Humphry 3
Cassey (see Causey, Cawsey), John 12
Castle, Tho. 23
Castons, Robert 5
Casum, James 41
Cate, Robt. 43
Catetope, Fra. 26
Causes Cleare 12
Causey 12; Natha. 12(3); Nathaniell
   9;
Causeys Care (Cleare) 19(2)
Cave, Patrick 11
Cavnah, Arthur 45; Gerraud 45
Cawker, John 2, 6
Cawsey (see Cassey, Causey), John 1 2
Cerley, Francis 45
Chaddocke, Henry 20
Chainey, Jno. 32
Cham 15
Chamberford, John 53
Chamberlaine, Edward 38
Chamberlayn (see Chamberlaine, Chamberlayne) William 85
Chamberlayne (see above), William 86;
   Wm. 90

98

Chamboone (Chamboon), Widow 52; Gideon 50(2); 52, 89
Champaine, Elizabeth 55
Champee, Mitchell 50
Chandler, Ann 23; Arth. 12; Batt. 35, 52; Joel 71, 86; Joseph 90; Ralph 23; 71
Chanler, Sarah 63
Chapell (see Chaple, Chapple), Tho. 24
Chaple (see Chapell, Chapple), Thomas 16
Chaplin, John 36
Chaplyn, Robt 8
Chapman, Humphry 19; Jon. 5; Roger 10; Tho. 42
Chapp, Wm. 46
Chapple (see Chapell, Chaple), Thomas 16, 17
Charles, Thomas (Tho.) 27, 28, 30
Chastain (see Chastaine, Chasteane, Chastiene), 59, 67, 83, 84, 87, 88; Mary 62; Peter, Junr. 62; Stephen 48, 52, 57, 60, 76(2), 77, 83, 85, 88, 91; Jane 62
Chastaine (see Chastain, Chasteane), 79; John 48, 52; Peter 48, 52; 62 Stephen 51(3)
Chasteane (see above), Stephen 44
Chastiene, Stephen 44
Cheldnedge, Wm. 12
Cheton, Marke 11
Cheyny, Robert 5, 10
Chiccahomany (see Chickahominy river and swamp), 73
Chickahominy ( see above), 23, 25
Chickahominy path 35
Chicohominy (see Chickahominy river and swamp, 61
Childers, Abraham 47; Lemon 26; Philemon 28; Philmon 32; Philemon, Junr. 52
Childs, Rich. 8; Richard 10; Henry 64, 87;
Chiles, Nich. 23
Chilton, 30; Edwd. 27
Chinkapin Island 38

Christian, Charles 47, 58, 71, 72, 73, 75, 80(2), 81(2), 87; James 44, 56, 62, 70, 71; Thomas 38, 40, 44(2), 56, 61, 70, 71(3), 80, 82; Thomas, Senr. 34
Christy, Jane 21
Chumley 61; Francis 59
Clappe, Francis 62
Clapton (see Clopton) Walter 57(2)
Clare, Brdget 32; Katherine 38
Clark 45, 58; Christopher 55; Mary 25; Richd. 21, 27; Tho. 28; Wm. 46; Zach. 38
Clarke (see above), 55; Allanson 33; Alleson 42; Benja. 28; Christopher 55; Daniell 15, 17; Eliz. 8; Fra. 12; John 5, 22, 26, 36; Robert 26; Uriah 3; William 44, 60, 91
Clasper, Thomas 39
Clatworthy (Clattworthy), Walter,34,37
Clay, Henry 76(2), 80, 81, 87; John 5(2)
Clayes, Wm. 17
Clayson, John 45
Cleavely, Fra. 30
Cleer, Jno. 24
Cleft, William 24
Clement, Sara 21
Clementson (Clemetson),Sigfred (46) 2
Clerk 47, 59(2), 63; William 60;
Clerke, Richd. 23
Cliffe, Nich. 9
Clifford, Mary 30
Clifton, Eliz. 32; Thomas 53
Clobe, David 13
Cloke, Robert 42
Clopton (see Clapton), Walter 57
Coaker, Charles 43
Cobbs, Susan 42; Susannah 52
Cock (see Cocke) 25, 32, 63; Capt. Senr. 36; Bowler 71, 72, 83; Danll. 30; James 35, 42, 52;Mary25; Nathaniel 45; Richard 30, 33, 35, 57, 65; Richard, Junr. 42; Rich. Sr. 15; Stephen 34; Thomas (Tho.) 23, 24, 27(2), 29, 30, 36, 38(2); Thomas, Junr. 33; Thomas, Senr.30; Walter, 39; Wm. 36, 47

Cocke (see Cocke) 14(2), 20, 65, 86;
    Benjamin 64, 65; Bowler 68, 70,
    74, 83, 89; James 39, 77; James
    Junr. 79; James Powell 65; John
    65; Richard (Rich.) 5, 8, 10, 11,
    13, 21, 25, 33, 64, 65; Richard,
    Junr. 45, 64(4); Richard, Senr.,
    15, 21, 38(2); Thomas (Tho.), 23,
    24, 25, 26(2), 31, 36; Thomas,
    Junr. 33, 35; Thomas, Senr. 39;
    Walter 39; William (Wm.) 47, 59
Cockes, Hugh 2
Cockrum, James 19
Cocks, Jonathan 28
Coddle, Abraham 53
Colchester, Jone 8
Cole, Ann 11; Geo. 54, 56; John 31;
    Jon. 24, Jno.26, 29; Mary 20;
    Robert (Robt.) 2, 6; William 68
Cole Pit Road 48, 54
Colegrove, Wm. 43
Coleman, Ann 18; Robert 6; Samuel 87
Coleson 23
Coley, Francis 82
Collaine, James 34
Collett, Mary 42
Colling, Anne 27; Avis 27
Collins, Anne 30; Avis 30; Hen. 2;
    John 44; Richard 34;
Colson 33, 35
Come, Jane 38
Coming, Alice 46
Conner, Timothy 47, Winefred 33
Constable, Jane 45
Constantine, Henry 54
Conway, Thomas 73
Conwey, Thomas 73
Cook, Jno. 29, 47; John 57; Robt. 30
Cooke, Barth. 3; George 29; John 10;
    Jon. 5; Mary 24; Miles 10; Richard
    5, 10; Tho. 2; William (Willi.,
    Wm.) 4, 7(4), 11; Edwd. 15
Cookney, John 42
Cooper, Cha. 24; Rich. 25; Tho. 25;
    Thomas 91; Wm. 8
Coram, Wm. 53
Corben, Nic. 21
Corbet, Jone 46

Corderoy, Barbara 21
Cormacke, Dan. 14
Cornish, Antho. 32
Cosam, John 43
Cosby, Wm. 28
Cottril 67
Cotton, Jno. 21
Cotrel 61
Coulchester, Jno. 24
Court House 22
Covell, Savell 29
Cowed, Edwd. 29
Cowlishaw, David. 56
Cow Taile Quarter 15
Cox 59, 84; Bartholomew 75, 78, 90;
    Frederick 76, 79, 80; George 79,
    80; Henry 79(2); Hugh2; Jane 26,
    29; John 14, 22, 29, 39; Jno. 18,
    19, 25; Jon 11; Mary 24; Matthew
    (Mathew) 58, 79, 81, 82; Nicholas
    24, 61(3), 74, 89; Richard 38,
    47, 63; Stephen 87; Tho.8; William
    (Wm.) 4, 5, 8(2), 11, 24, 45, 69
Coxe, Hugh 12; William 7
Coxon, Wm. 16
Crabb, John 40; Mary 40
Craddock, Robert (Robt.) 7(2), 8(2),
    18, 22
Cranny, Porter 28
Crawford, Andrew 47
Crawley, Rich. 29
Creasy, William 91
Creed, Ellenor 21
Creede, Wm. 31

CREEKS
    Allens 65
    Almonds 15, 20, 28, 40
    Angelo 80
    Angoler 82(2)
    Baileys 2
    Baylyes (Baylys) 19, 91
    Bear Garden 64
    Beaver Dam (Beaverdam) 43(2), 44
    (2), 45(2), 48, 53(2), 55, 56(2),
    57, 61(3), 64(4), 65, 70, 71, 79,
    80, 82
    Beech 75

100

CREEKS (continued)
  Michune (see above) 87
  Michunck 86
  Mill 44, 45, 46, 53, 78(2), 85, 90
  Monakin (see Manacan, Manakin) 54,
    (2), 56
  Moyses 22
  Muddy 65, 70(2), 72, 74, 75(2),
    81, 82(2), 83(3), 84, 85,87(3)
  New Bremo 79
  Nevils 74
  Old Johns 83
  Old Mans 10(2), 12, 13, 15, 17, 18
  Oldmans (see above) 8
  Owens 83
  Poplar 15
  Powhite 41
  Procters 54
  Proctors (see above) 41, 92
  Queens 12, 13, 15, 16, 17, 18, 19
  Raccon 91
  Randolphs 78
  Reedy 41
  Rockfish 80
  Shaccoe (Shacko, Shoccores) 27
  Shacko (see above)27, 30
  Shaccores (see above) 24
  Stony 69
  Stovals 75
  Swift 34, 42, 54(2), 55(2), 60,
    61(2), 62(3), 65, 66, 68, 71,
    81, 83, 86(2)
  Three Mile 1, 4, 37
  Tuckahoe (also Tuckaho) 31, 33,
    35, 39, 42, 44, 45(2), 47(3),
    52, 53, 55(4), 56, 58, 59(4),
    61(3), 62, 63(2), 64, 67(4), 69
    (2), 72(4), 73, 74, 77(2), 78
    (3), 81, 84, 90(2)
  Turkey 55
  Turkey Island 7, 8, 9(2), 10, 11,
    12, 13, 14, 15, 33
  Two Mile 1(2), 3, 6(2), 10, 11,
    19, 32, 35, 37, 40, 47
  Ufnom 28
  Wattkins 12
  Westham (West Ham) 30, 33, 35,39,
    41, 59, 61, 67,

CREEKS (continued)
  Wild Boar (also Boare) 71, 80, 85
  Willis 58, 60, 78
  Willses 44

Creswell, Isac (also Isaac) 24, 29,
  33, 35
Crewe 20
Crewes 14
Crews, James 15; Mary 16
Crispin, Eliz. 24
Croft, Hen. 5
Croker, Geo. 24
Crome, Rich. 14
Crommie, Walter 39
Crooke, Thomas 61
Crosby (Crosbye) 11, Hen. 2; Tho. 5;
  Thomas 8, 10, 11
Crosdale, Roger 43
Crosse, Peter 26
Crouch, Robert 12
Crowder, Edw. 40
Crump, Edw. 16; Giles 6
Crutchfielde, Peter 54; Saml. 54
Cuddy, Jno. 27
Cummins, Roger 28
Cunegen, Timothy 65
Cuninghorm, Jon 8
Cunningham, 82, 84; James 84
Curd 71, Edward (Edwd.) 53, 57(2),
  63(3), 64(2)

Curles 3, 4(2), 6(2), 9(2), 10, 11
  (2), 13, 33, 37
Curell, Edward 19
Curtin, Eliz. 24
Custilly, Alice 65; Anna 46

                  D
Dacres, Jno. 24
Daine, Mary 55
Dale, Jon. 9; Susan 28; Sir Thomas 2
  (3), 4(2)
Dangerfeild, Peter 25
Dangerfield (see above) Peter 27
Daniell, Ja. 25
Darby (see Dawby) Jno. 24; John 26,
  56

102

Darlow, James 27
Dauxe, William 5
Davehill, Ed. 28
David, Peter 48, 50
Davies, Capt. 22; Jno. 18, 25; John
22; Wm. 34
Davis, Abell 23; Anne 30; Capt. 5,
25; Edwd. 46; Hugh 30, 35; John
5, 7(2), 8, 11(2), 22, 27, 37(2),
45; Jone 16, 20; Lucy 13, 15;
Mary 11(2); Owin 16; Robecca 29;
Robert (Robt.) 19, 38, 56; Sarah
38; Thomas (Tho.) 24, 46
Davy, Welch 27
Dawby (see Darby), Jno. 24
Dawkes, Henry 1(2); William 1(4), 2,3
21
Dawly (see Darby), Jno. 24
Dawson 84
Dawson, Gregory 38; Jonathan 3; Tho.
40; Thomas 64, 66, 68, 82; Will-
iam 6
Day, Joseph 44; Robt. 23, 24
Deacon, Gilbert 36; Thomas (Tho.) 4,
24
Dean, Richard 66, 82, 84, 90
Deane, Hanah 28; James 38; Wm. 5
Dearelove, Richard 37
Deep Bottom 22, 26, 33, 35, 40
Deeds, Julius 30
Deer (Deere), Tho. 15, 23
Dehall (Dehull, De Hull), Vincent 4
Dehull (see above), Cornelius 4
De Hull (see above), Cornelius 11(2)
Deker, Gilbert 44
Delahay (Delahaye), Gringall, 6, 11,
Sarah 6(2)
Demsey, Eleanore 44
Demson, Rowland 19
Denby, Ralph 56
Denham, John 38, 42
Denly, Ralph 56
Dennis, Richard (Rich.) 16, 54
Denson, Thomas 84
Dent, Catherine 46
Dep, Peter 78
Depuy, Barthotomew 76, Francis 67
Derfee, Jno. 53

Derrick, Francis 10
Devall, Jon. 11; John 11
Devils Wood Yard 47
Devin, Tho. 32
Dewe, Richard 34
Dewitt, Jacob 7
Dibdell, John 22
Dicer, Tho. 24
Dick, George 29
Dickenson, Richd. 46
Dickerson, Mary 56
Dickson, John 53
Diggs, Dudley 78
Diggs Hundred (Digs his hundred) 2, 9
Diggs, Mary 23
Dillon, Sarah 34
Dillwait 51
Dimock, Martin 6
Dioret, James 51,
Dishon, Abra. 53
Ditno, Barbara 88
Dittnoy (see above), 85
Dittwoy (see above) 85
Ditway (see above) 67, 76(2), Mary 88
Dixon, Francis 24; Jno. 30; Peter 45;
Richard (Rich.)3, 31; Wm. 92
Dobbs, James 13
Dobson, Seth 14
Dobye, Wm. 45
Dod, William 33
Dodd, Jon. 11
Dodge, Glowd 61
Dodson, Wm. 16
Dogg Point 83
Dogoe, Glowd 46
Dollard, James 44
Donnevan, Danl. 42
Doobees, Jon. 9
Dood, Anne 38
Doran, Lott 42
Dorgill, Arthur 47
Dorman, Roger 23, 27,
Dormer, Eliza. 24; Roger 30
Doubty, Mary 8
Douglas, Charles 34, 40
Dover, Edward 31
Downes, Fr. 9
Drakeford, Ann 14, Wm. 14

Draytonn, Harthorne 39
Drinkwater, Jon. 8
Drowgen, Wm. 24
Drummer, Eliz. 23
Drunkard, Lyddia 21
Drury, Jno. 24; Mary 22
Dry Bottome 23
Duch, Jon. 8
Duckett, James 14
Dudley, Charles 40
Dudly, James 28
Duff, John 38
Dugon, Catherine 46; Daniel 46
Dule, Richd. 41
Duncan 88
Duncomb, Jno. 31
Duncum, An. 24;
Duncumb, Herbert 32
Dunen, Antho. 52
Drunkert, Richd. 54
Dupea, Peter 77, 85
Dupee, Bartholomew 49, 54; Francis 51
Dupen, James 11
Dupra, Francis 87
Dupree, Thos. 43
During, Mary 23
Dutoi, Peter 57
Dutoy, Peter 48
Dyer, Mary 53, Phill. 24

E

Eakens, James, Junr. 34
Eakins, James 55
Eale, Samuel 40
Earle, John 39
Easely, Warham 71(4)
Easley (see above) 58; Robert 41;
   Warham 71; Warran 76
Easly 58, 81; Robert 41; Warham 73,
   88(2), 89
East, Thomas 26, 37; Tho. 54; Tho,
   Senr. 39
Eaton, Fra. 31
Eaven, Owen 55; Cha. (2)
Eavins, Thomas 60
Echolls, James 31
Edgar, Charles 11
Edger, John 29

Edlo (see Edloe, Edlow, Edlowe)Mrs.11
Edloe, Alice 2, 3, 4, 5(2), 7(2), 9;
   Capt. 13, 14; Mathew 5(2); 22
Edlow , Mathew 15
Edlowe, Alice 18; Mathew 5
Edmonds, Howell 6; Tho. 22

Edsell, Tho. 41

Edward, Tho. 25
Edwards 80; Hugh 39; Jno. 23(3), 30,
   40; John 9; Jon. 2; Thomas 82;
   Wm. 32, 46
Elam 34; Gilbert 44; Martin 22, 44;
   Martyn 33; Wm. 24
Elder, Anne 31; Tho. 32
Elderkin, Jno. 43(2); John 33
Elders, Mary 54
Eless, John 52
Elk Island 44(2), 45, 58, 66, 69
Elkes, John 16
Ellam (see Elam), Martin 22
Elleston, Edward 34
Ellet, Peter 20
Elliot, Humphry 21; Robt. 30; Thos.
   28
Ellis, Edward 3; John 61, 62, 67(2),
   John 77

Ellit, Hanah 28

Ellom, Robert 3
Elon, Phillip 26
Else, Ellis 22
Elton, Ed. 13; Edward 36
Ely (Elye), Joane 5, 10
Emerson, Jno. 25
Emetson, John 29
England, Wm. 15
English, John 42
Enroty, Darby 24
Epes, Capt. 36; Francis 35, 36, 52,
   70, 76, 77
Epperson, John 56
Epps, Capt. 12, 19
Eps, Francis 35
Eseley, Robert 54
Esely, Robert 41
Esquire, John 9
Estly, Robt. 24

104

Eustace, Downes,6
Evans 58; Charles 41, 42(2), 44(2),
58, 78; Dan 5; Daniell 10; Edw
ard 8, 10, Edw. 23, Edwd. 41;
James 8, 39, Jno. 27, 32; Robert
(Robt.) 17(5); Thomas 59(2), 78;
Wm. 21
Evard, John 54
Evelyn, Mary 21
Ever, Jno. 32
Everett, John 28
Everingha, Jeremie 21
Everton, Tho. 23
Eves, Jno. 32
Exon, William 54

F

Facy, Hannah 39
Fairface, Jno. 31
Falconer, Richard 9
Fanell, Willi. 19
Farcee, John 51
Farham, Jane 29
Farlar, John, Junr. 40
Farned, Edwd. 46
Farrar, Jno. 20, 25, John, Junr. 40;
Thomas 38, 55, 57, 59, 60, 62;
William 6, Wm. 16, 21, 23, 42
Farrer, William 3
Farsy, Francis 77, 83
Farthing, Bartholomew 6; Barr. 91
Feaser, Morgan 47
Featherstone, Wm. 40
Feild, John 15
Felkes, Walter 16
Fellows, Ambrose 56, Robt. 33
Fenner, Daniel 46
Ferne, Jane 28
Fernett, Edwd. 25
Ferrell, Richard 32
Ferres, Richard 26, 28, 29
Ferris (see above) Rich. 3, 28; Wm.
28
Ferryman, John 41
Feuray, Jno. 32
Fewson, Edwd. 6
Fidler, Wm. 43
Field, John 27, 28; Peter 68; Thomas
28

Fifield, John 42
Filbrough, Tho. 24
Fillmore, Edwd. 39
Finch, Edw. 26; Jno. 28, John 91
Finney, William 56
Finny, Mrs. 90
Fish, Jona. 22
Fisher, Anthony 34; Elizabeth 22,
Eliz. 26; Jno. 23, John 22; Jo-
seph 22; Mary, 22, 40; Sarah 22;
Wm. 22(3)
Fisholl, Jno. 21
Fitchcomb, Nicholas 44
Fitzjarrell, Elizabeth 66
Flag, Henry 16
Fleete, Robt. 11
Fleets Quarter 13
Flegg, Hen. 23; Margat. 23
Fleming 68; Charles 44(3), 53, 54,
57; John 89; Richard 37
Flesh, Wm. 22
Fletcher, Valent. 5, Valentine 10
Flinch, Danll. 26
Fling, Mary 46
Floide, And. 23
Flood, David 8; Richard 11
Flournoy, Francis 60, 62(3)
Florenoy, Jacob 49(2)
Floyd, George 56(2), 85, 90; Margt.
15, Marg. 23; Martha 39; Walter
23; Wm. 29
Foker, John 4, 6
Fonville, John 50
Forcuran, John 51, 56
Ford, Ale. 45; Peter 62, 65, 77;
William 73, Wm. 42
Fludd, Martha 9
Flynt, Robert 34
Forgott, Margary 15
Forshew, Hugh 11
Fossatt, William 34
Fossell, Rich. 24
Fossett, Kath. 24
Foster, Cha. 34; Eliza. 6; James 11,
16; John 38; Patrick 30; Phillip
5; Rich. 22; Tho. 23, Thos. 45
Fouke, John 2
Four, Daniel 48

Foure 49; Daniel 49; Peter 48, 51
Fowler, Bartho. 33; Bartholomew 35;
    Beata 21; Edwd. 31; James 2; John
    35, 52
Fox, Lawrence 36
Fox Slash 60
Frame, Jon. 6
France, Jon. 6
Frank, Eliza. 32
Franking, Thomas 65
Franklin, Mary 13; Richd. 28
Frayle, Tego 11
Freeman, George 55, 62, 69; Henry 39
French, Benj. 45; Katherine 60
Friend, Thomas 84
Frignale, Danll. 29
Fry, John 38; Tho. 15; William 13
Fryth, Robert 12
Fuckett, Gill 30
Fuer, Sam. 13
Fulks, John 41
Fullmow, Edwd. 39
Funk, Eliza. 32
Fustins, Ferdinando 16
Fute, Robt. 9

G

Gage, Mary 24
Gaineford, Jno. 21
Galen, Elizabeth 63
Gallier, John, Junr. 77; John, Senr.
    77; Mathew 77
Gardner, Edward 13, 14, 18; Jno. 24;
    Martin 30, 31(2), Rachel 44
Garford, Ruth 45
Gargaine, Eliz. 5
Gargame, Ellis 10
Garner, Dorothy; John 6; Rich. 6
Garnett, Sarah 43;
Garrett, 22; Jno. 23, John 11; Wm. 20,43
Garthrite, Samuel 54; Ephraim 37
Garthwright (see above) Michael 86
Gaten, Elizabeth 63
Gay, Ann 15; Mary 25
Geavodan, Anthony 48(2)
Gee, Gilbert 66
Geer, Edwd. 38
Gemston, John 36

Gentleman, Wm. 44
Gerant, Peter 71
Gerrard, Peter 19; Rich. 20, Richard
    22
Gerrulld, Kath. 32
Geverson, Wm. 45
Gevodan, Anthony 49(2)
Gibbin, Eliz. 20
Gibbins, Ellin 66; Esther 46
Gibson, Jon. 6
Gilcrest, Robert 68
Giles, William 26, Wm. 29, 42;
Gill, Henry 43, 55; Stephen 46
Gilley 39
Gilly 64
Gipson, Peter 54
Gitshill, John 45
Glaney, John 40
Glas, Mary 19
Glass, Dark 48
Gleab (Gleabe, Gleeb) 2, 6, 21, 32,
    35, 50
Glenister, Francis 54
Gload, David 15
Glover, Jno. 23; Sarah 5
Goadton, Anthony 54
Gobble, Hezekiah 45
Bobell, Wm. 44
Godfrey, Mary 30, 31
Godfrye, Jno. 2, John 9
Goff, Abra. 25
Goffe, Jno. 17; Mathew 17(2)
Gold, James 29; Wm. 27
Golding, William 68
Good, Edward 19; Jno. 29, John 34;
    Samuel 34, 41
Goodall, Rich. 3
Goodman, Jno. 35
Goodwin, Charles 53; Hana 24; Richd.
    46; Samll. 12
Goolsby, Thomas 86(3)
Goose, Abra. 23
Goram, John 34
Gording, William 61
Gory, Claude 50(2), 51, 52(2), 89
    Peter 56
Gosling, Mary 16
Gosse, Christopher 5

Gough, Mathew 10
Gower, Abell 22, 26, 27; Jno. 28; Wm. 22
Gowry, Wm. 28
Grace, Wm. 31
Granger, John 39
Grant, Antho. 28; Thos. 44
Graunt, James 16
Gray Ann 23; James 46
Grayne, Elizabeth 9; James 9; Rowland 9
Grayve, Elizabeth 9
Great feild 2
Great Rocks 33, 40
Greedewell, Robt. 52
Greeke, Rich. 6
Green 21, 38; John 45, 63; Robt. 30 (2); Thomas 19
Greene 15; Jane 29; Jno. 31; Robert 2, Robt. 31(2); Samll. 24; Susan 21; Wm. 8
Greenhaugh, Jno. 25
Greenhough (see above), Jno. 14, John 13(2);
Greenleafe, Robert 2, 3, 6; Susan 2
Greet, Elianor 6
Greete (see above), Alice 6; Richard 4, 6
Gregory, Ja. 19; Tho. 8, 19
Grewmarrin (also see Grewmeren, Groomarin, Groomerin, Grumarine, Grumartin, Grumeren, Grummeren, Grumurren), Gilly 54
Grewmeren (see above) Giley 39
Grey, Robt. 23
Griffen, John 19
Griffin, Jer. 29; Richard 39, Richd. 33
Grigg, James 59
Grimson, Jno. 21
Grindole 52
Grinwell, Margaret 57
Grizell, Humphry 3
Groom 72, 83; Daniel 58, 65, 70, 84
Groomamarin (see Grewmarrin), Gylly 27
Gront, Jno. 21
Groomerin (see Grewmarrin), Gilly 27
Grose, Anne 39

Grout, Jno. 21
Groves 31
Grumarine (see Grewmarrin ), Giles 90
Grumartin (see above), Gilly 72
Grumball, Jno. 29
Grumeren (see Grewmarrin), Gilly 30, 32
Grummeren (see above), Gilley 31
Grumurren (see above), Gilly 45
Gryer, Eliza. 28
Guilham, John 11; Thomas 11
Gully, Tho. 16
Gulton, John 19
Gun, John 56, 58, 66, 79
Gunn, James 46
Gunter, Jno. 16
Gurganey, Ann 6; Edward 6
Gurrant, Daniel 87
Guy, Ann 23
Gyles, Nich. 15; Rebecca 25, 28; Wm. 24, 29
Gyllom, Hen. 6

## H

Haborne, Robt. 25
Hacker, Edward 27
Haddelisey, Jno. 25
Haeles, Benj. 31
Haile, John 85, 86
Hailes, John 76
Haines, Eliz. 23; Robt. 20
Hair, Timo. 32
Halchard, Wm. 31
Hales, Lewis 29; Tho. 24
Half Sink 32, 36
Hall, Edwd. 42; Hen. 31; Jno. 23; Mathew 31; Peter 56; Robt. 32
Hallam 13
Hallom (see Hallum), Mrs. 10, 11 Ann 8, 9, 10; Robert 3(2), 7, 8, 10
Hallome (see above), Frances 11; Robert 11
Halloway, John 3
Hallum (See Hallom, Hallome), Robert 3, 5(2)
Haman, John 7

Hennick, Robt. 42
Henrick, Marg.
Henrico Parish 21
Henry, Jno. 23, John 41
Heper, Jno. 21
Herbert, Jno. 30
Hewanno, Ruth 22
Hewes, Margarett 18; Richard 4, 11;
   Tho. 21, 23
Hewett, John 5
Hewit, Thos. 44
Hewlet, John 44
Hews, Henry 42; William 53
Hexon, Ralph 11
Heyman, Mrs. 11
Heymans, Mrs. 12
Heynes, Mary 6
Heyward, Rand. 5
Heywood, Roger 14
Hicary Points 58
Hickman, James 16
Hicks, Hen. 23, 27(2)
Hicksoe, Jno. 28
Hickson, James 16
High Hills 36
Higson, Ralph 9
Hill, Alice 32; Edward 34, Edwd. 14;
   Francis 47; Isaac 31;Mary43; Rich 5,
   Richard10;Tho. 29, 30, Thomas 31
Hilliard, Wm. 45
Hilton, Tho. 32
Hind, Jno. 16
Hine, Jno. 16
Hinton, Edwd. 20; Geo. 16; Wm. 5
Hitchcox, Hen. 11; Richard 3
Hives, Margtt. 17
Hix, Daniel 59(2), 63; Marmaduke 74,
   81, Matmaduke 74
Hobbs, John 9
Hobby, Lar. 61
Hobson, William 52
Hoccadie, Wm. 13
Hockles, Wm. 41
Hodges, John 85; Saml. 43; William
   69(2), 88, Wm. 40
Hodkins, Abra. 24
Hoe, Rice 18
Hoes, Margtt. 17

Hoggatt 81; Anthony 72, 81; Philip 82
Holden, Roger 30; Wm. 24
Holder, Abra. 30
Holeman 63; James 58, 59, 62, 77
Holland 87; Edward 3, 5, Edwd. 3;
   Michael 62(2), 69(2), 70(4), 78
   (2), 82, 84, 85, 88, 91; Michell
   71; Peter 38
Hollaway, Susan 31
Hollinsby, Eliz. 24(2)
Hollon 84
Holloway, Peter 2
Hollum (see Hallom, Hallum), Eliza-
   beth 4; Robert 4
Holly, Eliz. 26
Holman, James 74(2), 75; Robert 9
Holmes, Anne 46; Eliza. 45; Jno. 28;
   Richard 42
Holt, Mary 44
Homes, Peter 5
Honor, Sara 42
Honour, Sarah 60
Hooe, And. 8
Hooke, Edwd. 6
Hopkins, Arthur 88, 89; Hen. 31;
   Italy 18
Hopps, Robert 11
Hore, And. 8
Horgott, Mar. 23
Hormell, James 31
Hormer, James 3
Horney, Mary 39
Horse, Francis 54
Horsepen 79
Horsley 82; Robert 82, 85(2)
Horsmandine 19
Horsnell, James 31
Horton, Danll. 32; Isaac 5, 10
Hosier, Saml. 40
Hosock, Jno. 24(2)  Hoton, Eliza. 32
Houghton, George 16; Leonard 7
House, Ann 25
How, Humphry 38; Richard 19
Howard, Allen 80; Eliz. 24; Ja. 24;
   Willi. 24; Wm. 24
Howarth, Thomas 54
Howe, William 3
Howell, Henry 6; James 53; John 6,

34; Tho. 12
Howman, Jon. 6
Howse, Wm. 26
Howtree, Mary 11
Hoyle, Susan 29
Hubort, Jno. 28
Huccoby, Tho. 24
Huddlecey 65

Hudsey, Peter 7

Hudson, Ben. 24; Charles 47, 61, 69,
    76, 77, 83, 90
Hudspeath (Hudspith), Ralph 80, 88
Hudspith (see above), George 76;
    Ralph 54, 64, 76
Hues, Jon. 6; Margtt. 17
Huett, John 10
Huffe, Mary 5, 15
Huggins, John 56
Hugh, Danll. 23
Hughes, Anne 33; Ashford 74, 75(3),
    82, 83, 85, 87, 88; Jose 29; Otho.
    29; Rebecca 29; Robert 64, 72, 83;
    Stephen 74, 83
Hughlett, Wm. 14
Hughs, Darcy 31; Sarah 31
Hugins, Mary 38
Hulett, Anne 31
Hull, Tho. 31
Humphries, Fra. 15; Tho. 15; Wm. 15
    (2), 23
Humphry, James 13; John 91
Hunt, Jno. 21, Jon. 24; Ralph 73;
    Samll. 31; Tho. 20; William 18
Hunter, Wm. 32
Hurim, Nowell 11
Hurst, Wm. 46
Hurt, Wm. 12
Hutcher 28
Hutchins, Isaac 8; Nicholas 38, 43;
    Will. 30
Hutchinson 72, Nicholas 47; Robt. 53;
    Thomas 53
Hutton, Tho. 21
Hyde, Robert 38
Hyres, Rich. 21
Hyyes, Rich. 21

# I

Inch, Fra. 31
Indian Feild 18
Ingram, Roger 29
Irby, William 45
Irish, Jone 19
Irwin, James 32
Isbell, John 40
Isar, Timothy 16
Ive, Jonathan 41
Izard, Mrs. 31, 37; Frances 26;
    Francis 72; Patrick 20

# J

Jackson, Abra. 20; Eliza. 11; Ja. 35;
    James 30, 40; Jane 30; Jno. 28,
    John 40; Joseph 86; Ralfe 68;
    Rebecca 23; Sar. 23; William 54,
    65
Jacob, Martha 11
Jamerson, John 32
James, Cha. 23; Francis 86, 88; John
    33; Richard 19; Robert 3; Wm. 29
James City County 34, 72
Jambou, Gideon 77(2)
Jarret, Robert 29(2)
Jarrett, Robt. 14
Jax (Jux), Eliz 5
Jefferson 58; Capt. 56; James 9;
    Peter 77; Thomas 41(2), 54, 81
Jeffries, Wm. 20
Jenings 69; Edmund 59; Ralph 23
Jenkins, Edmond 18
Jennings, Edmund 31; Mary 72
Jervis, Robt. 20
Jesop, Wm. 29
Jevedon 85
Jevodan, Anthony 68
Joanes, Amy 21
Johnes, Wm. 9
Johns, William 33
Johnson 85; Abraham 31; Benjamin 64,
    71, 87; Catherine 40; Charles 90
    (2); Daniel 90(2), 30, Danll. 31
    (2); Eliza. 38; Esther 24; Fair-
    hair James 46; Jacob 37; Jacques
    20; James 55(2), 90; John 5, 38,

Meredith 13
Lantthorpe, Jno. 25
Lasher, Eliz. 21
Lattimore, William 43
Laughton, Leon 4
Laurence (see Lawrence), James 17;
    Jane 24; Wm. 17, 19;
Lauthorp, Jno. 32
Lavean (Laveau), Adam 63
Lavillian, John 49(2), 78
Lawne, John 25
Lawrence (see Laurence), James 17;
    Martin 56; Thomas 29; Wm. 17
Lawson, George 62; Jonas 69(2), 82;
    Wm. 43
Lax 75; William 81
Leach, James 40; Jno. 25
Lead, Amos 43(2), 47, 53, 69, 90;
    Jno. 20, John 22; William 43, Wm.
    43
Leading, Hugh 23
Leake, Philip 38
Leasam, John 34
Leath, Jno. 25
Leather, Robt. 40
Lee, Eliza. 45; John 72
Leech, Fra. 24; Thomas 39
Leey, Wm. 43
Legg, Margt. 19
Legran, James 54, Peter 76, 77
Legrand (see above), Daniel 54, James
    54; John 54, 81; Peter 54(2),
    Peter, Senr. 54
Le Grand (see above) Peter 90
Leigh, William 1, Wm. 32;
Leinch, John 39
Lester, Ed. 16
Lestrange, Jno. 21
Levell, Richard 12
Levereau (Liverean), Moize 54; Ury 54
    (2), Vry 54
Levia, Peter, 54
Lewd, Rich. 6
Leweas, Edward 61
Lewellin 14; Daniell, 11, 37, Danll.
    15; David 18; Jon. 8
Lewellyn (see above) Daniell 11
Lewin, Steven 22

Lewis, Charles 70, 86, 87; Jane 54;
    John 23, 25, 69; Jone 56; Mary
    40, 43; Richd. 40; Robert 5; Ste-
    ven 22; Tho. 3, Thomas 5; William
    59, Wm. 28, 53
Leyden, John 26
Liburne, Tho. 30
Licheston, Jon. 5
Licking 79
Licking Hole 85, 88
Lidgold, Henry 29
Lifeholy, Marke 45, 53
Liggon (see Ligon) 26; Tho. 21, 23,
    42(2)
Light, Emlin 39
Lightfoot, Major 75; John 44
Ligon (see Liggon), Mary 41; Matthew
    55, 59, 70, 77, 79, 85(2); Rich-
    ard 34, 55; Tho. 16, 21; Wm. 41
Likes, David 81
Lile, James 31
Liles 83; David 89
Lilley, Jno. 24
Lilley Valley 8, 11, 24
Lilly Valley (see above) 36
Limber, Martha 43
Linch, John 45
Linney, Wm. 23
Linsley, Math. 23
Lipscome, Susana 35; Nicholas 35
Liptrot, Edmd. 43
Liscom, Jonas 40
Lisle, James 31, 32; Tho. 11
Lisse, Geo. 24
Lister, Humphry 20, 40
Little, Fra. 26
Little Guinia 86
Little Licking Hole 74
Littlefeild, Robt. 21
Littleworth, Jone 60
Liveran, Moses 47, 50
Liveran (see above), Moses 47, 51
Lluellin (see Lewellin), Daniel 12
    (2)
Lock, Tho. 13
Locket, Thomas 80(2), 83
Lockett (see above), Thomas 79
Lockey, Cha. 28

Logan, Alexander 82, 84
Logen (see above), Alexander 66
Lomess, Nathl. 53
Long, Eliza. 32
Long Falls 84
Long Feild (Long Field) 2(2), 6, 7,
    9, 11, 18, 22, 35, 37, 53
Long, Jane 18; Jon. 8
Lorange, Frances; 56; Francis 50(2),
    52
Lord Island 8
Louth, Jno. 32
Love, Dorothy 38; Tho. 5
Lovedere, wm. 24
Low, Peter 8
Lowder, Josh. 32; Mary 44; Tho. 24;
    Wm. 16
Lowe, Tho. 10
Loyd, Cornelius 4; James 42; Tho. 31
Ludwell, Phill 14; Tho.,20, 21(2),
    22, Thomas 14, 21
Luellin (see Lluellin, Lewellin),
    Daniel 12, 13(2), Danll. 18; David
    18
Luffe, Mary 10
Lunado, John 51
Lupton, John 9, 13
Luquedoe, John 91
Lyborne, Thomas 26
Lydall, Mary 40
Lyes, John 53
Lygon (see Ligon, Liggon), Mathew 81
Lyle (see Lile), James 28
Lyles, John 52
Lynes, John 44
Lynn, Mary 33; George 33

# M

Maborne Hills (see Mamborne, Mamburne)
    15
Macartee, Daniel 46
Macarty, Margaret 37
Maccarrell, Archaball 45
Macdarmott, Owen 32
Macey, John 9
Macham 65
Machunck 86
Mackallam, Danll. 41

Mackartyham, Danll. 41
Mackary, Ja. 24
Mackassey, John 46
Mackculla, Charles 41
Mackdaniel, Alex. 38
Mackenny, Alexander 30, 31
Mackentush, James 47
Mackergoe, Jno. 21
Macklane, Allen 46
Mackully, Chas. 42
Mackwell, Alex. 24
Macon, John 74, 75
Maddem (see Maddin), Edward 11; Mary 33
Maddin (see above), Edward 13, 14,
    18
Maden, Rosamond 40
Madison, Edward 14
Magnum Lapis 58
Mahook 67
Main Road 75
Major, Phi. 8
Makevary, Gilb. 21
Malby, Ann 22
Mallet 87; Maryan 49; Stephen 50, 91
Mallett (see above), Martin 58; Ste-
    phen 44
Maloone, Anthony 48
Mamburne Hills (see Maborne) 10
Man, John 38, 66, 70(2), 80, 82;
    Robert 66
Manaclith, El. 23
Manakin Towne 42, 44, 45, 46, 63,
    71, 76
Mane, Nathaniel 76
Mann, Tho. 23
Mansfeild, David 31
Marchbanks, Georg 70
Marches, John 43
Mark, Mathew 53
Markham, Susan 3, 6; Thomas 3, 6, 9, 13,
    14, 15, Tho,. 25
Marrain, Gilly Grew (see Grewmarrin)
    59, 84
Marsh, Jno. 28; Nicholas 29, 33,
    Nicho. 42; Richd. 21; Robt. 16;
    Wm. 21
Marshall, Alexander 80; Angilo 56;
    Ester 21; Phill. 28; William 38

Marshbank, George 77
Marshbanks (see above), George 81
Marshen, Wm. 5
Marston, Wm. 5
Marston, Joane 23; Tho. 31
Martin 61; Capt. 2,6,9, 37,64; And.
    24; John 10, 47(2), 49, 50, 55,
    56, 65, 70, 72, 75; Margaret 56;
    Martin 67, 77, 81; Nathan. 3; Nic.
    21; Rich. 29, Richd. 30, 31; Robt.
    32; Tho. 5, Thomas 29(2), Thos. 43
Martyn, Robert 19
Mascall, Maiden 45
Mascoll, Rich. 2, Richard 9
Mason, Geo. 53; Jo. 23; Peter 12; Tho.
    22, Thomas 12; Wm. 20
Massey, John 38
Massie, Capt. 72(2); Charles 72(2)
Matherell, William 8
Mathers, Kath. 33
Mathew 67
Mathews 81; Capt. 22, 25; Edward 26,
    Edwd. 22(2), 32; Morris 24; Thos. 30
Mathy, Mary 40
Matoone (see Mattoon, Mattoone), An-
    thony 51
Matthews (see Mathews) 71, 79, 87, 90
    John 40; Morris 24
Mattoon(see Matoone), Anthony 50; 77;
    Jacob 89
Matoone, Anthony 49, 52
Mawborn Hills (see Mamborne) 37
Max, Edward 77, 85; John 77, 85
Maxe, Edward 79; Edward, Junr. 79;
    Nathaniel 76, 79(3); William 79
Maxey (see above), John 86; Nathan-
    iel 77, 86, 90; Edward 90; Wil-
    liam 90
May, John 43; Peter 38; William 65,
    Willm. 54; Maybury, Fra. 25
Mayden, Jon. 13
Mayes, William 90
Mayo 74, 87, 89; William 81, 84, 85,
    89
McDaniel, Margt. 44
McKenny, Colen 56
Mcklamar, Mary 65
Mclawny, Margaret 65

Meads, Xper. 24
Meares, John 14
Mecarty, Denis 63
Meclare, Jno. 47
Meclary, John 62
Medane, Arth. 47
Medly, Georg 18
Meeds, Anne 44
Meeler, Tho. 26
Meeres, John 14
Mekeney, Alexander 31
Mekes, Roger 21
Mercer, Robt. 23
Meredith 69; Thomas 62
Meres, Jno. 18
Merie, Peter 24
Merridae 23
Merritt, Wm. 20
Merryman, John 81, 82, 84, 85, 87
Mesem, Sara 21
Michaux 57, 67, 78, 89; Abraham 42;
    90; Jacob 67, 90; John 89
Micheaux (see above) 72; Abraham 75,
    81;
Michell, Tho. 31, 34
Micraugh, Owen 31
Middle Spring Bottome 22, 23
Midlemore, Geo. 13
Middleton, Eliza. 46, 48; John 48
Miles, Arth. 24; Humph. 13, 16
Miller, Andrew 13; Dorothy 13; Jno.
    11, 47; Wm. 24
Millford, Dennis 31
Mills, Anne 45; Humph. 16; John 5;
    William 87
Millton, Richard 5
Milner, Jno. 20, John 22, 25, 28;
    Willi. 24
Milton, Richard 12
Mims, David 68(2); Thomas 45, 70(2),
    Thos. 53
Minetree 50
Minifie, Georg. 10
Minns, Isaac 39
Minor, Thomas 38
Missheux (see Michaux), Abraham 49,
    55, 76
Misshiux, (see above), Abra. 54

114

Misshuex (see Michaux), Abraham 48
Mitchell, Edwd. 42; Hen. 31; Jno. 56
   Jo. 19; Mary 45; Mill 42; Tho. 30,
   31
Mock, Math 25
Mole, Jno. 28
Moltmain, Nich. 45
Mongyes 36
Montfort, Thomas 38
Moodey, Daniel 56
Moodry, Daniel 56
Moody, Hump. 31
Moor, Bernard 20
Moore, James 31; Leonard 1; Nath. 2,
   9; Nice. 23; Rebecca 16; Tho. 23;
   William 63
Mooreman, Andrew 68(2), 69
Morant, Ja. 25
More, And. 23; James 32, 47; Jno. 23
Moreman 70
Morethorpe, Tho. 3
Morgan, Anthony 75; Edwd. 44; Evan 8;
   James 47; Jane 34; John 9, 34, 53,
   Jon. 4; Peter 37; Tho. 2, 9, 11;
   William 10
Morgrove, Jane 28
Moriset, Peter 51
Morley, Geo. 31; Sym. 5, Symon 10
Morlin, Jon. 5
Morrill, Lewis 50
Morris, Edwd. 29, Ed. 32; Eliza. 34;
   James 39; Jno. 34; Lionell 25, 31,
   Lyonell 26; Robt. 2; Roger 27;
   Sarah 48; Tho. 5, 31
Morriset, Peter 49
Morse, Thomas 82, 89; William 89
Mory, Tho. 23
Mosby 74; Benjamin 88; Richard 66, 73,
   88, 89, Robert 73(2)
Moseby, Benjamin 82; Edwd. 45; Rich-
   ard 84; Robert (2)
Moseley, Arthur 61, 80(2), 83, Arthur,
   Jr. 76, Arthur, Junr. 80(2)
Moses 63
Moss, James 54, 62; Tho. 21, Thomas
   72, 84; William 72, 74, 75, Wm. 42
Mount My Lady Feild 42, 92
Mount Peloin 29

Mount Pelom 29
Mugeden, John 66
Mulkey 78
Mullin, Patrick 74
Mullinax, Sarah 59
Murcell, Tho. 35
Murffy, Jane 46
Murfy, Timothy 56
Murrell, Thomas 82
Murry, John 56
Myles, Jno. 16

## N

Nanny, Hugh 31
Napier, Booth 81, Bouth 56
Nash, Michael 66
Neale, Morris 23
Neck of Land 1(2), 2, 10, 13, 32, 35
Nellei, Edward 22
Nelson, Mary 40
Nett, Nicholas 10
Nevel, James 89
Nevil, James 64, 75(2), 91
New, Edmund, 57, 71, 74; Edward 67;
   Tho. 24
New Kent County 55, 65(2), 72(3),
   73, 75(2), 81, 90
New Kent Path 26
New Kent Road 24, 25, 27, 30, 32
Newby, Samll. 31
Newcomb, Edmd. 39; Mary 39
Newell, Jno. 32
Newjant, Kath. 32
Newlet, John 44
Newman, John 2, 40; Richard 11;
   Thomas 57
News, Edmon 80, Edmond 81, 89,
   Edmund 89
Newton, Ann 34; John 31; Wm. 21
Niccols, Rebecca 26
Nicholas, Jon. 3
Nicholls, Fra 44; Thomas 38
Nichols, Edwd. 23; Frances 43, 60;
   James 43; Thos. 46; Walter 8
Nicholson, John 62
Nobbs, Anne 27
Noble, Miles 13
Nobles, Anne 24

Noland 72, 90; Agnes 78, 89; Thomas 89
Norey, Alex. 3
Norgs 23
Norris, Jno. 21; Roger 30; Wm. 28
North, Hen. 21; Jno. 23, 24, John 3
Northerne, John 5
Nowellin, James 57
Nuckles, Samuel 84
Nutt, John 53

O

Oage, Matthew 48, 79, 86
Oake, Wm. 33
Oakely, Jno. 26
Oates, John 56
Oatley, Wm 35
Oge (see Agee, Oage), Matthew 66(2), 68
Oggs, Thomas 9
Oglebey, Charles 46
Oglesby, Richard 82
Ogleoy, James 34
Old Feild 18
Old Path 19
Old poetan Path 42
Old Road 75, 83
Oldey, John 40
Oliver, Nich. 5, Nicholas 10; Tho. 19
Omooney, Timo. 40
Oneale, Byran 37
Oposum 30
Orton, Sarah 31
Orts, Cornelius 28
Osborne 92; Edward 3(2); John 42
Osbourn, Eliz. 21
Oswald, Andrew 43
Otme, Wm. 24
Oughnom brook 25
Overton, Jno. 30; Sarah 30
Owen 82; John 76(2), 78, 79; Jone 31; Joseph 54; Margt. 45; Richard 11; Robert 31; Thomas 72, 73(2); Wm. 31
Owens, John 79, 82
Owin, Col. 15, 38; Simon 16
Oystershell Landing 22

P

Packenton, Eper 23
Packer (see Parker), Elizabeth 2, 4, 7; Thomas 1(4), 7
Page, Eliz. 24; Richd. 25
Pagester, John 38
Paine, Joseph 78; John 29; Josia 80; Thos. 43
Pall, Tho. 31
Palmer, Edward 13, 39; Eliza. 39; Wm. 24
Pamunkey Path 15, 38
Pandle, Henry 10
Paniteur, John 50, 52
Panituer, John 50
Parcost, Tho. 5
Parcroft, Thomas 10
Pardoe, Jno. 31
Parentan, Isaac 50
Parentau, Isaac 50, 51(2)
Parish 66, 90; John 72
Parke, Jno. 16; Richard 23
Parker (see Packer) 7; Elizabeth 2, 4, 56; Hannah 53; Hellena 38; Jon 9; Luke 53; Owen 31; Richard 20, 79(2), 89; Thomas 1(4); Parker's Path 37
Parkson, Ralph 14
Parrott, Wm. 31
Parry, Samll. 12
Parsons, Hen. 24; Jno. 24
Partin, Robert 12(2), Robt. Jr. 18, Robt. Junr. 14, Robt., Senr 14, 18
Partree, Mary 38
Partridge, Jno. 31; Wm. 16
Passiful, Elizabeth 44
Paterson (see Patison, Patterson, Pattison), David 82
Patison (see above), John 46
Pattent, Eliz. 13
Patterson (see Paterson), David 80, 81(2), 91
Pattison (see above), David 43, 58; Davis 47, Hen. 2
Pattman, Tho. 19

Paulett (see Pawlett), Chiddock 8;
   Thomas 8
Pawlett (see above), Marmas 4; Tho-
   mas 4
Payne, George 75, 82, 85, 91; Josiah
   85
Payton, Tho. 31
Peach, Honor 31
Peacock, Michaell 11
Pead, Jon. 6
Peake, Robt. 35
Pearson, Tho. 5
Peckington, Xpher. 27
Pegg, Joseph 38
Peirce, Henry 38; Morgan 21
Peirson, Christian 31
Peldon, Tho. 16
Pemston, John 35
Penery, Eliza. 43
Penfeather, Robt. 24
Penhorne, Christo. 6
Pennull, Jno. 18
Penquit, Wm. 32
Pequoucky Path 30
Perault, Charles 51
Penticon, Jane 44
Penton, Tho. 19
Perault, Charles 51
Perce, Francis 19, 37, Wm. 19
Peren (see Perin, Perrin), Richard 29,
   Thomas 29
Perfitt, Noba 3
Perin (see Peren, Perrin), Thomas 42
Perkins, Constant 58, 66; Constantine
   61(2), 80; Nicho. 23, Nicholas 11,
   28
Perlue, Nath. 20
Perne, John Peter 73
Pero, Daniel 87
Perrin 36; Ann 40; Richard 22, 36, 42, 91
Perrott, Susan 25
Perry, Capt. 8; Eliz. 38; Henry 10(2)
   Mrs. Perry 8; William 10(2)
Person, Thomas 10
Pertue, Nath. 20
Perue (see Perne), John Peter 73
Petercue, Alice 23
Peters, Charles 54

Peters, Edwd 36
Peterson, David 67; Hen. 23; Jno. 23
Pettis, Step. 5
Petto, Edw. 29
Petts, Edw. 29
Peury, Eliz. 43
Pew, Henry 29, 38, 47
Pewe(see above) Henry 29
Peynoucky Path 30
Phelps 78; John 73, 88; Robert 8, 10
Phillipps, Georg 9; Richard 8
Philips, Geo. 31
Philpot, Jon. 13
Philpott, Tho. 21
Phips, Eliz 28
Pick, Jno. 24
Pickiner, Mary 21
Pickinoky Road 27
Pidgen Land 39
Pidgeon Land 42
Pidiston, Sam. 12
Piges Slash 54
Pigg Slash 37
Piggott, Mary 19
Pilkington, Wm. 45(2)
Pimasioes Feild 4
Pindale, Thos. 43
Piney Slash 33, 34, 36(2)
Piper, Tho. 40
Pirnell, Eliz 24
Pistor, Charles 39; Christian 39
Pistote, Cha. 24
Place 23, 27, 28; James 3, 4, 8, 10,
   17; Rowland 20, 38
Plant, John 41
Platt, Gilbert 2, 21
Pleasants 33(2), 35, 45, 58, 62, 84,
   Dorothy 53; John 25, 26, 29, 32,
   33, 35(2), 36(2), 38, 39, 41(2),
   43(3), 44, 45, 46(2), 47, 48(2),
   53; 56, 58, 63, 64, 66, 84, 88,
   (2); Joseph 36, 41, 43, 44, 45,
   48(2), 56(2); Thomas 54
Pledge, John 33; Nich. 91
Ploke, Robert 42
Plum, John 45
Plumer Peter 18
Plummer (see above) Peter 16, 18

Pocoshock 41
Point of Rocks 44
Poke, Robt. 46
Polly, Samuel 34
Polwen, John 63
Polwin, John 45
Pomonkey Path 21
Ponder, Thomas 9
Poplar Brooke 21, 37
Porter, Jno. 21; Thomas 90; William
    26(2),31, 37, William, Junr. 26,
    Willm. 21, Wm. 21, 45
Posey, Fr. 6
Potteete, Georg 19
Potter, Charles 43; John 46; Joseph
    39
Potts, Tho. 43
Pouder, Thomas 9
Povall, Eliza. 40; Robert 40, Robt.
    Junr. 40
Povey, Robt. 30
Powel, Roger 64(2);
Powell, Hopkin 24; Hugh 2; James 31;
    Margaret 5, Margarett 10; Thomas
    12
Power 78
Powers 78
Powhetans Tree 1
Powhite feilds 30
Powhite Path 26
Powle, Ann63
Powndle, Henry 5
Pratt, Andrew 7; Jon 6
Price, Daniel 74, 87, Daniell 31; Geo.
    16; Howell 22; Jane 31; John 5, 8,
    9, 13, 61, 64, Jon. 6; Kath. 28;
    Mathew 9; Morgan 16; William 57
Prichard, Jos. 42
Pricklove, Geo 5
Pride, Halcoat 80(2), 83; John 61, 65,
    79, 80, 83, 86
Prideman, Robert 32
Prier, John 71, 80
Prior, Nicholas 30
Prise (see Price), Hoell 18
Proctors 34,
Procters 40
Prosser, Thomas 83

Prouinsall, Anthony 46
Prout, Peter 26
Provinsall, Bernard 54
Pruett, Henry 27, 28
Pue, Henry 32
Purnell, Wm. 2
Purnell, William 9
Pyconockney Path 59
Pylar, Wm. 12

Q

Quin 78, 90
Quinell, Mary 46

R

Radford 20; Francis 17, 20, 21, 22,
    37; John 38, 64, 69
Rains, John 41
Raley, Charles 83
Ralfe, James 31
Ramsey 31; Wm. 16
Randall, Adam 29
Randolph 29, 60; Col. 39, 67; Major
    70; Henry 20, 21, Henry, Junr. 55;
    Richard 76(2), 77, 80, 85; Thomas
    57, 58, 59(2), 60, 61, 62, 71, 75
    (2), 81, 83(2), 86, 87; William
    25, 35(2), 37(3), 40, 42, 59,
    76(3), 78, 79, 80(2), 81, 82(2),
    86, 87, 88, Wm. 33, 36(3), 46
Raner, George 60
Ranger, Wm. 30
Rapean, Anthony 79
Rapeen (see above), Anthony58
Rappeene (see above), Anthony 45
Rapine (see above), Anthony 51, 52
Rattenbury, Henry 42
Rawson, Charles 38
Rawsonsey Neck 37
Ray, John 12, 56; Tho. 31
Rayes, Margaret 23
Rayley, Charles 83; Thomas 74
Rea, Margt. 38
Read, John 3; Tho. 16; Will. 56
Reade, Wm. 31
Reathworth, Moses 52
Red Bank Falls 88
Red, John 46; Wm. 46

118

Red Water 23, 42
Reddey, James 3
Redford (see (see Radford), Francis 20, 28, 29
Redman, James 32
Reed, Wm. 47
Reener, Elianor 39
Reest, Moses 28
Reeves, Francis 33
Regan, John 65
Reives , Francis 40
Relfe, Jane 29
Remey (Remmy, Remy), Abraham 49(4)
Renno, Stephen 48, 49
Renols, Abraham 29
Rent, Mary 53
Resons, Mathew 42
Reyalls, Robert 53
Reynols, Jane 29
Ribot, Francis 46, Jane 46; Jno. 46; Maria 46; Martha 46; Nicho. 46; Susanna 46
Rice, Carleton 54; Henry 12; Isabell 26; Thomas 45
Rich, Jno. 26; Thomas 80
Rich Levell 14, 18
Richard, Tho. 12
Richards, Edwd. 27, 30; Eliz. 24; Jno. 31; Oliver 33; Will. 23, William 33, Wm. 23
Richardson, Alex 31; Edward 29, Edw. 31, Edwd. 23, 30; Hen. 34; Jno. 20; Melch 25; Sarah 38; Tho. 11 Wm. 6
Richeson, Barnaby 10; Edwd. 56
Rickason, Reb. 26
Ricroft, Richard 19
Ridely, Danll. 21
Rider, Willi. 8, William 10
Ridge, 78
Ridley, Ann 9; William 10
Ridly, Ann 2; Wm. 8
Right, John 72
Rigot, Sam. 16
Rigsby, James 6
Rite, Isabell 26

RIVERS
Appamattox 76(8), 77, 78, 79(5), 80(6), 81, 82(2), 83, 86, 87 (2), 88, 89
Chickahominy 13, 28, 29, 34, 36, 72
Fluvanna 61, 64, 74(3), 75(2), 76 77, 79(2), 80(2), 82, 85, 86 (4), 88, 89, 90(3), 91
Hardwar 77
Mattapony 46
Pamunkey 43, 53, 67
Powhatan 75
Rivanna 57, 65(2), 75(2), 78, 82, 83, 84, 85, 86, 87(2), 88, 90 (2), 91
Rock Fish 77, 80
South 88

Rivis, Edward 59
Roades, George 54
Roane, Charles 22
Roatch, John 34
Roberts, Fr. 5; Griff. 5; James 6; Jon. 9; Jonas 31; Jone 31; John 57, John, Junr. 42; Roger 62; Thomas 33, 38
Robertson, John 36, 45; Patrick 28; Tho. 42; Wil. 48
Robins, Alex. 28; Arthur 33; Hen. 8, John 33; Thos. 33
Robbinson, James 39; Wm. 47
Robinson, Francis 21; Jab. 12; Jno. 23, 27, 47; John 39, 43(2), 90 Patrick 6; Tho. 4, 42, Thomas 19
Rock Castle 53, 57, 68, 81
Rock Island 90
Rock, Mary 65; Thomas 66
Rocky Island 60, 75
Roe, Margaret 31
Rogers, Eliz. 22, 26; Jarvis 21; John 23, 43; Ralph 38; Richd. 31; Tho. 5; Wm. 5, 10, 19, 26, 38
Rookings, Sara 31
Rose, Addam 21; Hugh 53; Margery 21; Morrice 5, 10; Wm. 8

Rosse, Adam 15, 23
Roundabout 11, 19, 20, 22, 25, 28, 33,
    39
Roundabout Slash 16, 20, 21, 37
Rowly, William 9
Royall, Capt. 34; Ann 7; Henry 7;
    Joseph 7, 9, 11(2), 14(2), 18, 36
    (2); Katherine 11; Thomasin 7
Ruarke, Mary 66
Rucell, Robert 39
Rudds, Peter 23
Ruggles, An. 31
Rumbold, Charles 33
Runalds, Henry 87; William 83
Runnals, Henry 69

RUNS
    Beachen 38
    Bridge 38
    Cattaile 15, 21, 27, 38
    Cold Water 54
    Coles 36
    Cornelius 25(2), 28(2), 36
    Cowtaile Quarter 21, 38
    Deep Run 28(2), 32, 47, 55(2),
        65, 67, 68, 73
    Drinking 73
    Edwly. 15
    Fishing 13, 15, 17, 35
    Gillies 27
    Gravilly 77
    Grindalls 22, 34
    Grindons 26
    Licking Hole 57
    Mill 23, 70
    Miry 47
    Mongoies 23
    Moses 19
    Myry 26
    Old Town 35, 39, 52
    Possum 40
    Proctors 22
    Rockey 38, 58
    Seder 13
    Seller 13, 15, 17, 20
    Spring 54
    Southern 20
    Stony 59

RUNS (continued)
    Strawberry Hill 34
    Three Mile 25
    Treasurers 46, 57, 82, 84
    Widdows 26

Russel 59(2); Charles 62
Russell 47, 58, 63; Charles 42;
    Eliz. 19; Robt. 56; Wm. 38
Ryall (see Royall), Joseph 3, 5
Ryalls (see above), Joseph 12

S

Sabotte, Peter 50, 52(2)
Sacony 68
Salle, Abra.43, Abra., Junr. 43,
    Abraham 43, 47, 48(2), 49(2),
    55; Jacob 43; Oliver 43; Peter
    87; William 81
Salsbury 16; Robert 5
Salt, Ben. 24, Benja. 24
Saltrea, John 11
Sampson, Francis; Jno. 30; Wm. 42
    (2);
Sampson's Slash 29, 33, 40
Samson, Francis 66
Samson's Slash 35
Sanders, Edward 29; Eliz. 37; James
    31, 66; Joan 30; Jno. 16, John 66,
    67(2), 82, 89, 90; Thomas 66
Sands, James 27
Sandy Lick 79
Sappony Path 61
Sassin, Francis 50, 53
Saunders, John 81, Wm. 29
Savage, Bartho. 31; Grace 24, 27
Sawkins, Jane 33; John 33, 40
Scarburgh, Chas 32
Sclater, John 90
Scofeild, Anne 32
Scoot, Chr. 45
Scot 87; Edward 76; Samuel 83
Scott 70, 72, 81, 83; Col. 70(2);
    Andrew 74; Edward 58, 63(2),
    74, 89(3), 90(2), Jane 23, Jno.
    21, John 74; Joseph 64, 82; Wal-
    ter 41, 61
Scutt, Elizabeth 69

Smith, Kath. 16; Marg. 23; Mary, 23, 28; Obadiah 72, Obediah 64, 73(2); Richd. 28; Robert 40, Robt. 53; Tho. 3, 27, Thomas 39; William 62, Rev. William 85, Wm. 27
Smithes, Thos 43
Smiths Bay 13, 14, 25
Snelling, Joan 21
Snugg 40
Snuggs, Robert 61
Soane, Samuell 62; William 35, 60, Wm. 30
Soanes, Wm. 38
Soblet, Abraham 48, 50(2); Peter 50, 76, Peter Lewis 52
Sobriche, Ann 79(2); Gaspard 79, Gaspard, Junr. 79; Jacob 79; Mary 79; Susanna 79
Soleager, John 52
Somerscales, Ser. 32
Sorrell, Tho. 23
Sotone, Mary 16
Souch, Peter 24(2)
Soullie, Nicholas 49, 51, 83, 85, 88
South, Peter, 24; Robt. 25
Southall, Wm. 45
Southerland, George 77, 88
Southfeild, Jno. 24
Soward, John 40
Spaidman, Robt. 45
Sparkes, Phill. 16
Spear, John 83, 89; Robert 83
Spearman, Jno. 26
Spears, James 73; John 67, 68
Spence, Ringin 47
Spencer, Margery 16; Peter 45; Sarah 32; Wm. 38
Spendlowe, Ralph 13
Spense, James 39
Spillman, Wm. 38
Spinke, Robert 8
Spits, Mary 44
Sprigge, Elizabeth 38
Spring, Tho. 23
Sproson, Abra. 21
Spurlock, William 72, 88
Squire, Walter 27
Stanard, Wm. 24

Stanaway, Will. 19
Stanbrig, Tho. 22
Standley, William 46
Stanford, Jno. 30
Stanley, Wm. 25
Stanly, Tho. 26
Staple, Eliza. 53
Staples, Margt. 38
Stapp, Joshua 30
Starling, John 26
Start, Jno. 31
Steer, Jno. 21
Stegg 27; Col. 19, 21; Tho. 15, Thomas 5, 13, 15, 17(2), 18, Thos. 13
Stell, Tho. 41
Step, Josha. 31
Stephens, John 57, 66; Tho. 27, 29, Thomas 28; Wm. 34, 44
Steele, Mary 38
Stevens, Wm. 17
Stevenson, Christ. 7
Steward, Charles 3, Jno. 19, 23, John 55
Stewart, Wm. 44, 60
Stiball, Richd. 32
Stibbins, John 40
Stiff, Jno. 18
Stile, Wm. 20
Stiles, Mary 39
Stills (see above), Mary 39
Stingston, John 46
Stith, Maj. 34; Drury 40; Jno. 24; Wm. 24
Stoaner 77
Stock, Robt. 24
Stockes, John 40
Stone, Francis 7; Geo. 31; James 4; John 55(2); Mary 17; Oliver 31
Stoner, Daniel 75, 81, 82, 86
Stoney Point 32, 36
Stoone, Tho. 45
Storey, Wm. 23
Story, Hannah 45; Jno. 31
Stoval, Bartholomew 81, 89(2); George, 85, 89; John 89
Stovall (see above) 66, 86; Bartholomew 47, 67, 70, 71, 74, 76,

Stowers, John 34
Strange 24
Stratton, Edward 27, 33, 34
Street, Anne 28
Streete, Fra. 13
Stringer, Jno. 21; Mary 24
Strong, John 28, 62
Stuart, John 22
Stutfeild, Jno. 24
Subly, Charles 44
Sucker, Wm 12
Suewell, Mary 33
Suillman, John 34
Sulie, Nicholas 79
Sullivan, Alice 46; John 34; Timothy
    46
Sunter, Spethen 60
Suttle, Nicho. 42
Swaine, Margt. 27
Swaley, Daniel 40
Swallow, Geo. 28

SWAMPS
    Ashen 23, 42
    Bare 32
    Chickahominy (Chiccohominy,Chic-
        ahominy) 15, 21, 23, 24, 25, 29,
        30(3), 31(2), 32(2), 34, 36(3),
        38, 43, 60, 62(4), 63, 69, 73

        (2), Chickahominy Main 26(2)

    Cross 68, 84
    Curles 33
    Horse 32
    Neca Land 43
    Persimon Island 17
    Roundabout 28, 29
    Three Mile
    White Oak 26(2), 28, 32(2), 37,
        39, 41, 42

Swanley, Ann 30
Swann, Marg. 23
Sweet, Isaac 45
Sweft, Thomas
Swift, Tho. 9; William 88
Swifton, Wm. 40
Swillifant, Mary 32

Swine, Margaret 27
Swinfeild, Philip 40
Sykes, Jane 31
Symes, John 80
Symons, Jno. 21

T

Tabitha, Tab 40
Tabor 70, 71(3), 74; John 68, 85
Tabour (see above) John 74
Talbot, Rich 14
Talbott, John 11(2)
Tally, Eliza. 3; Elias 8
Tannar (see Tanner), Edwd. 22;
    Joseph 22; Martha 22; Mary 22
Tanner 23; Joseph 39, 77, Joseph,
    Junr. 79; Thomas, Jr. 86
Tate, Jno. 16, John 16
Tayler (see Taylor) 28; Adam 29;
    James 75; Jno. 29, John 85;
    Martha 29; Thomas 28
Taylor (see above), Dorothy 19;
    Elizabeth 60; Francis 19; James
    74; Jno. 18, John 74; Nicho. 45;
    Robert 12; Tho. 11, 20, Thomas
    14, 19, 20, 29, 39, 53
Taylour (see above), Thomas 15
Temple, Jno. 33; Robt. 24
Ternden, John 24
Terrell, Math. 23; Rich. 24
Terrey, Jonas 32
Thomas Abig. 23; Alice 46; Daniel,
    69, 81; Henry 43, 44; John 4,
    7, 11, 33, 45; Joseph 33, 75(2)
    Margarett 6; Philip 80 ;
    Phillip 76, 79; Wm. 6, 11, 32
Thompson, Ann 16; Elinor 55; Eliz.
    29; Geo. 45; Ja. 24; Robert 34,
    37, Robt. 36; Walter 31; Wm. 43
Thomson, Eliz 39
Thorne, Philip 43
Thornhill 72, 81; Mary 24
Thornton 64, 66, 74; John 57, 70
Thosatt, William 34
Thrift, Eliz. 25
Throgmorton, Wm. 42
Thurston, Edward 12
Thweat, John 36

Timber (see Tymber) Slash 14
Tindal 88; Thomas 88
Tindale (see above), Thos. 44
Tindall (see above), Thomas 56, 59
Tinson, widow 81
Tiplady, Isabella 38
Tisdale, Thomas 42
Toby, Jno. 34
Tolwin, John 45
Tombs, Rich 4
Tomkins, Wm. 14
Tompson (see Thompson), Edwd. 5;
    Georg 4; James 5, 10; Maurice 4
Tomson (see Tompson) Jno. 15
Toppin, Geo. 24
Totero Town 74(2)
Totier 90
Towell, Jon. 8
Towers, Wm. 6
Townes, William 90
Towns (see above), William 69
Trebue, Anthony 54; Jacob 90; Kath.
    54
Trenchman, Michaell 23
Trent, Henry 23(2), 29, 33(2), 35(2),
    41; John 66
Tribue, Anthony 49(3), 54(2), 60, 61
Trotman, Jno. 33
Trowell, Jos. 26
Truelove, Eliz. 21
Trussell, Jon. 8
Trustum, John 45
Tuckahoe (see Creeks) 78
Tucker, Jane 34; William 4
Tuder, Joan 40
Tuffin, Edw. 33
Tullett, Hannah 40; John 40
Tullit (see above) John 61
Tundal (see Tindal), Thomas 69
Turkey Island 10
Turner, Hen. 25, Henry 37, 85, 90;
    James 18; Jno. 31, 35; Robert 6;
    Susanna 30; Thomas 5
Turney (see above), Hen. 25
Tunstall, Owen 31; Rich. 22
Turpen, Michael 38
Turpin (see above), Michael 14, 18,
28; Tho. 41, Thomas 54, 58, 77, 79

Tustin, Edw. 33
Twyne, Thomas 38
Tye, Lambert 30, 31(2)
Tymber (see Timber) Slash 20
Tyre, Charles 23; Hen. 23

## U

Ubank, Stapleton 31
Ufenum (Ufnam, Uffnam, Uffnum, Ufnom,
    Ufnum, Upnim, Upham) Brook 26,
    31, 32, 41, 44(2), 47, 59, 61,
    63, 66, 71, 72, 73
Underhill, Edward 20
Urwin (see Irwin), James 28, 32
Utley, John 67(2)

## V

Vaden, Henry 66
Valker, Dan. 19
Vallow, Judith 78
Valton, Jno. Ja. 38
Vanderhood 75; Henry 77
Varling, Richard 16
Vase, Rich. 4, 7
Vaughan, Eliz. 19
Venis, Eliza. 31
Venne, John 14
Vincent, William 9, 10
Vinter, Iz. 20
Virgany, Edward 2
Vissell, Francis 3

## W

Wadds, Tho. 56, Thomas 39
Waddy, Tho. 56
Wade, Jno. 32; Richard 60, 65(2),
    74; Thomas 5
Wading Place 22
Wadkins (see Watkins) 39; Henry 26,
    33; Thomas 56, 57, 60;
Wadson, John 26, 28, 31, 37, 73(2);
    Robt. 54
Wailes, Thomas 26
Waite, James 43
Waites, Wm. 21
Wakam, Mary 24
Waker, Tem. 23
Waklin, Anth. 5

Waldron, Wm. 45
Wales, Tho. 33
Walker, 62; Danll. 28; Geo. 28; Jane
13; John 57; Tho. 40, Thomas 74,
76, 77
Walkner, Wm. 16
Wall, Geo. 42(2), 54; Richard 4, 6
Waller, Benj. 77; John 73
Wallis, Ellinor 16; Jno. 24
Walters, Edwd. 42; Henry 40; John 67
Walton 30; Henry 41; Thomas 82;
William 82, 85
Wamack (see Womack, Womacke) 83;
Abraham 89, Abraham, Jr. 84
Wamblin, Anth. 10
Wanklin, Anth. 10
Waraner, Math. 6
Ward, Edward 15; Grace 4; John 1, 4
(2), Jon. 7; Richard 6; Robert 11,
14; Seath(Seth) 1, 3(2), 5, 7, 11,
20(2), 80(2); Silvester 19; Wil-
liam 9
Ware Bottom 23
Ware 74; Caleb 46; Edward 15; Peter
78; Tho. 26; Valentine 59, 63
Wareing, Jacob 25
Warren, Fra. 25, 31, Francis 28, 32;
Garratt 23; Isaac 23; Jno. 24;
Thomas 2; Wm. 38
Warrener, Jno. 20
Warrick 41
Warwell, Robert 7
Warwick County 68
Waterhouse, Samll. 11
Waterridge, Jno. 22
Waters 77; Walter 31; William 85,
Wm. 24
Watkins (see Wadkins) 9, 75, 77;
Benjamin 58; Henry 12, 16, 26;
Morgan 5; Thomas 47, 81, 86
Watkinson, Hen. 25
Watson (see Wattson) 73(2), 77, 88,
89; Jno. 30, John 27, 47, 59, 63,
72(3), 73; Joseph 55, 59; Tho. 24
Wattals, David 45
Watts, Jno. 23, 27; Thomas 44; Wil-
liam 61
Wattson (see Watson) John 24, 25

Waylett, John 20
Weare, Tho. 26
Weatly, Mary 40
Weaver, John 11; Robert 40
Webb, Capt. 40; Giles 33(2), 35(2),
39, 40, 59; Hannah 44; Henry 68,
80, 87(2); John 40; Mary 23,
Merry 84, 85; Tho. 23
Webber, Philip 90, Phillip 72;
Webster, Thomas 35
Welch, SAMLL. 24; Tho. 32
Weldy, William 67, 91
Wells, John 9, Jon. 7; Jos. 25;
Thomas 24, 27, 30, 33
Welsh, Ellin 46; Jno. 31; Mary 91
West, Capt. 55; James 42; John 5;
Nathaniel 55; Will. 42, Wm. 24,
32, 42
Westham 31, 39
Westoby, Jno. 31
Westopher (see Westover) Parish 34
(2)
Westover (see above) 4, 5, Par. 38
Wetherlee Gilbert 46
Wethers, Wm. 43
Weyanoke (see Weynock, Weyonoke) 8
Weyat, Henry 32
Weynock 16(2), 17(4), 18(2), 19,
Weyonoke (see above) 12
Whadsey, Peter 4
Whaley, Jno. 46; John 40
Wharton, Tho. 24
Whatley, John 43
Whattin, John 5
Wheeler, Antho. 24; Hen. 32; Thomas
8, 18; Wm. 24
Whidow, Clement 12
Whitby, Richd 56
White Oake Land (see White Oak
Branch, White Oak Swamp) 36
White, Charles 8, 10, Chas. 24; Ell.
23; James 22; Jno. 24; Joane 30;
John 15, 20, 22, 39, 54; Jon. 13;
Michael 66; Neale 13, 15; Tho. 17,
31, 53; Tim. 20; William 10; Wm.
5, 35
Whitebread, John 43
Whitfeild, Richd. 2

125

126

Wortham, Jno. 21, John 34
Wragg, Ja. 23
Wright, Elizabeth 5; Gilbert 32;
   Hugh 21; Jno. 32; Othelr. 24;
   Richd. 41; Robt. 21; Wm. 13, 45
Wyat, Henry 27
Wyatt (see above) 25; Henry 26
Wyett (see above), Henry 25
Wynn's Col. Quarter 21
Wyyon, Antho. 5

**Y**

Yates, Tho. 20
Yeardly, Sir Georg 9
Yeates, Geo. 42; Jno. 21
Yernsher, Edmund 28
Yéurnon, Corn. 23
Young, Anne, 48; Dorcas 23; Eliza-
   beth 60; Henry 53; James 42, 63;
   John 19; Rachel 27
Yowell, Eliza. 32

---

## ADDITIONS to INDEX

Bagly, Jon. 92
Bailie, Thomas 91
Batchelers bancke 91
Bowling, James 21; John 38
Branch, Christopher 91
Bullock, Joane 91
Burford, Wm. 91
Cock, Rich. 92
Coxendale 91
Currant, Robert 91
Curtis, Eliz. 91
Dennington, Oliver 91
Dixon, Wm. 92
Everedge, William 91
Fearing 91, 92
Greere, Susan 21
Hoveller, Jeremiah 91
Jenings, Richard 91
Kilbye, Henry 91
Lawley, Thomas 91
Maxney, Charles 91
Melder, John 91
Norton, Jeremy 21

Oliver, Nich. 91
Osborne, Thomas 91, Thomas, Junr. 91
Pack, Christ. 92
Perrin, Richard 91
Proctors Cr. 92
Pullum, Edmund 91
Quash, Francis 92
Robinson, Hum. 25
Rush, Jon. 92
Shaddock, Jon. 7
Shamapoke 41
Somersale, Thomas 91
Stanton, Robt. 92
Stubbs, Izabell 91
Thorneford, Samll. 91
Tydder, Hugh 5
Wadkines 39
Waldrom, Tho. 92
Wall, John 91
Walthall, Henry 62
Weyan, Jon. 91
Williams, Edward 91
Willis, Eliz. 91

# Rent Roll of Virginia
## 1704-1705

A true and Perfect Roll of all the Lands held of her Maj[tie] in Henrico County
**Aprill 1705**

### A

| | |
|---|---|
| ANDREWS THOMAS | 396 |
| ASCOUTCH MARY | 633 |
| ARCHER JNO | 335 |
| ADKINS JNO | 125 |
| ARCHER GEO | 1738 |
| ALDY JOHN | 162 |
| AKINS JAMES Sen[r] | 200 |
| ASHBROOK PETER Sen[r] | 200 |
| AKINS JAMES Jun[r] | 218 |
| ALLIN WIDD[o] | 99 |

### B

| | |
|---|---|
| BYRD Esq[r] | 19500 |
| BOLLING ROB[t] | 500 |
| BOLLING JOHN | 831 |
| BEVILL JOHN | 495 |
| BRANCH X[to] | 646 |
| BLACKMAN WM | 175 |
| BRIDGWATER SAM | 280 |
| BOWMAN JOHN Jun[r] | 300 |
| BOWMAN EDW[d] | 300 |
| BRANCH BENJ | 550 |
| BROWN MARTHA | 893 |
| BULLINGTON BENJ | 100 |
| BOWMAN LEW | 65 |
| BULLINGTON | 144 |
| BEVELL ESSEX | 200 |
| BAUGH JOHN | 448 |
| BAUGH JAMES | 458 |
| BURTON ISAAC | 100 |
| BOTTOM JOHN | 100 |
| BAYLEY ABR | 542 |
| BROOKS JANE belonging to | |
| WM WALKER New Kent | 550 |
| BRASEAL HENRY | 200 |
| BRAZEAL HENRY Jun[r] | 300 |
| BURTON ROB[t] | 1350 |
| BURGONY JOHN | 100 |
| BRANCH JAMES | 555 |
| BURROWS WM. WM BLACKWELL | |
| New Kent | 63 |

| | |
|---|---|
| BRANCH THOMAS | 540 |
| BAILEY THOMAS | 251 |
| BRANCH MATTHEW | 947 |
| BURTON WM | 294 |
| BULLINGTON ROB[t] | 100 |
| BROADNAX JNO Jr | 725 |
| BEVERLEY ROB[t] | 988 |

### C

| | |
|---|---|
| CHEATHAM THO | 300 |
| COX BATT | 100 |
| COX JOHN | 150 |
| COX GEORGE | 200 |
| CHAMBERLAINE Maj. THO | 1000 |
| CHILDERS ABR. Sen[r] | 368 |
| CANNON JOHN | 108 |
| COX WM | 300 |
| CHILDERS AB[r] Jun[r] | 100 |
| CLARK WM | 333 |
| CLARK JOHN | 300 |
| COX RICH[d] | 300 |
| CARDWELL THO | 350 |
| CROZDALL ROGER | 200 |
| COCK WM | 1535 |
| COCK RICH[d] Sen[r] | 2180 |
| CHILDERS PHILIP Sen[r] | 50 |
| CHILDERS PHILIP | 300 |
| CHILDERS THO | 300 |
| CARTER THEOD | 75 |
| COCK Capt THOMAS | 2976¼ |
| COUZINS CHARLES | 362 |
| CLERK ALONSON | 604 |
| COCK JAMES | 1506 |
| CURD EDW[d] | 600 |
| COCK RICH[d] | 476 |
| COCK JNO | 98 |

### D

| | |
|---|---|
| DIXON NICHOLAS | 150 |
| DODSON WM | 100 |

128

DOUGHLAS CHARLES ............ 63

**E**

EDW<sup>d</sup> THO ................... 676
ENTROUGHTY DERBY ........... 200
EALAM ROBT ................... 400
ELLIS JOHN ................... 217
EAST THO Sen ................ 475
EAST THO .................... 554
EAST EDW<sup>d</sup> ................... 150
EPES Capt FRAS .............. 2145
EVANS CHARLES ............... 225
EALAM MARTIN ................ 130
EPES ISHAM, EPES FRA. Jun<sup>t</sup>.
 each 444½ acres ......... 889

**F**

FIELD PETER Major ......... 2185
FARRAR Capt WM .............. 700
FARRAR THO .................. 1444
FARRAR JNO .................. 600
FOWLER GODFREY .............. 250
FERGUSON ROBERT ............. 230
FERRIS WM ................... 50
FRANKLIN JAMES Sen ......... 250
FRANKLIN JAMES Jun ......... 786
FERRIS RICH<sup>d</sup> ............... 550
FARMER HENRY ................ 100
FORREST JAMES .............. 138
FORREST JOHN ............... 150
FEATHERSTONE HENRY ......... 700
FARLOE JOHN Sen ............ 100
FARLOE JOHN Jun ............ 551
FAILE JOHN ................. 240

**G**

GILLEY GREWIN ARRIAN ...... 2528
GEE HENRY .................. 435
GOOD JOHN Sen .............. 600
GARTHWAITE SAML ............ 50
GARTHWAITE EPHRIAM ........ 163
GRANGER JOHN ............... 472
GILL JOHN .................. 235
GOOD SAM<sup>l</sup> ................. 588
GOWER JAMES GRIGS Land .... 500

**H**

HILL JAMES ................. 795
HOLMES RICH ................ 100
HARRIS THOMAS .............. 357
HARRIS TIM<sup>o</sup> ............... 250
HILL ROSAM<sup>d</sup> ............... 1633
HOBBY LAWRENCE ............. 500
HATCHER JOHN ............... 215
HASKINS EDWARD ............. 225
HATCHER EDWARD Sen ......... 150
HUNT GEO ................... 200
HUGHES EDWARD .............. 100
HANCOCK SAMUEL ............. 100
HOLMES THOMAS .............. 50
HAMBLETON JAMES ............ 100
HUTCHINS NICH<sup>o</sup> ........... 240
HATCHER BENJ Sen ........... 250
HATCHER WM Jun ............. 50
HOBSON WM .................. 150
HATCHER WM Sen ............. 298
HATCHER HENRY .............. 650
HANCOCK ROBERT ............. 860
HARRIS MARY ................ 94
HALL EDWARD ................ 184
HERBERT Mrs ................ 1360
HUDSON ROBERT .............. 281

**J**

JONES HUGH ................. 934
JEFFERSON THOMAS ........... 492
JONES PHILIP ............... 1153
JORDEN HENRY ............... 100
JAMSON JOHN ................ 225
JACKSON RALPH .............. 250

**K**

KENNON ELIZABETH ........... 1900
KNIBB SAMUEL ............... 209
KNIBB SOLOMON .............. 833
KENDALL RICHARD ............ 400

**L**

LIPTROLL EDWARD ............ 150
LEWIS WM ................... 350
LESTER DARENS .............. 100

129

| | |
|---|---|
| LADD WM .................. | 70 |
| LIGON ELIZABETH Widdow | 1341 |
| LIGON MARY Widdow | |
| LAFORCE REU .............. | 100 |
| LOCHETT JAMES ............ | 50 |
| LOWND HENRY .............. | 516 |
| LOCKITT BENJ ............. | 104 |
| LIGON RICHARD ............ | 1028 |
| LIGON HUGH ............... | 150 |

**M**

| | |
|---|---|
| MANN ROBERT .............. | 100 |
| MATTHEWS EDWARD .......... | 330 |
| MOSEBY ELWARD ............ | 150 |
| MOSEBY ARTHUR ............ | 450 |

**N**

| | |
|---|---|
| NUNNALLY RICHARD ......... | 70 |

**O**

| | |
|---|---|
| OSBOURNE THOMAS .......... | 288 |
| OWEN THOMAS .............. | 68 |

**P**

| | |
|---|---|
| PERKINSON JOHN ........... | 622 |
| PERRIN ANN ............... | 500 |
| PLEASANTS JOHN ........... | 9669 |
| PARKER WM ................ | 100 |
| PARKER NICH .............. | 500 |
| PLEDGE JNO ............... | 100 |
| POWELL ROBERT ............ | 150 |
| PEICE JOHN ............... | 130 |
| PLEASANTS ................ | 1709 |
| PORTER WM ................ | 305 |
| PEIRCE WM ................ | 175 |
| PEIRCE FRANCIS ........... | 312 |
| PAINE THOMAS ............. | 300 |
| PORTLOCK ELIZABETH ....... | 1000 |
| PERO HENRY ............... | 350 |
| PATTRAM IRA .............. | 778 |
| PRIDE WM Sen ............. | 1280 |
| POLLARD THOMAS Sen ....... | 130 |
| PERKINSON SETH ........... | 50 |
| PINKITT WM ............... | 192 |
| PINKITT THOMAS ........... | 300 |
| PATTISON JOSEPH .......... | 500 |
| PORTER JOHN .............. | 100 |
| POLLARD THOMAS Jun ....... | 235 |

| | |
|---|---|
| POLLARD HENRY ............ | 235 |
| PINKITT JOHN ............. | 215 |

**R**

| | |
|---|---|
| ROBERTSON GEO ............ | 1445 |
| RAGSDAILE GODFREY ........ | 450 |
| RAWLETT PETER ............ | 164 |
| RUSSELL CHARLES .......... | 200 |
| ROWLETT WM ............... | 200 |
| ROWEN FRANCIS ............ | 148 |
| ROBERTSON JOHN ........... | 415 |
| ROUCH RACHELL ............ | 300 |
| ROBERTSON THOMAS ......... | 200 |
| RUSSELL JOHN ............. | 93 |
| ROYALL JOSEPH ............ | 783 |
| REDFORD JOHN ............. | 775 |
| RANDOLPH Col WM including | |
| 1185 acres swamp ......... | 9465 |

**S**

| | |
|---|---|
| STEWARD JNO Jun .......... | 902 |
| SCOTT WALTER ............. | 550 |
| SOANE Capt WM ............ | 3841 |
| STANLEY EDWARD ........... | 300 |
| SNUGGS CHARLES ........... | 400 |
| SEWELL WM ................ | 59 |
| SMITH HUMPHREY ........... | 40 |
| SHARP ROBERT ............. | 500 |
| STOVALL BARTHᵒ ........... | 100 |
| SKERIN Widdow ............ | 75 |
| STEWARD DANIELL .......... | 270 |
| SMITH OBADIAH ............ | 200 |
| STOWERS Widdow ........... | 200 |
| SARRAZIN STEPHEN ......... | 120 |

**T**

| | |
|---|---|
| TANCOCKS Orphans ......... | 1230 |
| TRENT HENRY .............. | 224 |
| TURPIN THOMAS ............ | 491 |
| TURPIN PHILIP ............ | 444 |
| TURPIN THOMAS ............ | 100 |
| TURNER HENRY ............. | 200 |
| TAYLOR THOMAS ............ | 475 |
| TANNER EDWARD ............ | 217 |
| TRAYLOR EDWARD ........... | 100 |
| TOTTY THOMAS ............. | 260 |
| TRAYLOR WM ............... | 730 |

**V**

| | |
|---|---|
| VEDEN HENRY .............. | 100 |

| | |
|---|---|
| WOODSON JOHN ............... | 4060 |
| WILLIAMS ROBERT ........... | 300 |
| WOODSON ROBERT Jun ........ | 1157 |
| WARD RICHARD .............. | 300 |
| WATSON JOHN Sen ........... | 1603 |
| WALTHALL WM ............... | 500 |
| WALTHALL HENRY ............ | 832 |
| WHITBY WM ................. | 215 |
| WATKINS HENRY Sen ......... | 100 |
| WEBB JOHN ................. | 100 |
| WATKINS THOMAS ............ | 200 |
| WOODSON RICH .............. | 180 |
| WOODSON Widdow ............ | 650 |
| WILLIAMSON THOMAS ......... | 1077 |
| WEBB GILES ................ | 7260 |
| WOOD THOMAS ............... | 50 |
| WATKINS WM ................ | 120 |
| WATKINS JOS ............... | 120 |
| WATKINS EDWARD ............ | 120 |
| WARD SETH ................. | 700 |
| WOOD MOSES ................ | 100 |
| WILKINSON JOS ............. | 75½ |
| WILKINSON JOHN ............ | 130 |
| WORSHAM JOHN .............. | 1104 |
| WOMACK ABR ................ | 560 |
| WILLSON JNO Sen ........... | 1686 |
| WILLSON JNO Jun ........... | 100 |
| WALTHALL RICHARD .......... | 500 |
| WORTHAM GEO ............... | 400 |
| WORTHAM CHARLES ........... | 90 |
| WOMACK WM ................. | 100 |

Total acreage:                     165814

Out of which must be deducted these
several quantities of land following Viz:

| | |
|---|---|
| THACOCKS Orphans Land ....... | 1230 |
| ALLENS Orphans Land ......... | 99 |

An account of Land that hath been
concealed:

| | |
|---|---|
| JOHN STEWARD Jun ............. | 2 |
| THOMAS JEFFERSON ............. | 15 |
| THOMAS TURPIN ................ | 10 |
| HENRY GEE .................... | 10 |
| STEPHEN SARRZEN .............. | 10 |
| Mr. LOWND .................... | 1 |
| JAMES ATKIN ................ | 32 |
| MATTHEW BRANCH ............... | 10 |
| JAMES FRANKLIN ............... | 360 |
| JAMES HILL ................... | 50 |
| ROSEMOND HILL................. | 33 |
| JOHN BULLINGTON .............. | 44 |
| BENJAMIN LOCKETT ............. | 4 |
| JOHN RUSSELL ................. | 23 |
| CHARLES DOUG ............... | 13 |
| Col. RANDOLPH ................ | |
| Careless Land ............. | 1049 |

The Quit Rent being 162719 acres.

A full & Perfect Rent Roll of all the Land held of her Majtie in Charles City
County this Present Year 1704.by Patents &c.

A

| | |
|---|---|
| ALIAT JOHN | 100 |

B

| | |
|---|---|
| BRADLEY JOSEPH ............. | 200 |
| BAXTER JOHN ................ | 250 |
| BISHOP ROBERT .............. | 200 |
| BEDINGFIELD THEO............ | 110 |
| BOTMAN HARMAN .............. | 100 |
| BURTON HENRY ............... | 100 |
| BURWELL LEWIS .............. | 8000 |

| | |
|---|---|
| BROOKS ROBT ................. | 150 |
| BLANKS RICHARD Senr ......... | 250 |
| BLANKS RICHD Junr ........... | 125 |
| BLANKS THO .................. | 125 |
| BRADFORD RICHD .............. | 1397 |
| BROWN MARMADUKE ............. | 100 |
| BRAY DAVID .................. | 230 |

C

131

| | | | | |
|---|---|---|---|---|
| COLE ROBT | 80 | | JAVOX JAMES | 100 |
| CODELL RICHD | 100 | | JORDAN EDWD | 100 |
| CLARK EDWD | 962¼ | | JUSTIS JUSTINIAN | 200 |
| CLARK DANIELL | 250 | | | |
| CLARK JOSEPH | 230 | | **L** | |
| CHRISTIAN THO | 1273 | | LOWLIN DANLL | 600 |
| COCK EDWD | 350 | | LAWRENCE JAMES | 100 |
| COCK RICHD | 975 | | | |

**D**

MANDERS JAMES ............... 100

| | | | | |
|---|---|---|---|---|
| DAVIS THOMAS | 200 | | MINGE JAMES | 1086 |
| DAVIS RICHD | 118 | | MONTFORD JEFFRY | 100 |
| | | | MARVELL THO | 1238 |
| **E** | | | MOODIE SAMLL | 82 |
| EDWARDS JOHN | 287½ | | MUSCHAMP JOHN | 80 |
| EPES LITTLEBURY | 400 | | | |
| EPES JOHN | 500 | | **N** | |
| ELE SAMLL | 682 | | NEW EDWD | 100 |
| EVANS JOHN | 800 | | NEW ROBT | 300 |

**F**

**O**

| | | | | |
|---|---|---|---|---|
| FLOYD GEO | 243 | | OWEN WM | 100 |
| FOWLER RICHD | 150 | | OWEN DAVID | 100 |
| FLOWERS SAMLL | 200 | | | |
| | | | **P** | |
| **G** | | | PARKER THO | 1667 |
| GUNN JAMES | 250 | | PARISH WM | 100 |
| GROSSE EDWD | 100 | | PARISH CHARLES | 100 |
| | | | PARKER JAMES | 160 |
| **H** | | | PARISH EDWD | 100 |
| HAMLIN JNO | 143½ | | PARISH JOHN | 100 |
| HILL EDWD | 2100 | | | |
| HAYNES NICHO | 125 | | **R** | |
| HARWOOD JOHN | 100 | | ROACH JNO Senr | 630 |
| HOWOOD JAMES | 200 | | RENTHALL JOSEPH | 270 |
| HATTLE SHARD | 112 | | RUSSELL SAMLL | 253 |
| HARWOOD JOSEPH | 659 | | ROPER JOHN | 220 |
| HARWOOD SAMLL | 350 | | ROYALL JOSEPH | 262 |
| HARWOOD ROBT | 312½ | | | |
| HUNT WM | 3130 | | **S** | |
| HUNT JOHN | 1500 | | SMITH OBIADIAH | 100 |
| HARMON ELIZB | 479 | | SAMPSON Widdo | 211 |
| HYDE WM | 120 | | STITH DREWRY | 1240 |
| HAMLIN STEPHEN | 80 | | STITH JOHN | 1395 |
| HAMLIN THO | 264 | | STOCKES JOHN | 476 |
| | | | STOCKES SILVANUS Senr | 250 |
| **J** | | | STOKES SILVANUS Junr | 550 |
| IRBY WM | 103 | | SPEARES GEO | 225 |

|   T   |      |   W   |      |
|-------|------|-------|------|
| TANNER THO ............... | 2000 | WYATT Widdo ............... | 800 |
| TARENDINE JOHN ........... | 150 | WOODAM THO ................ | 100 |
| TURNER EDWD............... | 195 | WAREN JOHN ................ | 54 |
| TROTMAN ANNE ............. | 120 |  |  |

|   V   |      |
|-------|------|
| VERNON WALTER ........... | 240 |

An account of what Land that I cannot get the Quit Rents the Persons living out of the County

| JOSEPH PARISH at Kiquotan | 100 | DANLL HAYLEY .............. | 200 |
|--------------------------|-----|----------------------------|-----|
| RICHD SMITH James Cty ... | 350 | WM LAGG Henrico Cty ....... | 100 |
|  | THO PARKER Sherif |  |  |

## New Kent County Rent Roll

A Rent Roll of the Lands held of her Maj[tie] in the Parish of St Peters and and St. Paulls. Anno 1704.

| A |  | B |  |
|---|---|---|---|
| ALFORD JOHN .............. | 240 | BOURN WM .................. | 140 |
| ALLEN RICHARD ............ | 550 | BRAY SARAH ................ | 790 |
| ALEX ABRAHAM ............. | 100 | BRADBURY GEO .............. | 100 |
| ALLEN ROBT. .............. | 100 | BROTHERS JNO .............. | 200 |
| AUSTIN ................... | 245 | BAYLEY JNO ................ | 80 |
| AUSTIN JAMES ............. | 700 | BECK WM Mr. ............... | 200 |
| AMOS FRAN ................ | 100 | BUTTS ALICE ............... | 150 |
| ASHCROFT THO ............. | 180 | BURNELL MARY Mrs. ......... | 2750 |
| ALDRIDGE JNO ............. | 250 | BASSETT WM. ............... | 550 |
| ATKINSON JNO ............. | 300 | BALL DAVID ................ | 200 |
| ANTHONY MARK ............. | 190 | BAUGHAN JNO Junr .......... | 300 |
| ANDERSON JNO ............. | 100 | BASSETT THO ............... | 350 |
| ANDERSON ROBT ........... | 900 | BLACKBURN ROWLAND ......... | 700 |
| ARISE MARGT .............. | 200 | BAKER CHRISTO ............. | 100 |
| AUSTIN RICH .............. | 50 | BEER PETER ................ | 100 |
| ANDERSON ROBT. ........... | 700 | BROOKS RICHD .............. | 85 |
| ANDERSON DAVID ........... | 300 | BURNELL EDWD .............. | 200 |
| ANDERSON RICH ............ | 200 | BROWN JNO ................. | 100 |
| ALLEN REYNOLD ............ | 205 | BULLOCK RICHD ............. | 450 |
| ALLVIS GEORGE ............ | 325 | BLACKWELL JAMES Junr ..... | 200 |
| ARON JOSIAH .............. | 200 | BROOKS ROBT ............... | 45 |
| AMOS NOCHO ............... | 50 | BULKLEY BENJ .............. | 200 |
| ALLEN DANIELL ............ | 250 | BLACKWELL ................. | 950 |
| ALLEN SAMLL .............. | 150 | BAUGHAN JNO ............... | 100 |
| ANDERSON JOHN ............ | 100 | BAUGHAN JOSEPH ............ | 100 |
| ASHLEY CHARLES ........... | 100 | BOSTOCK JNO ............... | 100 |

| | | | | |
|---|---|---|---|---|
| BOSTOCK WM | 80 | COCKER WM. | 1000 |
| BUMPUS ROBT | 100 | CASE HUGH | 100 |
| BURWELL LEWIS | 200 | CARLEY RICHD | 80 |
| BRYAN CHARLES | 100 | CHILES HENRY | 700 |
| BULLOCK EDWD | 450 | COOK ABRAHAM | 200 |
| BLALOCK JNO | 492 | CRUMP ELIZB | 80 |
| BAKER JNO | 130 | COLUM RICHD | 130 |
| BEARNE HENRY | 50 | CRUMP JAMES | 150 |
| BUHLY JNO | 225 | CRUMP ROBT | 150 |
| BOW HENRY | 200 | CLOUGH Capt. | 80 |
| BRADLEY THO | 255 | CHANDLER WM. | 300 |
| BARKER CHA | 100 | CHANDLER FRANCIS | 150 |
| BUGG SAMLL | 60 | CORDEY THO. | 150 |
| BASKETT WM. Esq. | 1250 | CURRELL ANDREW | 30 |
| BECK WM. | 433 | CROOME JOELL | 600 |
| BEARE JOSEPH | 150 | CRUTCHFIELD PETER | 400 |
| BARRETT CHRISTO | 60 | CHESLEY WM. | 500 |
| BAUGHTWRIGHT JNO | 250 | CRUTCHFIELD Junr | 400 |
| BAD SAMLL | 150 | CARLTON WM. | 140 |
| BANKS ANDREW | 50 | CHAMBERS GEORGE | 100 |
| BAKER RICHD | 80 | COX WM. | 350 |
| BOWLES JOHN | 500 | | |
| BUNCH JOHN | 100 | **D** | |
| BURNETT JNO | 150 | DOLERD WM | 50 |
| BARNHOWES RICHD | 1600 | DENNETT JOHN | 350 |
| BARBAR THO | 500 | DURHAM JAMES | 100 |
| BURKETT THO | 41 | DUMAS JERIMIAH | 250 |
| BATES EDWD | 50 | DEPREST ROBT | 350 |
| BREEDING JOHN | 300 | DODD JOHN | 300 |
| BREWER MARY | 100 | DABONY JAMES | 320 |
| BASSETT WM. Esq. | 4100 | DAVIS ELIZAR | 375 |
| BRADINGHAM ROBT. | 150 | DUKE HENRY Esq. | 325 |
| BAXTER JAMES | 90 | DIBDALL JNO | 800 |
| | | DARNELL RACHELL | 100 |
| **C** | | DUKE HENRY Esq. | 170 |
| COTRELL RICHD | 200 | DAVIS JOHN | 80 |
| CLARKSON DAVID | 200 | DAVENPORT MEST | 125 |
| CRUMP STEPHEN | 60 | DANIELL JOHN | 150 |
| CRUMP WILLIAM | 330 | | |
| CLOPTON WILLIAM | 454 | **E** | |
| CHANDLER ROBT. | 160 | EPERSON JOHN | 120 |
| CRUMP RICHD. | 60 | ELMORE THO | 300 |
| CAMBO RICHD. | 80 | ELMORE THO Junr | 100 |
| CRAWFORD DAVID Junr | 400 | ELLICON GARRATT ROBT | 520 |
| CRAWFORD DAVID Mr. | 300 | ENGLAND WM. | 490 |
| CHAMBERS EDWD | 235 | ELDERKIN JOHN | 300 |
| CLERK EDWD | 282 | ELMORE PETER | 100 |
| COLLETT THO | 100 | ENGLISH MUNGO | 500 |
| CLERK CHRISTO | 300 | ELLIS WM. | 100 |

## F

| Name | Value |
|---|---|
| FINCH EDWD | 300 |
| FORSTER JOSEPH | 800 |
| FORGESON WM | 507 |
| FLEMING CHARLES | 920 |
| FRANCIS THO | 150 |
| FREEMAN WM | 200 |
| FENTON Widdo | 270 |
| FISHER WM | 100 |

## G

| Name | Value |
|---|---|
| GOODGER JNO | 200 |
| GREEN EDWD | 200 |
| GIBSON THO | 370 |
| GARRAT JAMES | 375 |
| GONTON JNO | 250 |
| GLASS THO | 150 |
| GRAHAM THO | 250 |
| GLEAM JNO | 300 |
| GILES JNO | 120 |
| GENTRY NICHO | 250 |
| GARLAND EDWD | 2600 |
| GLASS ANN | 150 |
| GRANCHAW THO | 480 |
| GREENFIELD FRAN | 80 |
| GILLMETT JNO | 160 |
| GAWSEN PHILLIP | 50 |
| GILLMETT RICHD | 150 |
| GLASSBROOK ROBT | 400 |
| GADBERRY THO | 200 |
| GILL NICHO | 222 |
| GOSLING WM | 460 |
| GOODRING ALEXANDER | 100 |
| GILLS JOHN | 100 |
| GRINDGE RICHD | 225 |

## H

| Name | Value |
|---|---|
| HERLOCK JOHN | 320 |
| HILTON JNO | 300 |
| HUGHES JNO | 180 |
| HUBERD JNO | 827 |
| HOWLE JNO | 150 |
| HOWLE JNO Junr | 100 |
| HUGHES ROBT | 966 |
| HARRIS EDMD | 100 |
| HARRIS THO | 100 |
| HAWES HAUGTON | 850 |
| HARRIS HOHN | 146 |

| Name | Value |
|---|---|
| HILL JNO | 250 |
| HESTER FRA | 300 |
| HORSLEY ROWLAND | 250 |
| HORMAN ROBT | 300 |
| HUGHES REES | 400 |
| HILL SAMLL | 300 |
| HOLLED SAMLL | 100 |
| HARRELSTON PAUL | 360 |
| HARRIS WM | 125 |
| HARRIS BENJ | 100 |
| HORKEEY JOHN | 800 |
| HAIRY JOHN | 280 |
| HAISELWOOD JNO | 200 |
| HAISELWOOD THO | 150 |
| HOCKIDAY WM | 300 |
| HOLDCROFT HENRY | 95 |
| HOGG MARY | 140 |
| HARMON WM | 350 |
| HOGG JNO. Junr | 260 |
| HARRIS WM | 100 |
| HOPKINS WM | 200 |
| HOWLES JOB | 300 |
| HIGH JOHN | 100 |
| HANKINS CHARLES | 340 |
| HARRIS WM | 150 |
| HARRIS ROBT | 75 |
| HANDEY WM | 150 |
| HOGG WM | 200 |
| HASELWOOD RICHD | 100 |
| HARLOW THO | 230 |
| HUTTON GEO | 150 |

## J

| Name | Value |
|---|---|
| JACKSON THO. | 500 |
| IZARD FRAN | 1233 |
| JARRATT ROBT | 1600 |
| JOHNSON MICH | 40 |
| JONES JOHN | 100 |
| JOHNSON WM | 265 |
| JONES JANE | 200 |
| JOHNSON JOHN | 100 |
| JOHNSON EDWD | 150 |
| JENNINGS ROBT | 100 |
| JONES FREDIRICK | 500 |
| JOHES JOHN | 100 |
| JEEVES THO | 100 |
| JONES FRANCIS | 200 |
| JONES JOHN | 100 |

| | | | |
|---|---:|---|---:|
| JONES EVAN | 500 | MORRIS ROBT | 245 |
| | | MOSS THO | 430 |
| **K** | | MORGAN EDWD | 50 |
| KING ELIZB | 300 | MOON STEPHEN | 70 |
| KENBRO JNO | 540 | MAJOR WM | 456 |
| KEMBRO JNO Junr | 150 | MURROHO JNO | 100 |
| KEELING GEO | 1500 | MOOR JNO | 250 |
| | | MASEY THO | 300 |
| **L** | | MARTIN JOHN | 400 |
| LIGHTFOOT JOHN Esq. | 3600 | MASEY PETER | 100 |
| LITTLEPAGE RICHD | 2160 | MADOX JOHN | 300 |
| LOSPLAH PETER | 100 | MARTIN WM | 230 |
| LESTRANGE THO | 200 | MARTIN JAMES | 100 |
| LIDDALL GEO | 100 | MOSS JAMES | 720 |
| LAWSON NICHO | 200 | MOON THO | 65 |
| LEVERMORE PHILL | 1000 | McKING ALEXANDER | 170 |
| LEWIS JOHN Esq | 2600 | McKOY JNO | 300 |
| LAWSON JOHN | 50 | MERRIDITH GEO | 400 |
| LEWIS JOHN | 375 | MELTON RICHD | 290 |
| LOVELL GEO | 920 | MORREIGH JOHN | 110 |
| LOVELL CHARLES | 250 | MERFIELD JOHN | 210 |
| LEAK WM | 280 | MILLS NICHO | 300 |
| LOGWOOD THO | 100 | MASK JNO | 411 |
| LACEY WM | 500 | MEDLOCK JOHN | 350 |
| LACEY THO | 100 | MOOR EDWD | 65 |
| LACEY EMANUELL | 180 | McKGENE WM | 13½ |
| LUKE JNO | 150 | MERRIWEATHER NICHO | 3327 |
| LOCHESTER ROBT | 80 | MAGE PETER | 450 |
| LEWIS THO | 115 | MITCHELL WM | 512 |
| LEE EDWD | 120 | MARR GEO | 100 |
| LOCHESTER EDWD | 80 | MOOR ANNE | 75 |
| LAW JAMES | 100 | MUTRAY THO | 382 |
| LATON REUBIN. | 100 | MIRIDETH JAMES | 270 |
| LINSEY JOSEPH | 1150 | MOHAN WARWICK | 850 |
| LINSEY WM | 50 | MUTTLOW JAMES | 150 |
| LANE THO | 100 | MORGAN MATTHEW | 210 |
| | | MORRIS JOHN | 450 |
| | | MARKHAM THO | 100 |
| **M** | | MOXON WM | 100 |
| MILLINGTON WM Junr | 450 | MACKONY ELIZB | 250 |
| MITCHELL STEPHEN Junr | 75 | MEACON GIDEON | 270 |
| MILLINGTON WM | 200 | | |
| MOSS SAMLL | 200 | **N** | |
| MITCHELL THO | 300 | NUCHOLL JAMES | 300 |
| MEANLEY WM | 100 | NEAVES JAMES | 150 |
| MINIS THO | 200 | NONIA RICHD | 100 |
| MITCHELL STEPHEN | 200 | NORRIS WM | 100 |
| MOOR PELHAM | 125 | | |
| MARTIN THO | 100 | | |
| MARTIN MARTIN | 150 | | |

## O

| | |
|---|---|
| OSLING JOHN | 150 |
| OTEY JOHN | 290 |
| OUDTON MATT | 190 |

## P

| | |
|---|---|
| PAGE JOHN Junr | 400 |
| PENDEXTER GEO | 1490 |
| PATTISON DAVID | 300 |
| PARK JNO Junr | 300 |
| PARK JOHN | 200 |
| PEASE JOHN | 100 |
| PHILIP GEO | 100 |
| PENIX EDWD | 200 |
| PLANTINE PETER | 240 |
| PENDEXTER THO | 1000 |
| PYRAUL JAMES | 150 |
| PULLAM WM | 575 |
| PURDY NICHO | 200 |
| PAGE MARY Madm | 3450 |
| PERKINS JOHN | 120 |
| PAITE JERIM | 220 |
| PASLEY ROBT | 300 |
| PERKINS WM | 305 |
| PAIT JOHN | 1500 |
| PETEVER THO | 100 |
| PITTLADER WM | 147 |
| PICKLEY THO | 281 |
| PITTLADER THO | 295 |
| PETTY STEPHEN | 200 |
| PORTER JOHN | 100 |
| PETTY JOHN | 2190 |
| PARK COLL | 7000 |
| PURDY JOHN | 100 |

## R

| | |
|---|---|
| RAGLIN EVAN | 300 |
| RAGLAN EVAN Junr | 100 |
| RAGLIN THO | 100 |
| ROSS WM | 150 |
| RICHARDSON HENRY | 300 |
| RAYMOND JAMES | 80 |
| REYNOLD THO | 255 |
| REYLEY JNO | 100 |
| REYNOLDS JONAH | 50 |
| RHOADS CHARLES | 175 |
| REYNOLDS SAMLL | 820 |
| RICE THO | 300 |
| REDWOOD JOHN | 1078 |

| | |
|---|---|
| RULE Widdo | 50 |
| RICHARDSON RICHARD | 890 |
| RUSSELL JOHN | 550 |
| RICHARDSON JOHN | 1450 |
| RICHARD EMAN | 1250 |
| ROUND FREE WM | 100 |
| RANDOLPH Widdo | 100 |

## S

| | |
|---|---|
| STYLES JOHN | 200 |
| SMITH NATHLL | 82 |
| SANDERS WM | 40 |
| SPEAR ROBT | 450 |
| SANDERS JAMES | 60 |
| SCOTT JOHN | 300 |
| SCRUGG RICHD | 100 |
| STRANGE ALEXANDER | 450 |
| SMITH WM | 110 |
| SCRUGG JNO | 50 |
| SNEAD THO | 200 |
| SUNTER STEPHEN | 478 |
| SYMONS JOSIAH | 100 |
| SANDERS JOHN | 130 |
| STEPHENS WM | 100 |
| STANLEY THO | 150 |
| SANDIDGE JNO | 100 |
| SPRATTLIN ANDREW | 654 |
| SNEAD JOHN | 75 |
| SMITH JAMES | 80 |
| SEXTON WM | 80 |
| SIMS JNO | 1000 |
| SMITH ROGER | 300 |
| SHERRITT HENRY | 100 |
| SALMON THOMAS | 50 |
| SANDERS THO | 25 |
| SYMONS GEORGE | 125 |
| STAMP RALPH | 625 |
| STANOP Capt | 1024 |
| STANUP RICHD | 325 |
| SHEARS PAUL | 200 |
| STEPPING THO | 350 |
| SLATER JAMES | 700 |

## T

| | |
|---|---|
| TONY ALEXANDER | 170 |
| TOVIS EDMD | 100 |
| TURNER HENRY | 250 |
| TURNER WM | 250 |
| TURNER GEO | 400 |

| | | | | |
|---|--:|---|---|--:|
| THORP THO | 200 | | WILMORE JNO | 100 |
| THURMOND RICHD | 131½ | | WEBSTER JOSEPH | 80 |
| TUCKER THO | 700 | | WEST GILES | 200 |
| TURNER JAMES | 50 | | WHARTON THO | 270 |
| THOMPSON JAMES | 100 | | WILLIS FRAN | 134 |
| TULLY WM | 200 | | WADDY SAMLL | 150 |
| TURNER GEO Junr | 200 | | WILLFORD CHARLES | 100 |
| TATE JAMES | 160 | | WAID JAMES | 150 |
| TOWN ELIZB | 100 | | WHITE JNO | 320 |
| Thomasses Orphans | 500 | | WOOD HENRY | 100 |
| TINSLEY CORNELIUS | 220 | | WOODY SYMON | 50 |
| TYLER | 100 | | WOODY JNO | 100 |
| TINSLEY THO | 150 | | WINSTONE ANTHO | 310 |
| TIRRELL WM | 400 | | WINSTONE ISAAC | 850 |
| TAYLOR THO | 25 | | WOODY JAMES | 130 |
| TINSLEY JNO | 130 | | WINSTONE SARAH | 275 |
| TAPP JNO | 110 | | WATSON THEOPHILUS | 325 |
| TYRREY JAMES | 150 | | WOODSON JOHN | 600 |
| TYRREY ALEXANDER | 210 | | WALTON EDWD | 450 |
| THOMPSON Capt. | 2600 | | WOOD WALTER | 100 |
| TYREY THOM | 190 | | WATKINS WM | 50 |
| TAYLOR JOSEPH | 150 | | WILKES JOSEPH | 250 |
| TAYLOR LEMUELL | 212 | | WILLIAMS CLERK | 300 |
| TAYLOR THOMAS | 350 | | WILLIS STEPHEN | 500 |
| TWITTY THOMAS | 200 | | WILLIAMS THO | 100 |
| | | | WORRIN ROBT | 300 |
| **V** | | | WOODULL JAMES | 200 |
| UPSHERD JNO | 60 | | WALKER Capt | 400 |
| VAUGHAN WM | 300 | | WILSON JAMES | 60 |
| VIA AMER | 50 | | WHEELER JOHN | 75 |
| VENABLES ABR. | 100 | | WILLIAMS WM. | 100 |
| VENABLES JOHN | 200 | | WHITE JOHN | 190 |
| VAUGHAN JOHN | 250 | | | |
| VAUGHAN VINCENT | 410 | | **Y** | |
| | | | YEOMAN JOHN | 50 |
| **W** | | | YEOELL JUSITH | 150 |
| WINTBY JACOB | 250 | | | |

Quit Rents that hath not been paid
this 7 year viz.

| | | |
|---|---|--:|
| WINFRY CHARLES | RICHARDSON MAL: | 200 |
| WADDILL JNO | WM WHEELER | 150 |
| WALKER WM | COLL PARKES | 200 |

| | |
|---|--:|
| WINFRY CHARLES | 100 |
| WADDILL JNO | 40 |
| WALKER WM | 650 |
| WALTON EDWD | 150 |
| WILSON JNO | 200 |
| WADDILL WM | 375 |
| WARRING PETER | 88 |
| WINGFIELD THO | 150 |
| WEAVER SAM | 100 |
| WYATT ALICE | 1300 |
| WEST NATH | 6370 |
| WEBB MARY | 200 |

Lands that the Persons lives out
of the County viz.

| | |
|---|--:|
| COLL LEMUELL BATTHURST | 800 |
| ROBT VALKES | 500 |
| The Heirs of BRAY | 500 |
| JAMES MOSSE Sherriff | 173870 |

NRTH'R BAYLL THOS. CROSBY 1638
SAMUEL ALMOND. ALMOND CREEK
1638

THE MAIN COUNTY ROAD

ALMOND CREEK

THOMAS JORDAN 4C. 1716

DARBY TOWN ROAD

WHITE OAK SWAMP
II THOS. COCKE 1699

ISACK HUTCHINGS 1656
PETER LEE 1636
4 ORPHANS WM. COX C. 1630
FALLING CREEK

WORLD'S END

ANN HALLOM 1699
Corporation of Henrico Co. Corporation of Charles City
WESTERN BR. 1664

CORNELIUS CREEK—LILLEY VALLEY
THE MAIN COUNTY ROAD

DARBYTOWN ROAD

DUKE'S CREEK

14 WM. 15 JOHN
11 THOS.

JOHN BURTON 1672
RICH. PERRIN 1672
GEORGE PERRIN 1695
WM. COCKE 1698

ROB'T CRADDOCK AND JOHN DAVIES 1636 4 AFTER
JOHN BURTON 1649
ROGER CRADDOCK
WILLIAM COX 1636
JOHN BURTON 1665

112 THOMAS COCKE 1687
EDW. HATCHER C. 1658
JOHN PLEASANTS 1778

REEDY BR. EPPES DECOR 1717

FOUR MILE CREEK
WARREN 1635
MARY ANN GREEN (FORMERLY BAILEY)
ELIZ. DUNTON
RICH. DUNTON
WILLIAM HARRIS 1665
DR. 14TH 1669
RICHARD COCKE

MALVERN HILL
1 RICHARD COCKE 1670
11 THOS. COCKE 1699

KINGSLAND CREEK

ALIKE EMLOE 1636
JOHN COX 1665

CHRISTOPHER BRANCH "KINGSLAND"
1635, 1636, 1638, 1639, 1665
JAMES PLACE
THOS. BURTON 1656

ROUNDABOUT CREEK
HENRY JORDAN 1701
THOMAS JORDAN 1671
POWHATAN'S TREE
ROBERT BOLLINGTON 1678

THOMAS TAYLOR "TIMBER SLOAN" 1663

HENRY RANDOLPH THO.
SAM'L JORDAN 1635

ARTHUR JOHN

PROCTORS CREEK

ARRAHATTOCK
THOS. TAYLOR 1662
JOHN BOLLING 1706
FARRAR 1637
VARINA

JOHN WHITLOE 1713
TWO MILE BR.
NECK OF LAND

THOS. HARRIS 1635
SAM'L JORDAN 1622
"BREMO"
2 RICH'D COCKE 1665
3 RICH'D COCKE 1699
TEMPERANCE BAYLEY

CURLES

JAMES R.
TURKEY ISLAND
JOS.

THOMAS OSBORNE 1636, 1638, 1642

WM. SAMPLES 1652
ROB'T BURTON 1655
RICH. DULLINGTON

WILLIAM COXENDALE
FARRARS IS. formerly HENRICUS CITTY

JAMES RIVER

BERMUDA HUNDRED
FOX HILL 1660
WALTER EPPES
EPPES IS.

SHIRLEY HUNDRED

Corporation of Henrico Corporation of Charles City, 1618

JOHNSON CREEK

AMBROSE BOOTH 1699
JOHN BAUGH 1638
ABRAHAM WOOD 1639

JOHN BAUGH 1638

THE HENRICO CO. CROSSES CHARLES CITY CO. JAMES R.

JAMES

ASHTON CREEK

APPOMATTOX RIVER

JAMES

THOS. BAILIE 1635
SAMUEL JORDAN
TEMPERANCE BAILY
WM. BAILE
JOHN WOODLIFFE 1626

SWIFT CREEK

WM. CLARK 1636
WILLIAM HATCHER 1636-37

APPOMATTOX R.

SULLVIL RUN

CABIN RUN

CABIN CREEK

CATTAILER

CABIN CREEK

BAILEY CREEK

COLONIAL MAP
"CURLES OF THE JAMES"
IN
HENRICO COUNTY, VIRGINIA
WITH
JORDANS, COCKES,
RELATIVES AND NEIGHBORS

LOUISE HEATH FOLEY
and ROBERT J FOLEY
RICHMOND, VA

SCALE OF MILES:

SCALE OF ACRES:

(ONE SQ. MI.
OR 640 ACS.)

1 RICHARD COCKE 1664
11 THOMAS COCKE 1664
1R RICHARD COCKE 1664
16 RICHARD COCKE 1665

CHICKAHOMINY R.

CITY

WHITE OAK SWAMP (BY 1687)

1 THOS. COCKE 1675

RICHARD COCKE 1664

1652 CHAS CITY RD.

HENRICO COUNTY

CHARLES CITY COUNTY

CATTAIL RUN

T. RICHARD COCKE

1665
COCKE
1 CO. CREEK

CHARLES CITY CREEK

COCKE 1650

TURNER'S MILL

TURKEY ISLAND CREEK

RUMLEY MARSH

CHICKAHOMINY RIVER

11 R JAMES POWELL COCKE 1697

SALEM RUN

WEST RUN

EAST RUN

COLLINS RUN

BAYLEY
FORE 1638
PRICE 1628
BEFORE 1655
BALLOW 1654
RANDOLPH
1679

Shirley
MIDDLAND (52)

T. CREEK

ROYALL 1697

DAVILL LEVELLIN (by Co.) 1653 and 1653

1692 (AUPHERNA)

KIMAGES CREEK

KIMAGES HILL

JAMES POWELL COCKE 1677

11 R JAMES POWELL

IF JOHN COCKE
16 RICHARD COCKE

C. 1680
C. 1680

OLD MAN'S CREEK

CAPT. THOS. STEGG
1653
DAN'L
CLARKE
1662

COURTHOUSE CREEK

PARISH HILL CREEK

KEEBE CREEK

CAPT. THOS. STEGG
1653
DAN'L CLARKE
1662

STEPHEN HAMELIN
1650

HUGH COX
(OR COCKES)
1655
CAUSEYS
CARE

ASTON
K88

CARE

BERKELEY
HUNDRED

HERRING CREEK

WESTOVER

STEGGS CR.

TANKS
WEYANOKE

ROBT EVANS 1665
FRANCIS RADFORD
1665

RIVER

JORDAN POINT

CHARLES CITY CO.

JAMES RIVER

KITTEWAN CREEK

SAM'L
JORDAN 1620
CREEK

THOS. GAINES
1665

JOHN
ROLFE

BILLY CREEK

DICKERS

CHAPPEL CREEK

POWELL CREEK

FLOWERDIEU
HUNDRED

JOHN CANNON
1665

JOSEPH
HARWOOD
1665

JAMES RIVER

FLOWERDIEU HUNDRED CR.

ABRAHAM
PEARSEY 1624

GREAT WEYANOKE